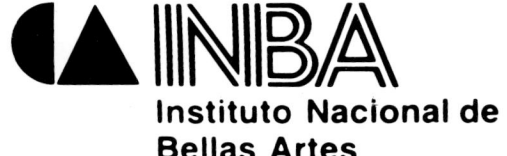
Instituto Nacional de
Bellas Artes

Photographers Credits

Pedro Hiriart, cover, 17, 19-23, 25-32, 34-35, 37-39, 41-43, 45, 47-55, 57, 59, 62 (left), 63, 66-67, 69-70 (lower), 71, 73, 75-77, 79, 81, 83, 93, 95, 97-101, 103, 105, 107-108, 110-115, 119, 127, 131-135, 137, 139, 141

Miguel Barbachan, 61, 62 (right)

Alberto Moreno, 65, 70 (upper)

Timothy Soar, 85, 87, 88, 89, 90, 91

Luis Gordoa, 123-125

Photographic Montage

José Muñoz Pedro 117, 129, 131

Models

Samuel Gabriel Vivar 57

Patricia Aguerrebere 119, 127

Perspective Views

Arturo Fajardo 120, 121

Editorial Director USA
Pierantonio Giacoppo

Chief Editor of Collection
Maurizio Vitta

Publishing Coordinator
Franca Rottola

Graphic Design
Paola Polastri

Editing
Martyn J. Anderson

Colour-separation
Litofilms Italia, Bergamo

Printing
Poligrafiche Bolis, Bergamo

First published January 1998

Copyright 1998
by l'Arca Edizioni

All rights reserved
Printed in Italy

ISBN 88-7838-033-4

González de León
Architecture as Art

Preface by
Teodoro
González de León

Introduction by
Mario
A. Arnaboldi

Contents

- 7   Preface *by Teodoro González de León*
- 9   Introduction *by Mario A. Arnaboldi*
- 15   Works
- 16   Banco Nacional de México Headquarters
- 24   Federal Law-Courts
- 36   Renewal of the National Auditorium
- 44   Fondo de Cultura Económica
- 56   Children's Museum
- 60   Site Museum at El Tajín
- 64   Hewlett-Packard Offices
- 72   Rufino Tamayo Square
- 78   Mexican Embassy in Belize
- 84   The Mexican Gallery at the British Museum
- 92   Arcos Bosques Corporativo
- 102   National Music Conservatory
- 116   Senate Building
- 122   Amsterdam House
- 126   Insurgentes Sur Office Block
- 136   Mexican Embassy in Berlin
- 142   Selected works
- 143   Biography

Preface

by Teodoro González de León

Architecture is a trade that we carry out through ideas and practice. Ideas constitute our personal vision of buildings. Practice modifies this vision, establishes boundaries and provides new ideas. Throughout my 48 years of regular practice, some ideas have disappeared, others have remained and new ones have emerged. The purpose of this preface is to comment briefly on these ideas.

I believe architecture is spatial configuration, construction and cultural representation. These three aspects are always present and inextricably linked. Space is shaped with volumes (volumes which wrap and unwrap space).

Space is shaped as a response to the climate and to site features and is also used to spread out human activities. I am interested in seeing buildings organized around "places" where people unavoidably meet around central spaces, such as patios or pedestrian streets, where users encounter each other and life sharing is the main form of interaction. Places where destiny unfolds, enriching our lives. In my recent works, I shape space by assembling different volumes into strictly calculated compositions which seem to be accidental. I am convinced, more than ever before, that it is through light - and the difficulties in managing it- that the composition of volumes is revealed. I believe, as Le Corbusier believes, that interiors exist only when they are flooded with light.

I am interested in handling access as an event: celebrating the place where visitors come into contact for the first time with these works. I have designed open lobbies which are arcades, which in turn, give us the opportunity to be in contact with the street. These open spaces are also clearances, insights of the city in architecture. In addition, I also believe that every building should establish a dialogue with the city. This is the greatest responsibility of architects working in huge and chaotic cities brought about by modern society. Our task is to ensure that every building is a benchmark identifying the place where it was constructed.

Talking about constructions, I am interested in showing how works can express the way they were executed, how they are supported and where their reinforcements lie. Works should express their tectonics (the poetry of their construction). In my works, I have avoided coatings: the structural materials make the facades. I am constantly searching for ways to reduce details. Concrete has been the prevailing material in my works, because it adapts itself to my formal aims and it responds to current technological developments in my country.

Building and shaping spaces are two of the three aspects of the architectural art. They require experience (Le Corbusier used to say that Mozart does not exist in architecture) and also, logical and rational thinking: they are a product of our awareness. But architecture inevitably carries within it the signs of the time and place where it was conceived. Architecture creates scenarios which represent our culture and with which we can identify.

The representations come from the subconscious, from our cultural background. This is the unscheduled part of architecture, the part which, when it becomes fine art, creates excitement that lasts beyond our age. It represents our age and has no spatial boundaries; it is international, but if it is genuine, its background is shot through with local expression.

It expresses the collective subconsciousness of each individual country.

The Architecture of Teodoro González de León

by Mario A. Arnaboldi

Whenever you admire the work of a great architect, you cannot help being amazed by the passion it exudes and the train of stylistic progress it displays. This is indeed the case with the works of architecture of Teodoro González de León, particularly those he designed between 1968 and 1996.

It ought to be pointed out right from the start that we are dealing with a true master of contemporary architecture: his projects mirror both his intriguingly original architectural models and his highly sophisticated constructions. González de León's architecture is the result of the kind of elaborate experimentation that goes into his paintings and of his natural ability to sketch out designs with great improvisation, gradually tempering them through his acute perception of forms. His work, in its entirety, is permeated with the expressive force of experimentation designed to construct form and space. The most intriguing thing of all is his determination to inject fresh life into sterile rationalism through the blistering modernity of his designs. This derives from both his practical experience and great love for a "trade" designed to serve man in general, rather than celebrate individuals.

As a dedicated disciple of Le Corbusier, González de León is a firm believer in the evolutionary development of architectural form. He actually draws on a technically correct approach to rationalism that manages to break free from the icy bonds of numbers and cold calculations, using his pen to give concrete form to the warmth of the Latin world and the force of South-American tradition. Obeying the tenets of Le Corbusier's school of thought, González de León seems to be following in his rationalist footsteps, drawing inspiration from nature to back up human labour.

González de León does not express his artistry like a landscape painter, who only depicts the external appearance of nature; he searches for its cause, scrutinises its form and living growth, thereby succeeding in forming syntheses that create genuine living organisms. Nevertheless, his work needs studying and analysing. We must be familiar with his work if we are really to come to terms with the latest developments in contemporary design; it is like getting to know a whole array of leading historical figures in architecture just by studying this one architect and his work. Making his acquaintance is just another way of nourishing our sacred love for the art of building. Teodoro González de León is forever showing just how much he deserves his place among the ranks of great architects, constantly inspiring all those who want to take up his legacy.

González de León also has the gift of transgressing the norms through simple diagonal strokes, as the forms he composes and designs he creates clearly exhibit a desire to be almost born again, as if he had some unknown DNA inside him which, as it reproduces, updates and injects fresh life into his works. As we analyse his design work, we cannot help being intrigued by the continual progress he has made and noticing that it clearly carries within it the entire process of architectural development of the age in which we live. The work of architecture that truly epitomises these cultural events in the evolution of design is unquestionably the Arcos Bosques Corporativo complex in Mexico City, both due to its sheer size and the spontaneous transparency of its basic design.

Given its scale, this work of architecture is actually a sort of small city. Incidentally, this and other projects designed by González de León have been on display at an exhibition organised by the Rufino Tamayo Museum of International Contemporary Art in Mexico City. The exhibition of González de León's work provided a great chance to analyse the intriguing originality of his architectural models, whose sophisticated construction features, as mentioned above, are, most unusually, actually inspired by his paintings.

González De León is an artistic narrator of forms and materials, which explains why the Arcos Bosques Corporativo project is such a richly expressive design that openly confronts the theoretical tenets of Le Corbusier with great erudition. González de León is a direct descendent of that warmly human vein of rationalism that was so successful in expressing its faith in the evolutionary development of architectural design. There can be no doubting the technical skill with which this contemporary master brings the coldness of rationalism and numbers to life. His architectural personality literally oozes with the underlying logic behind his own peculiar architectural method and idiom, as he shapes architectural space into stylistic narratives.

The most striking aspect of these designs is the debt they owe to Le Corbusier, as González de León strives to follow in his master's footsteps: the natural surroundings are the real inspiration behind images constructed within a carefully gauged framework. Yet, he never draws on a kind of "hyperreality" that only reveals the most obvious side of nature - i.e. the part nineteenth-century artists where so keen on, preferring instead to delve down to the causes, form and generative force behind things, forming syntheses that create genuine organisms. No school of architecture can afford to ignore his work, which provides everyone in the profession with new sources of knowledge and approaches to design. His method draws architectural rhythms from the logic of numbers, shaping them around spatial arrhythmias. It is a concrete example of the kind of deep respect for the art of architecture that is such a vital ingredient in our profession. The thematic contents of González de León's projects are the real key to the artistry of his architecture. His designs for offices, houses and sports facilities shape space into micro urban settlements which physically embody his country's real traditions. This is why he strives to create new behavioural patterns for the future. The roots of his architecture are deeply entrenched in the ground, as he constructs his service areas, storerooms and car parks, which are usually treated as marginal functions, in organised spaces which, as they emerge from the earth, together form a sort of "credo" of the Modern Movement, a vertical layering of the complexity of the urban environment. On a functional level, as both public and private structures, his works are designed to incorporate a carefully defined functional programme. Every project is treated like an authentic vertical or horizontal fragment of the cityscape with its own self-sufficient structure, capable of meeting the quantitative-qualitative demands of their urban surroundings.

González de León's works often incorporate a diagonal slash, as if to charge his projects with a different sort of three-dimensional dynamics geared to the surroundings through highly rationalistic and dissymmetrically rigorous designs. This is often expressed through materials used to give full force to his stylistic intentions which, through their diversity, draw on a basic pattern of forms to establish some sort of identity between the interior and exterior fabrics. He often uses glass, a transparent lightweight material, to exploit light in a strangely specific way and create a powerfully coherent sense of desecrating form. Teodoro González de León's work shows why he deserves his place among the great architects, thanks particularly to the agility with which he moves about his profession.

His work is also an inspiration for anyone keen to take up his legacy. It ought to be pointed out that, not only as an architect, but also as a painter or artist in the strictest sense of the word, he is always trying to perfect his own personal poetics. Thanks to his work, he has managed to gain his clients' respect, steering them clear from the idea of making an easy profit and encouraging them to focus on transforming the built environment. Gonzàlez de León is for ever striving to work for the community as a whole, something that clearly emerges from all his works of architecture and the messages they send out to his younger colleagues.

It is also worth noting that González de León usually manages to handle the negative aspects of rather absentminded clients who are still an influential negative force on the contemporary architectural scene.

His skill lies in the way he has tackled these problems with such dignity. He seems to firmly believe that that our profession could lay down the rules for change, if only it embodied the general will of the entire community.

González de León's design work strives to combine all the various disciplines of art and science. His artistry devises new ways of changing society; although, unfortunately, outside interferences sometimes affect his original ideas.

It is almost as if he were recycling the history of architecture: in other words, he attracts attention to those key features of "cultured" design aimed at continuing tradition.

His projects tend to suggest that architecture will continue to work along the lines of linguistic methodology, designed to inject fresh life into both design and the sober rules of town-planning, for a long time to come. This would seem to be the only way of transforming architectural space.

We cannot help wondering whether González de León would not be better advised to widen his stylistic horizons to embrace the entire territory, instead of confining them to just a few simple signs. Relationships, conversations, the power of the written and spoken word have been completely lost, communication no longer serves to raise the general standard and quality of life, but, on the contrary, consumerism now provides a model for speculating on society.

González de León is notable for the proper use he makes of signs; the way he uses "stone" to write is reminiscent of a letter Michelangelo wrote to Vasari in 1558 about his project for the Laurentian Library in Rome that marked the transition to a new era in style. This creative act of architecture, inspired by the sad modesty of a genius, delves back into the past. This is a clear allusion to the organic nature of González de León's work, as he struggles in the construction workshop and experiments, empirically, into building research. Herein lies the true force of experimentation and the legacy bequeathed to us by our ancestors, together with a clear sense of moving beyond matter, shaped by man, into the timeless realms of sacred universality, into a way of "feeling" architecture that is real battle between creation and power. These are the clearest features emerging from González de León's work and philosophical thinking, from the use he makes of its signs and symbols, and from the formal tools he employs to achieve these ends. His projects are ideally designed to show us how to control space so that it turns into a trace in time left by man.

The best way to analyse his architectural signs is to take a closer look at the tools he uses: models and sketches that never suffice to show just how feasible his constructions are.
He composes and combines various parts into a whole, but the real secret is just how he combines them and what he uses to do it. The tool he has used to create his designs is not so much his pencil as his very

heart and soul.

The sensations his projects draw out of reality literally envelop us and carry us off beyond mere images into a deeper experience of life. All this takes on a meaning that needs to be decoded, classified and assimilated, so that it becomes the common denominator in all his different ways of feeling. His seemingly endless wealth of knowledge is judge and jury of the stimuli reaching our brains and conscious awareness.

This universal process, common to us all, cannot be transcended; the difference lies in the extent of our desire or laziness in striving after such hard earned conquests.

González de León, as a designer, is well aware that, generally speaking, there is an average level of basic intelligence and knowledge. Love and humility are the key factors in determining just how marked the differences are.

Unfortunately, fears are often insurmountable obstacles manifested in a certain uneasiness about anything new, an inability to adapt to the unexpected and so on. Together this all creates a negative attitude to complexity. The fears implicit in his projects take the form of a certain refusal to engage, which can only really be overcome by being carefully analysed, counteracted and restrained.

The way he "cuts" through space determines how we actually observe architecture, actually bringing it to life. It is almost as if his works were instructing us that to train an architect to experiment we must first suffer in the flesh to make the mind immune as well, as part of one single process; a weak and fearful mind sullies and distorts our thoughts which, in this way, are filled with nothing but fear and danger.

González de León is clearly indicating that both man and society as a whole need something quite different; they need to feel safe and sound, through the work of those who have shown they can offer such security. New needs will inevitably emerge along unexplored paths capable of giving life back the kind of flavour that man still hungers for. His architecture really can achieve this goal through its strength and certainty. Of course, we will all find our own way of experiencing this feeling of certainty. It cannot be passed on like a scientific fact; it grows within us and can only be nourished through all those concepts based on reality. It is much harder to free the spirit of someone whose preconceived ideas actually derive from cultural shortcomings in the field of design. It takes determination and a strong will to achieve intellectual knowledge and architectural know-how; the efforts required to fill our souls with knowledge are immense.

St. Thomas Aquinas once said: "I must empty my soul so that God can enter in". Clearing the hearts and minds of anyone drawing near the work of a "master" is usually the task of images, critics, teachers, and even the press, as they teach how the art of design ought to be viewed, cleansing the intellect from the false legacy of the past and distracting us from academic fetishes.

It is up to them to open up our minds to these projects, their cultural connotations, underlying nature, and characteristic features, so that we can find within ourselves the strength to overcome our intellectual inhibitions.

González de León's work also teaches us to avoid the same old repetitive readings of models bereft of any evolutionary force, forcing us to follow the principles of perception common to all men that are at the very foundations of the science of design. The chance to analyse a complete collection of project designs of this standard allows us to grasp their true stylistic co-ordinates, which are: topology, margins, interaction-with the existing built environment, relations with artefacts, interaction with nature, scale, comfort, and a capacity to cater for high-tech cabling. These are the real features of González de León's architectural space.

The best way to elaborate on these "bullet points" - the list could go on for ever with his designs - is to draw on the idiom of the latest generations of architects as they prepare to enter the world of architecture.

González de León's work calls for a careful analysis of the psychology of vision that systematically controls every instant of perception and runs through our intricate system of mind and soul before providing the input for artistic creativity. These are the features of this collection of projects that cannot be found in the historical past, but in González de León himself as his own stylistic artistry enhances his cognitive capacities through a carefully gauged combination of signs. This "master's" skill and expertise seem to place him at the hub of a world that is splintering into a vast array of different disciplines and specialist fields of learning. This is the imaginary world of the industrial building process, evident even in these works of architecture, culture bursting out in all directions and interested only in brains capable of creating specialist programmes designed to make money.

This is exemplified by those American engineers who are capable of commissioning and controlling feasible operating systems through the individual parts of the system itself, but who, at the same time, are totally oblivious to any form of innovation.

We can only endorse Gropius's universalism when he says: "I believe that every ordinary human being is capable of understanding form. The real problem is not any eventual lack of creative ability, but rather finding the way to bring it into view".

It is also true that supplementing our knowledge is extremely important if we want to come to terms with everything involved in architectural design; even experiences need to be classified if they are to be placed at the right point along the path of design. González de León's determination to improve on our rather arid social system forces him to consider a radically new definition of creativity as embodied in contemporary society. He seems to be trying to ground new principles drawing on newly emerging scientific theories to create new avant-garde models capable of reconciling spirit and matter. Refusing to conform to the uninspired symbolic order dominating the contemporary scene, Gonzáles de León is capable of sparking off those contrasts that project his work onto the borderline between the rational and irrational, the static and dynamic.

Despite all these complex considerations, his work preserves that enthusiasm and simplicity that have characterised his whole career; González de León is clearly aware that there is no room for pedantry and presumptuousness in architecture, on the contrary, it is a simple, natural expression of man's inherent artistry. This is what separates those who feel that architecture is a way of giving free rein to their instincts, using it for their own personal ends, and those who treat it as a genuine mission. Such short-cuts have no place in González de León's design work; his pure instinct and conscience are ever present in his work without interfering with each other. These intimate qualities immediately attract our attention as we observe the gradual evolution in his stylistic experimentation, confirming the progress he has made throughout his career.

According to Cesar Pelli you have to be in your sixties to be a real architect. Unfortunately the confused state of our inspirationless society makes it hard to weed out those opportunists who are bringing a wave of moral ignorance into our profession. Only by drawing on the creative force in the works of architecture outlined here will we find the strength to carry on believing that our profession has any real future.

Teodoro González de León is now at the height of his creative powers but, alas, many of his designs are destined to remain at the drawing board. What a pity that his new projects will probably never get the chance to shine in all their splendour. Their perfect symbiosis of elegance, luminosity, composure and functionality would be real jewels for the towns and cities in which they could be built. González de León's work openly declares his admiration for such architects as Alvar Aalto and Mies van der Rohe, yet, like all those architects who grew up at the dawn of the Modern Movement, he is and always will be a disciple of
Le Corbusier. It is his ambition to bring these great names back in

vogue, believing as he does that they have been forgotten and buried in a past from which nothing can be salvaged.

González de León has been more successful than most in bringing his works to life by drawing on their mythological force. Few architects have shown his modesty and discretion. As Roland Barthes said "the relative insignificance of dullness is preferable to the intolerance of blandness". Blandness and dullness mark the boundaries between criticism and knowledge in all his works. A sense of blandness is mirrored in the realistic image of his work, gradually decoded by history. The "dullness" is hard to grasp, but it serves to break with rationalism as it is conventionally understood, in order to bring the hidden signs of architectural innovation to the surface.

His work seems oblivious to history and actually outside the realms of linguistic intricacy, although it does exude a certain way of reading "life" and hence "reality". Teodoro González de León draws on all his powers of seduction to rediscover these attributes and pass them on to anyone admiring the work of a true designer of human space. It is as if everything conceivably imaginable in the dreams of architectural design, in the socio-spiritual functions it places at man's disposal, and in the active imagination of its users, all vanish at the very moment you observe his "design". He manages to intrigue us in two separate ways: firstly through the image projected by his designs and then through their surroundings or in other words everything beyond mere image, such as the "timber" of the sound he instils in his architectural space, its walls, the light he lets flood into its spaces, and the weight of its structures as they interact with the outside. All this guarantees that his works of architecture are genuinely at people's disposal. To counteract hidden traces of the architecture of the past, González de León has incorporated a series of events into his work to instil a sense of mere conjecture. Judging by his work, González de León is neither docile nor compliant; he seems to be capable of hovering in a sense of lightness capable of contrasting the strangeness of popular idiom. Nevertheless, he has a much gentler and more compliant attitude towards the world itself, even the world of architectural image, although he is certainly keen to keep his distance.

Works

Mexico City, 1986-1989

Banco Nacional de México Headquarters

Owner
Banco Nacional de México

Architects
Teodoro González de León
Abraham Zabludovsky

Collaborator
José Maria Larios

Interior design
Luis de Regil

Structural design
Colinas de Buen, S. A.

Air-conditioning and electric design
Tecnoproyectos, S.C.

Hydraulics and sanitary design
G.H.A. y Asociados, S.A.

Construction area
13,640 sq.m.

The building is located in the old part of Mexico City, right at the corner of avenida Venustiano Carranza and calle de Palma. It is actually an extension of the Condes de San Mateo de Valparaíso Building designed by Francisco Guerrero y Torres in 1772.

This project clearly highlights González de León's great skill at handling a historical building, treating the past with great expertise without trampling all over it. His architectural style adapts perfectly to the gradual evolution of architectural design. Even the building facade fits in smoothly with the old building, adding something new of its own.

The design reiterates the same patterns and rhythms of the old columns. The facade stands at the same height as Condes de San Mateo de Valparaíso Building, leaving its own powerful imprint on the urban surroundings.

A corner tower completes the road front drawing on the same structural relations as the adjacent building.

The H-shape windows, typical of eighteenth-century Mexican architecture, are incorporated in González de León's own personal design style with great skill and cunning.

This enables González de León to leave the pattern of columns and openings as it is, providing the chance to repeat every other important feature of the Francisco Guerrero y Torres Building in a contemporary idiom. The "texture" of the facade is created out of a blend of white marble and red volcanic sand, both mixed with cement. This allows a sort of continuity between the new and old facades, without any clashing.

This is González de León's first project on such a historically important building and once again his expertise has injected the project with quality and style, enabling it to face up to any comparison with the city or its old works of architecture.

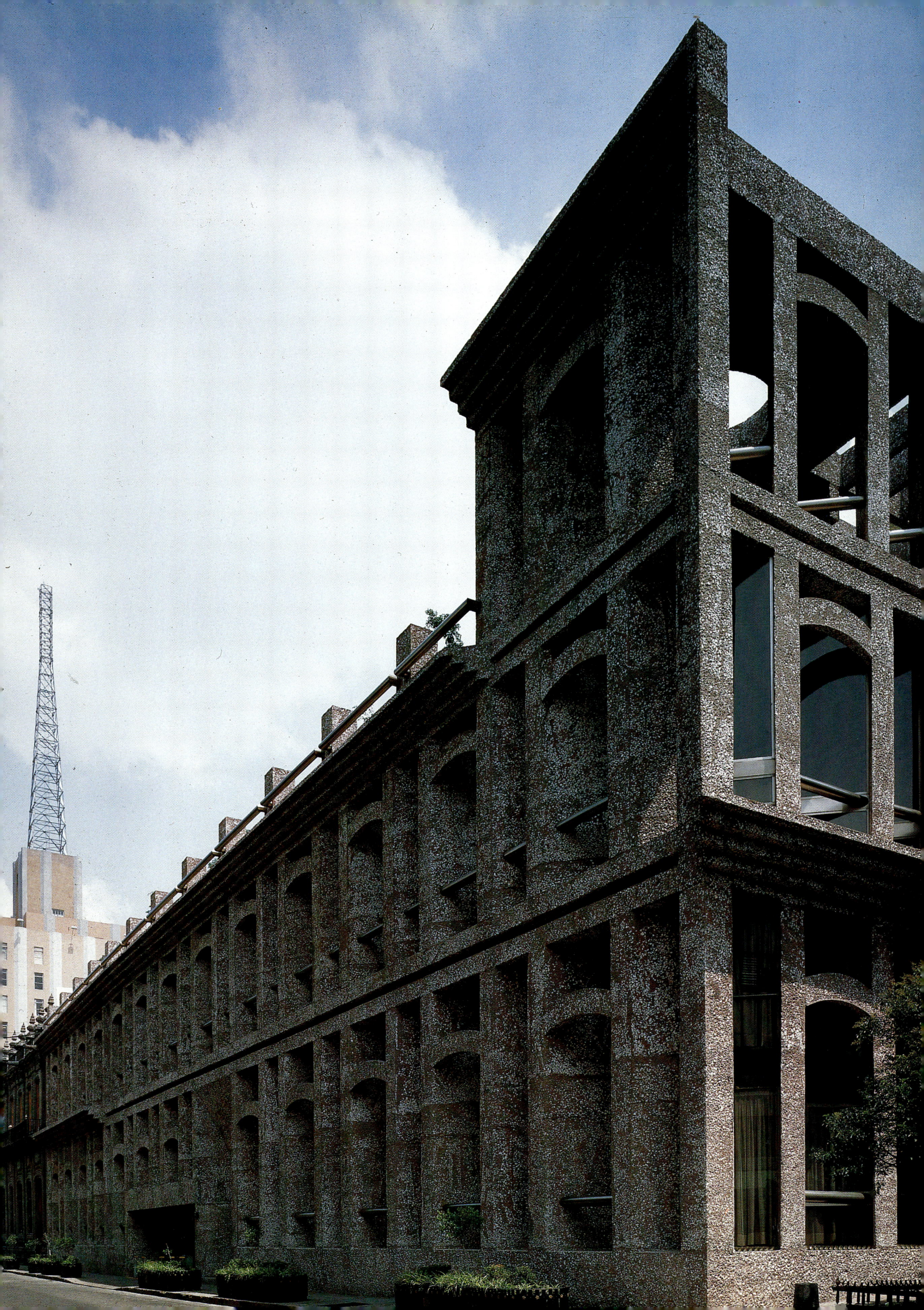

South elevation of the extension to the headquarters of the Banco Nacional de México. Below, ground floor plan and detail of the facade sliced through with cuts that evoke the pattern of windows on the Condes de San Mateo de Valparaíso Building dating back to 1772, to which the new extension is attached.

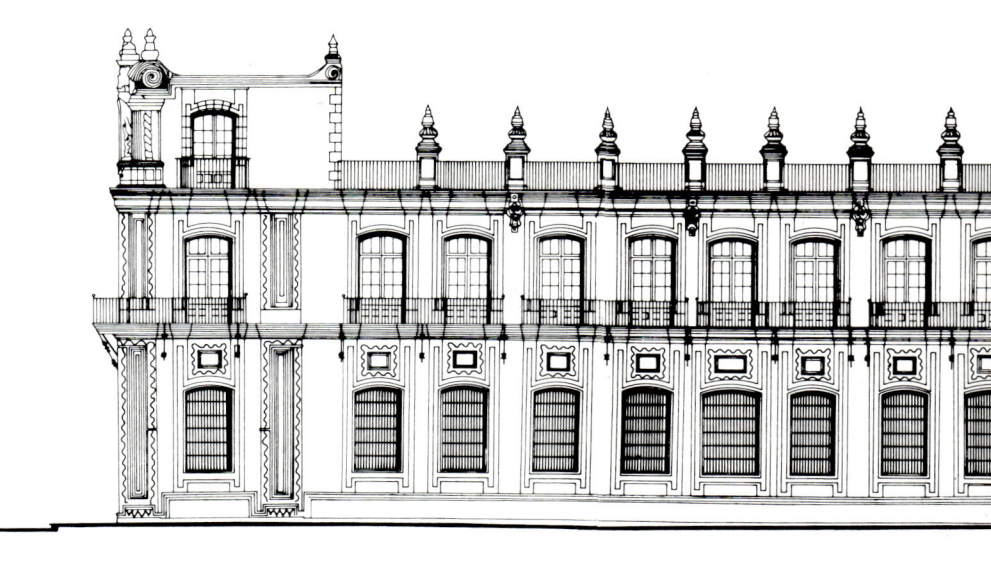

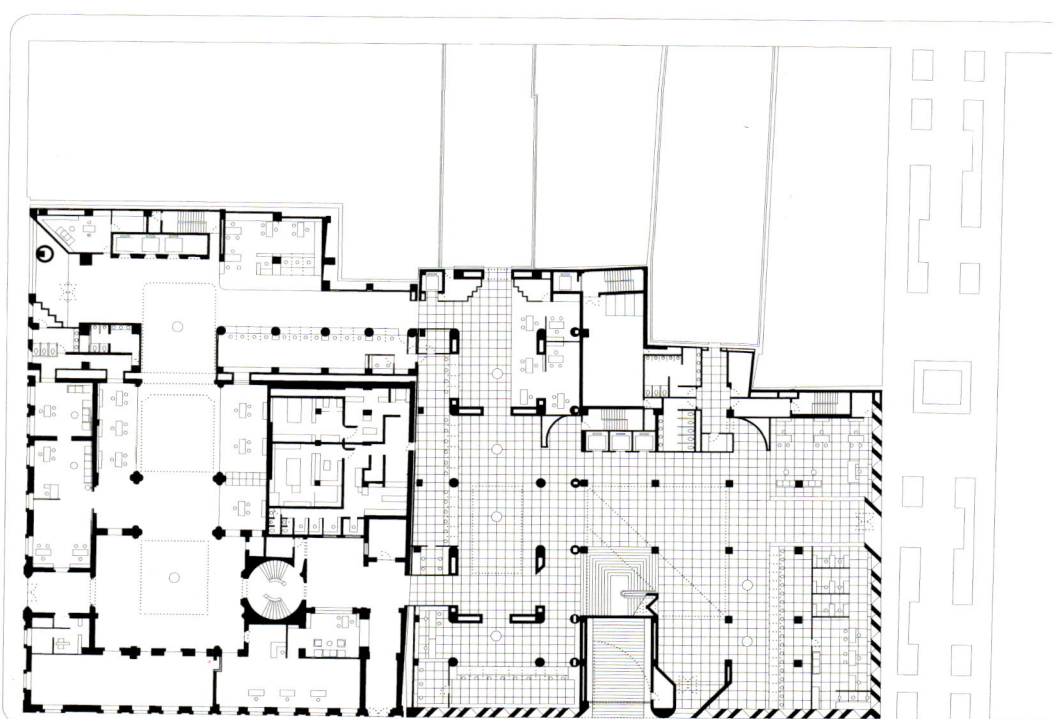

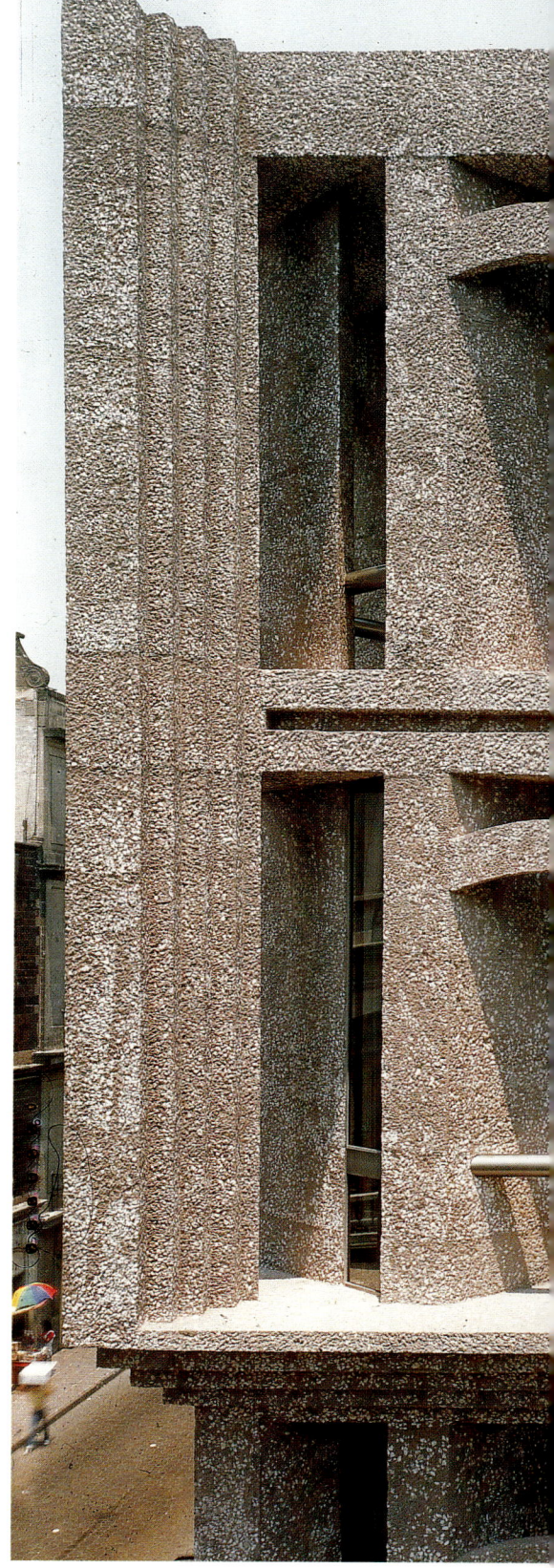

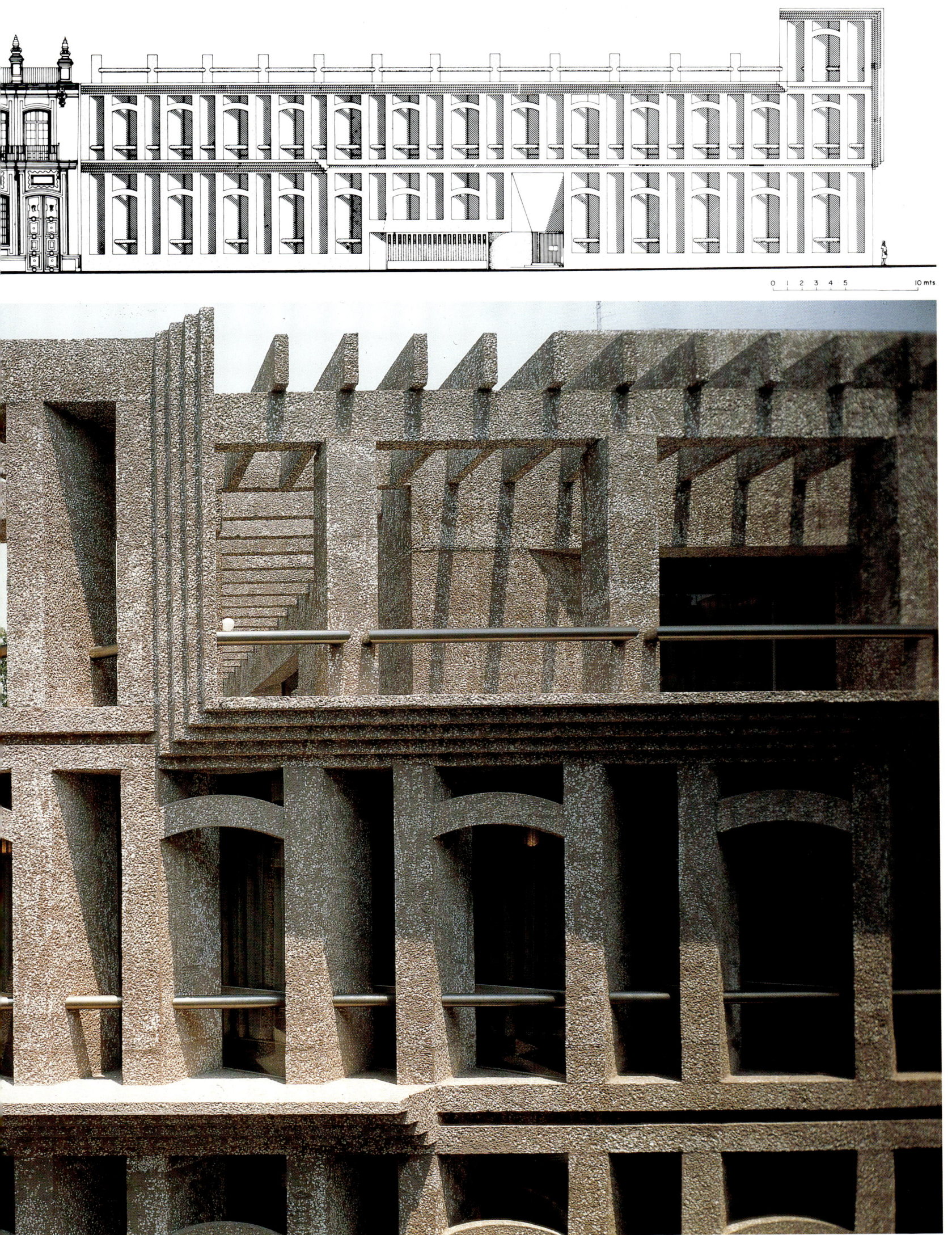

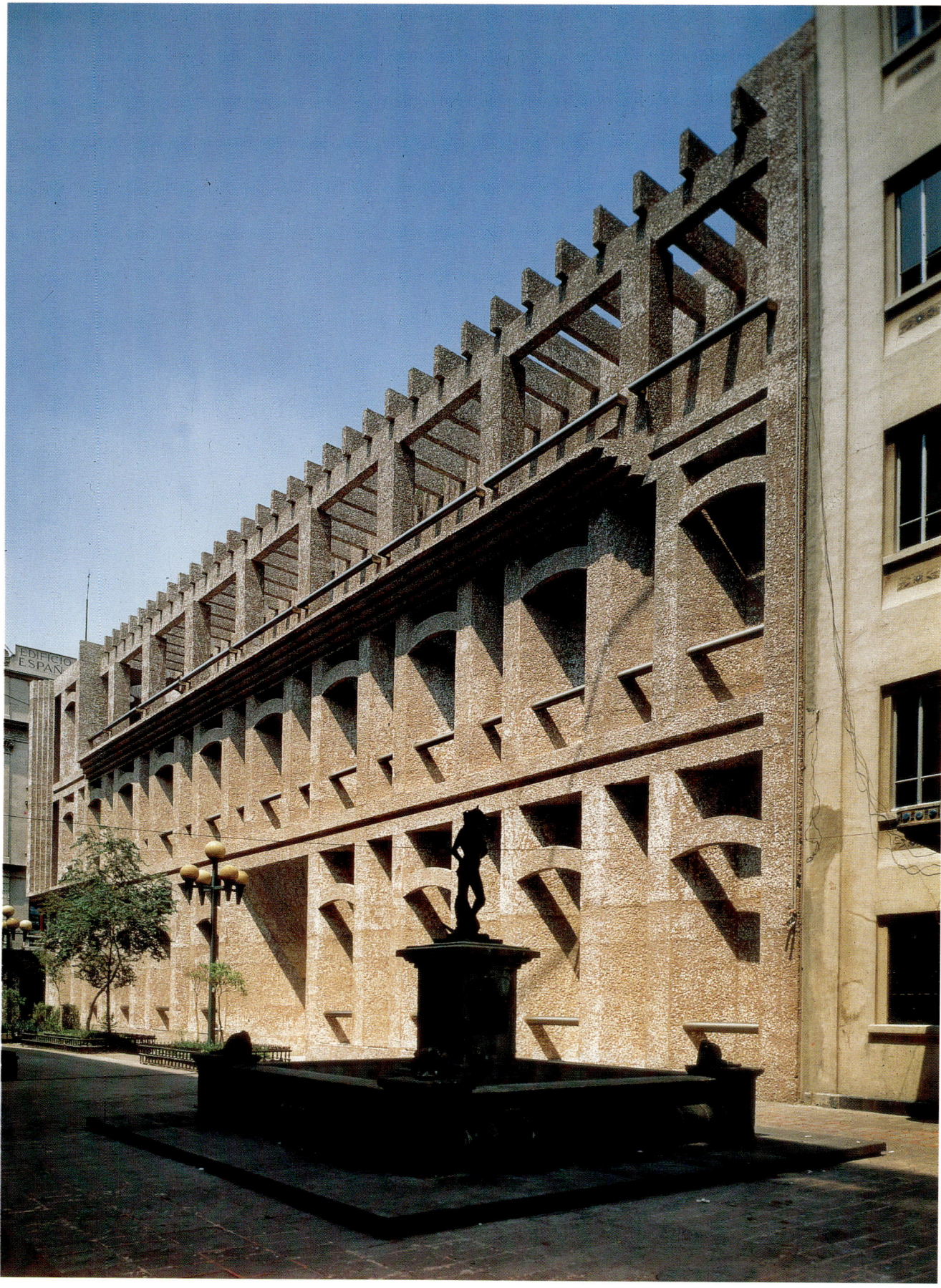

Detail of the facade along Calle de Palma. The texture of the facade is a mixture of white marble and red volcanic grains of sand mixed with cement. Opposite page, one of the stairways cutting through the interior lobbies.

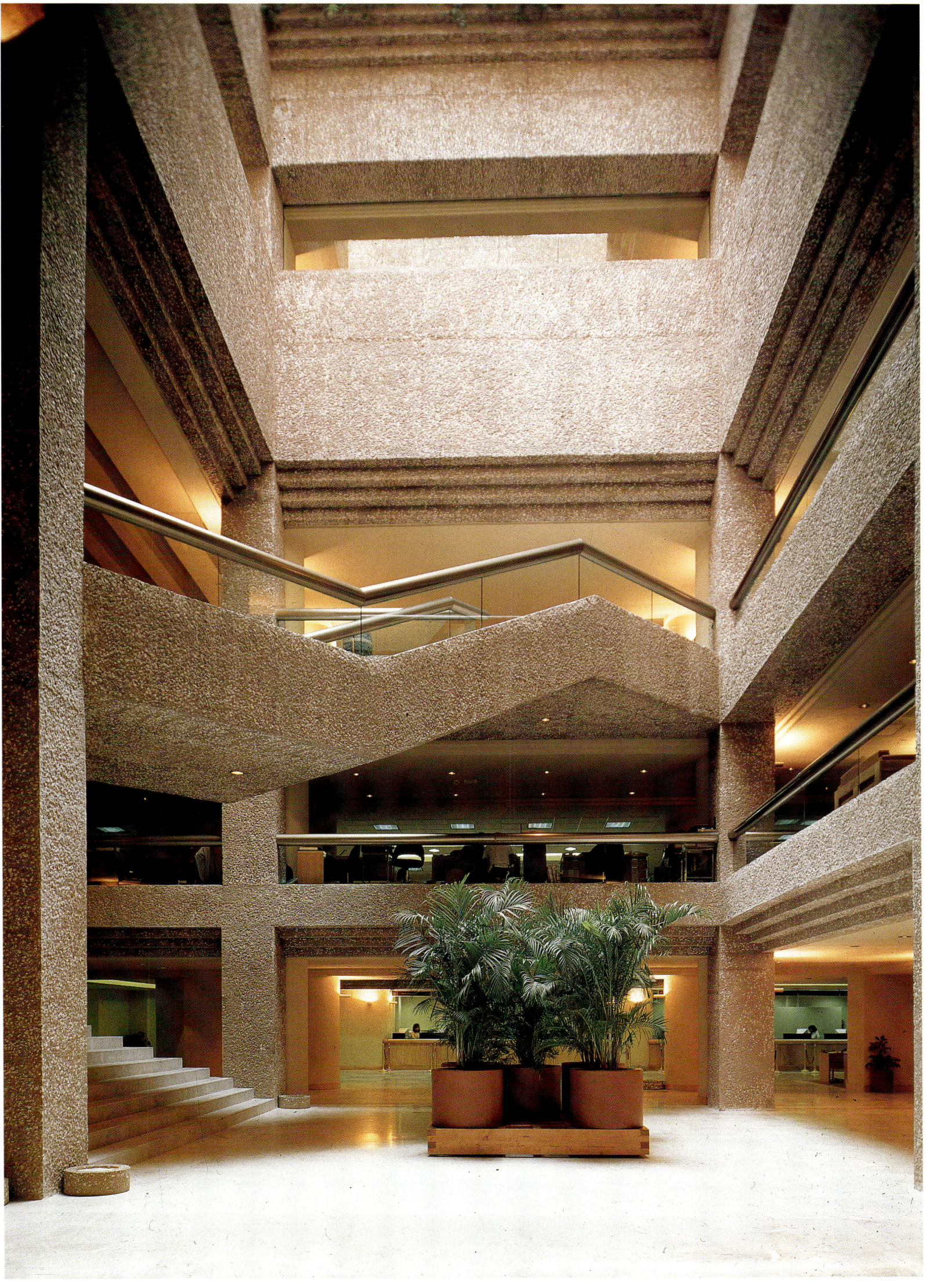

Details of the portico constructed on the building's upper balcony.

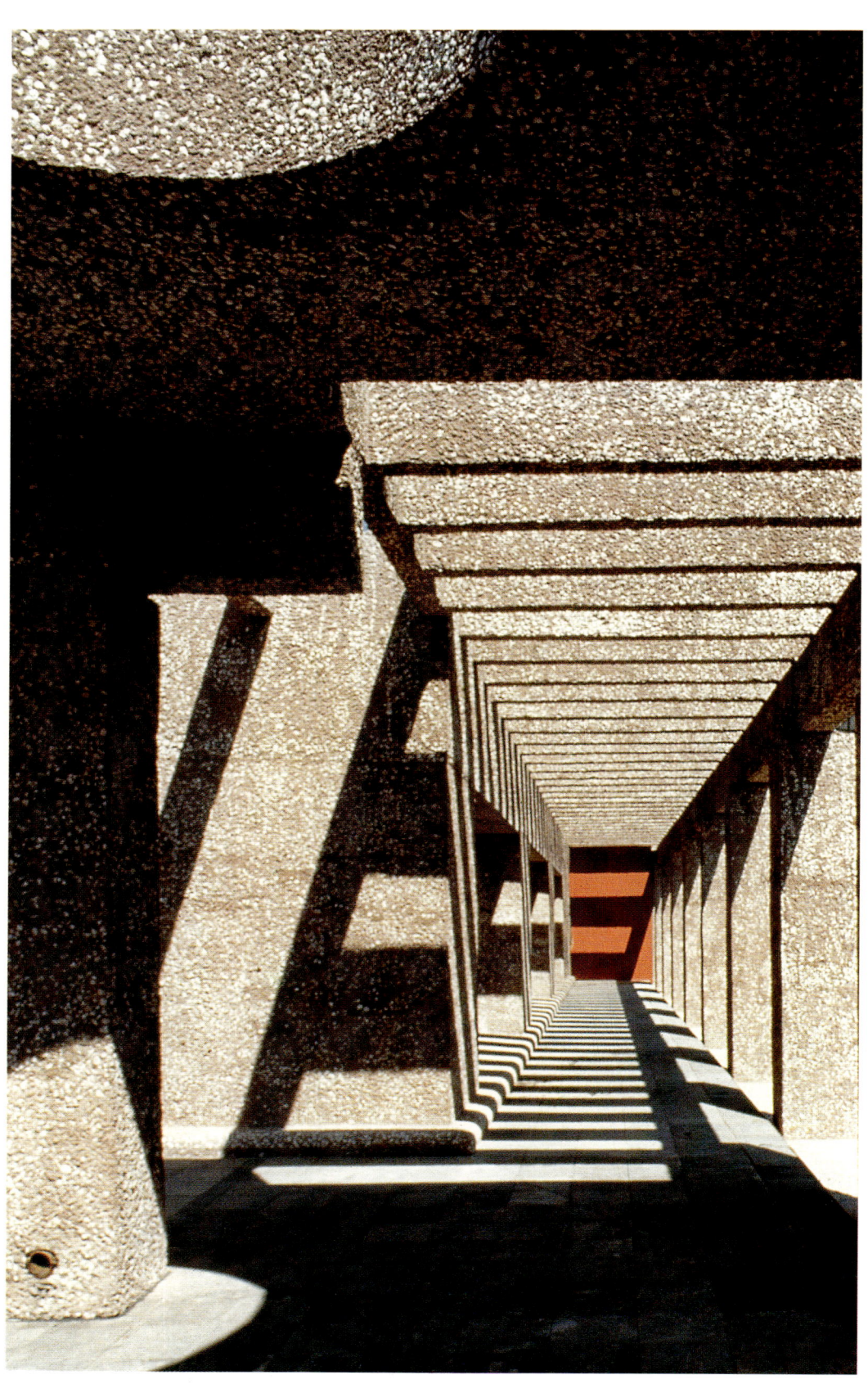

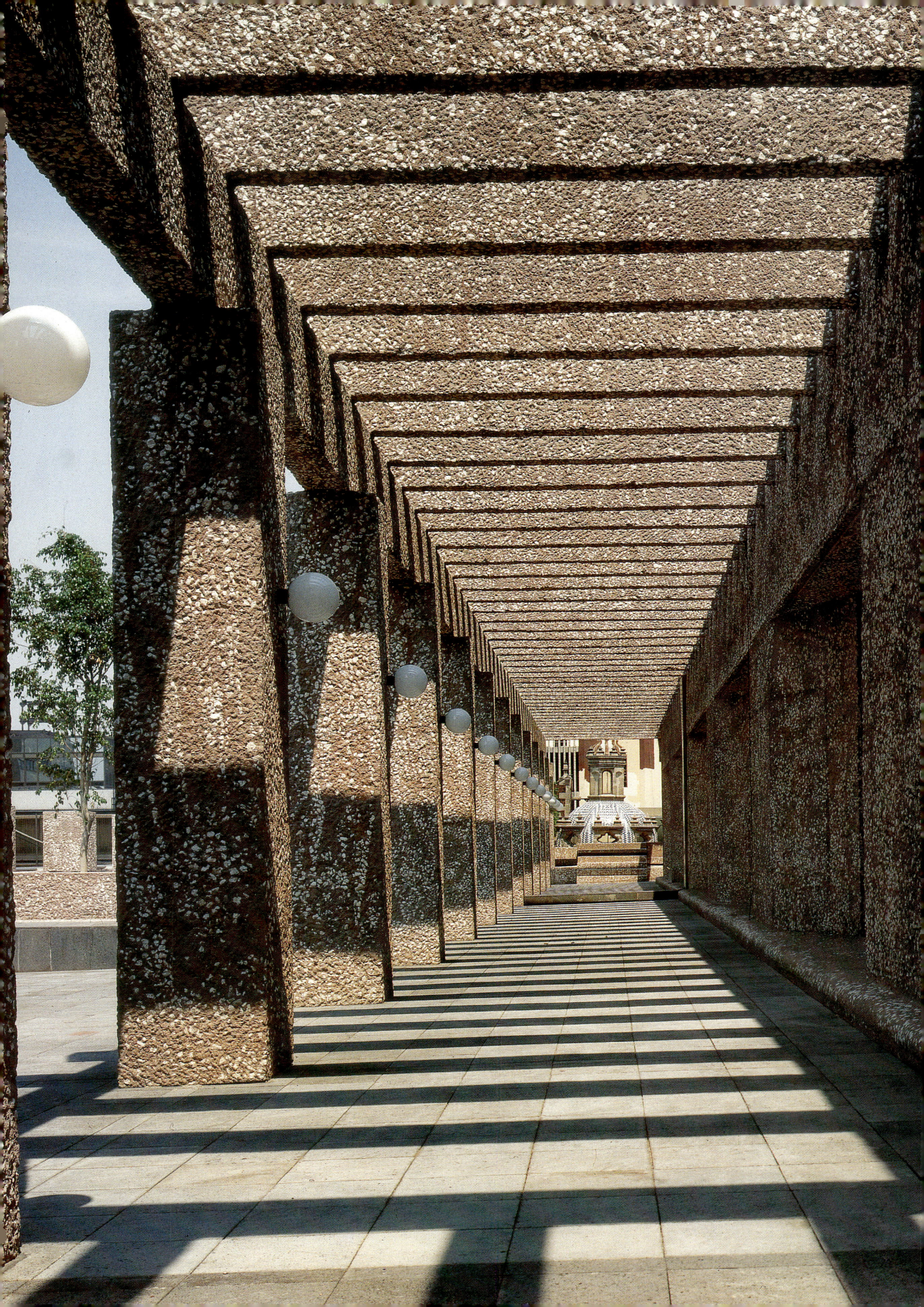

Mexico City, 1987-1992

Federal Law-Courts

Owner
Suprema Corte de Justicia de la Nación

Architects
Teodoro González de León
J. Francisco Serrano
Carlos Tejeda

Collaborator
Antonio Rodríguez

Interior design
José Ignacio de Abiega

Structural design
Diseño y Supervisión, "DYS", S.C.

Air-conditioning design
Tecnoproyectos, S.C.

Electric design
COESA

Hydraulics and sanitary design
GHA y Asociados, S.C.

Construction area
60,000 sq.m.

Designed along with J. Francisco Serrano and Carlos Tejeda the new Mexico City Law-Courts contains approximately twentyfour law-courts, thirtytwo legal offices, an auditorium, a library, and a complex service area.

The building is actually close to the city's main Law-House which was badly damaged during the earthquake in 1985. The building's four stories hinge around a central "path", 290 metres long, whose pattern of approximately 12-metre-tall columns form the building axis.

The ends of the building incorporate, on one side, the high-level entrance offering a panoramic view of the old part of Mexico City and, on the other side, all the various service facilities. Certain details of this project bring out González de León's elegant mastery of design.

The interiors are designed to jointly interact together independently and be as easy to move around as possible.

The interior spaces could indeed be described as meeting places for exchanging information, free from the bonds of any form of internal circulation.

González de León seems to have put his design expertise to much firmer use than usual, constructing a central axis to support the entire building structure. Transferred outside, this has a powerful, imposing impact on the cityscape.

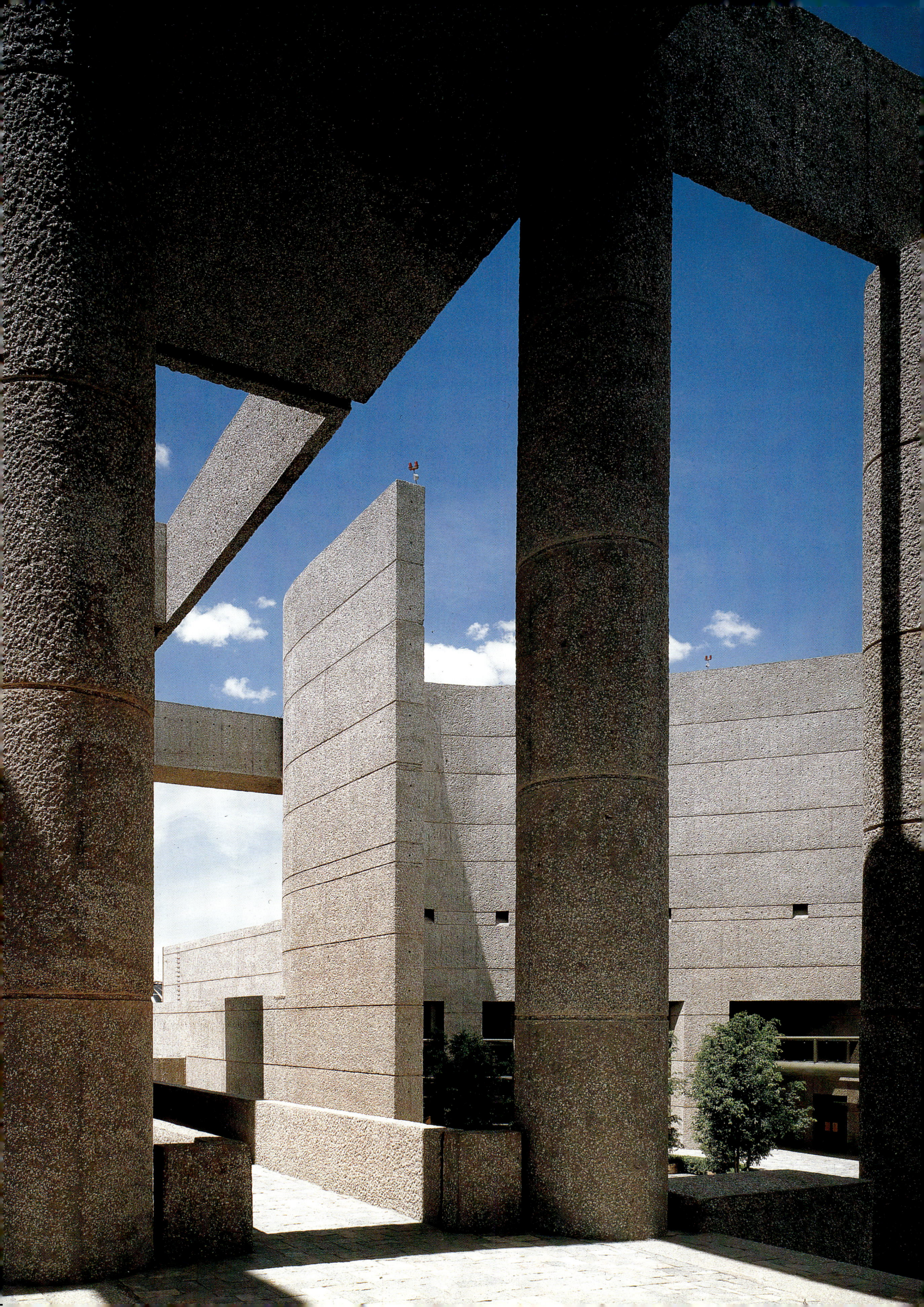

Below, site plan. Right and opposite page, two of the building entrances opening onto the 290-metre-long central "path" forming the building axis.

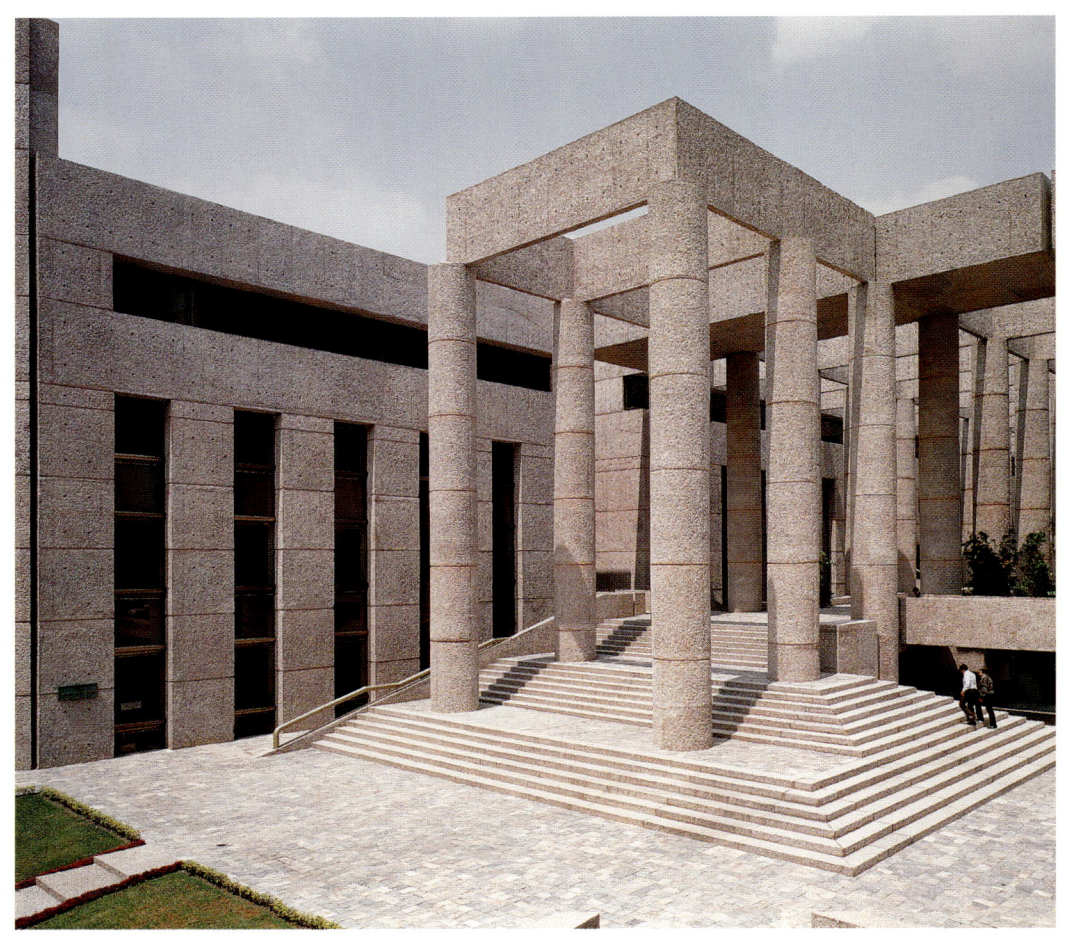

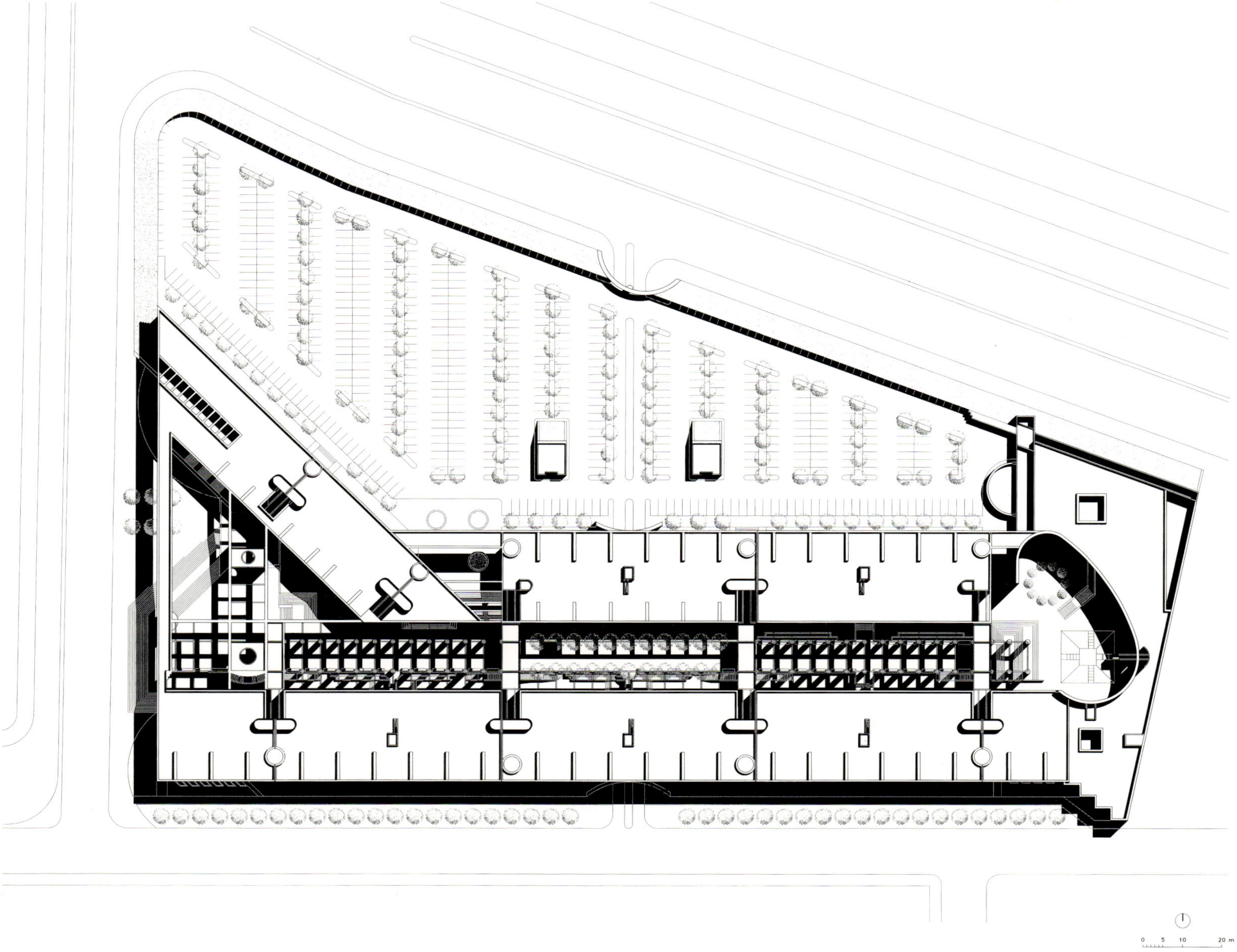

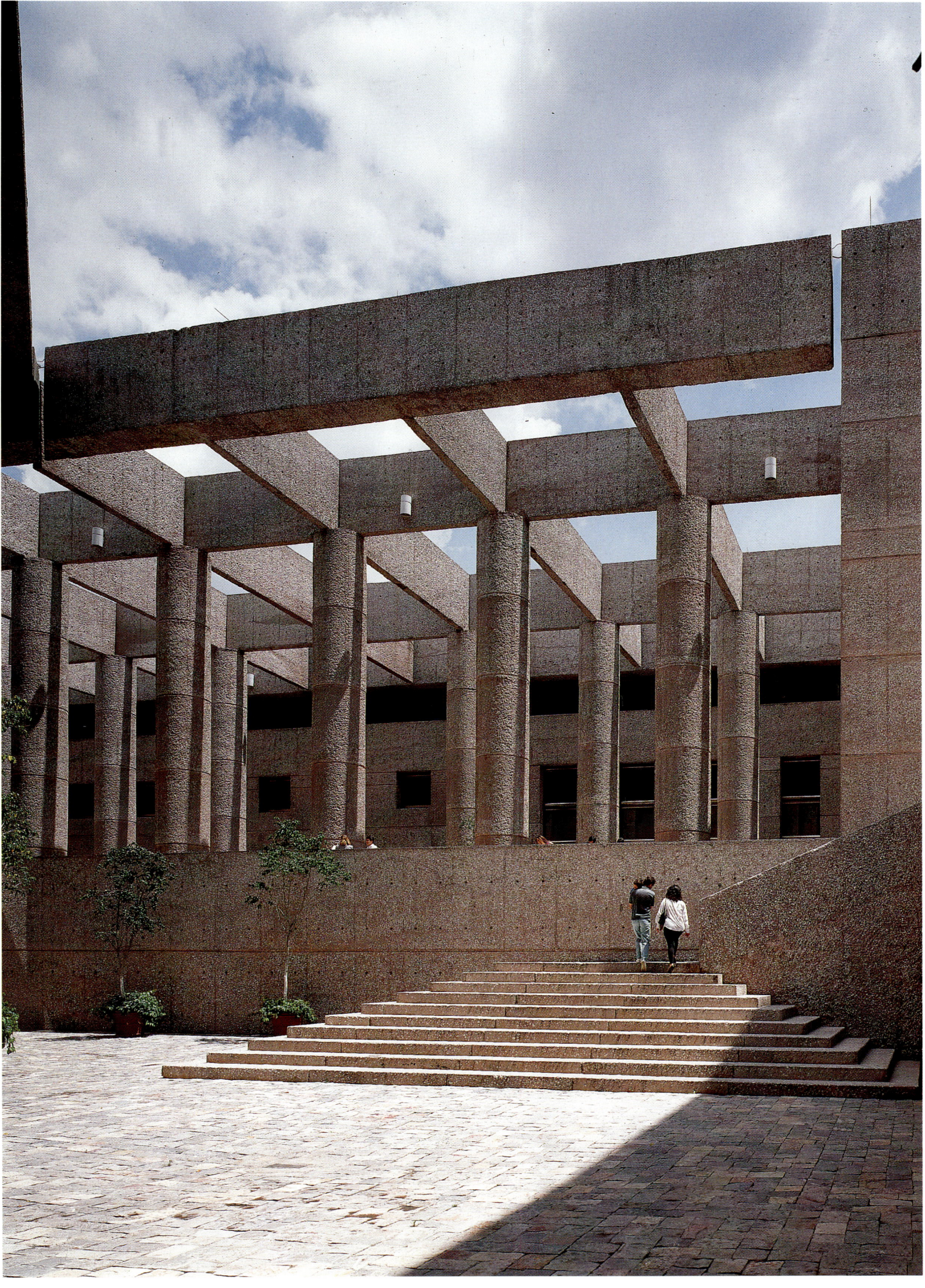

Below, outside entrance to the building. Bottom of page and opposite page, the end section of the central axis.

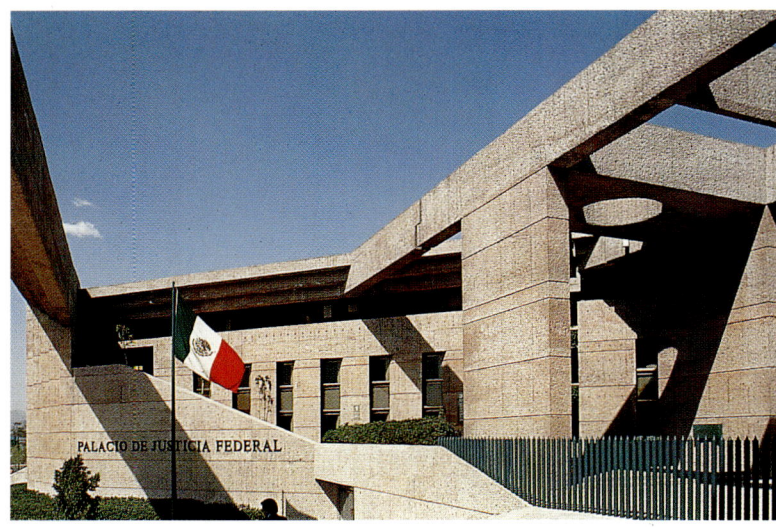

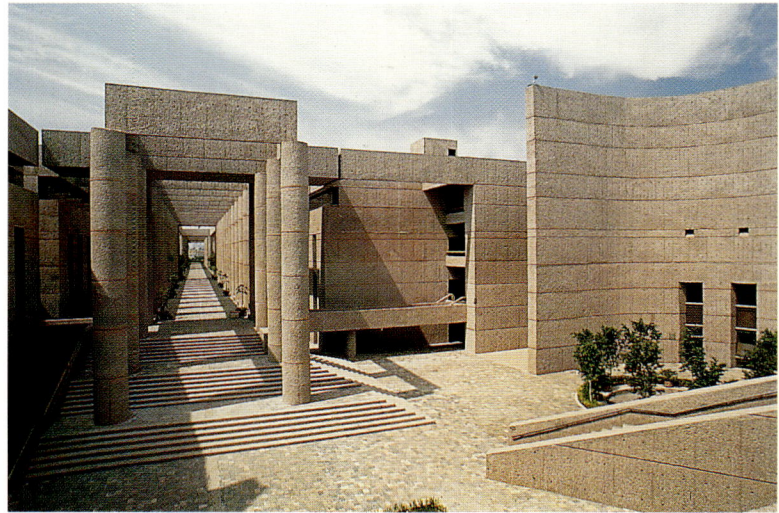

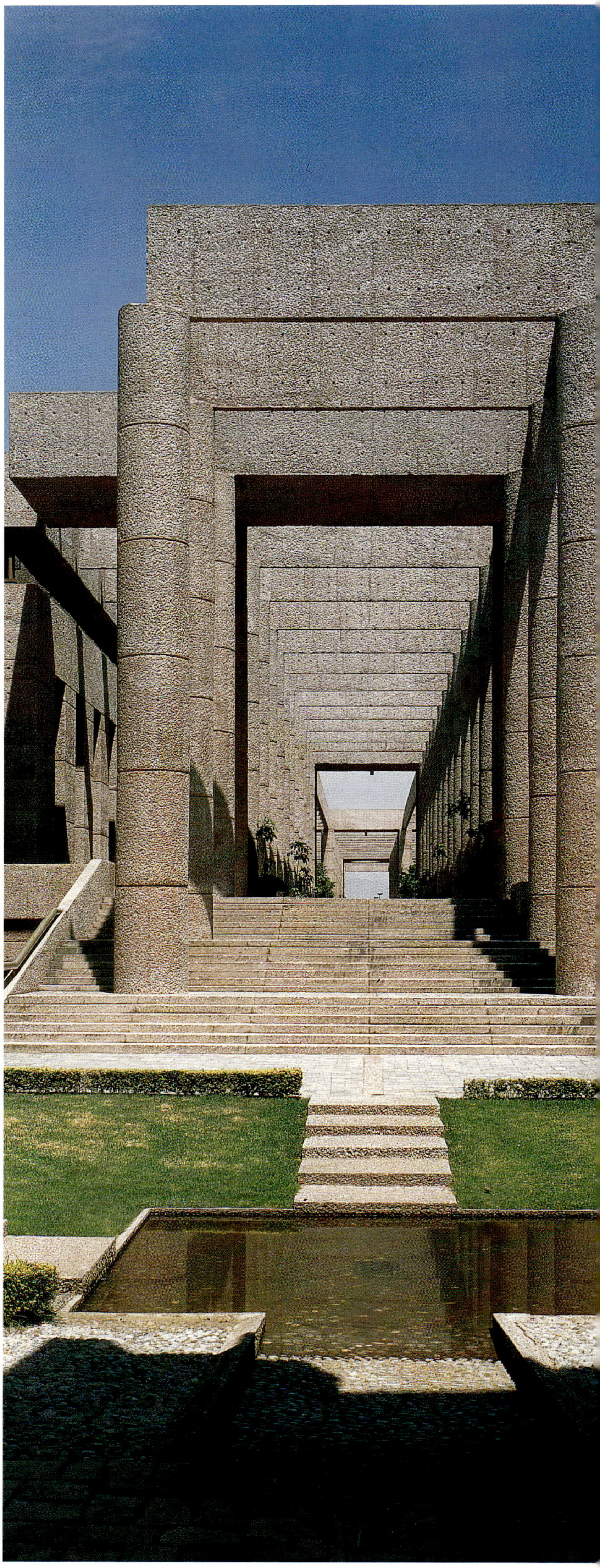

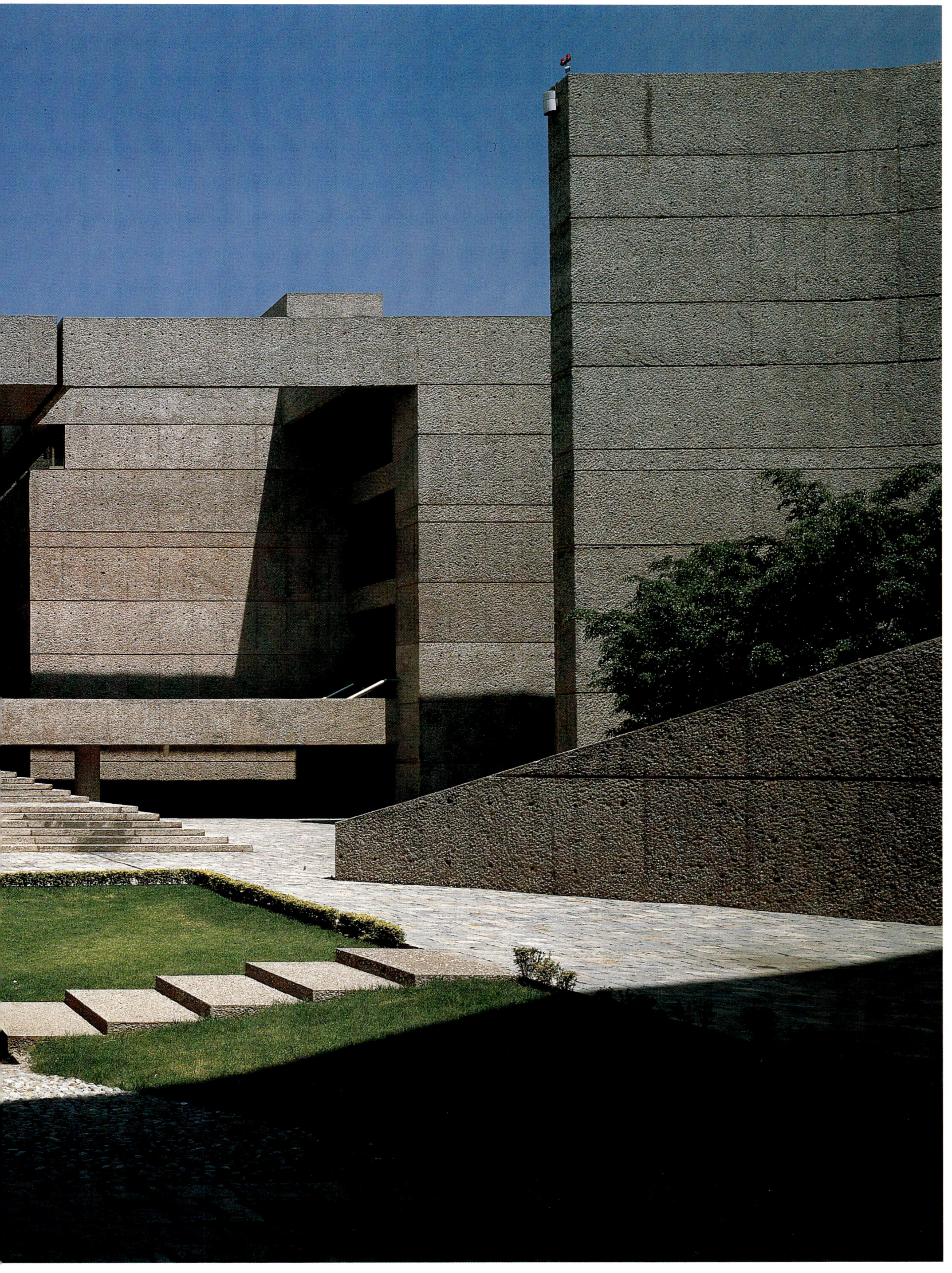

The main facade showing the monumental building entrance.

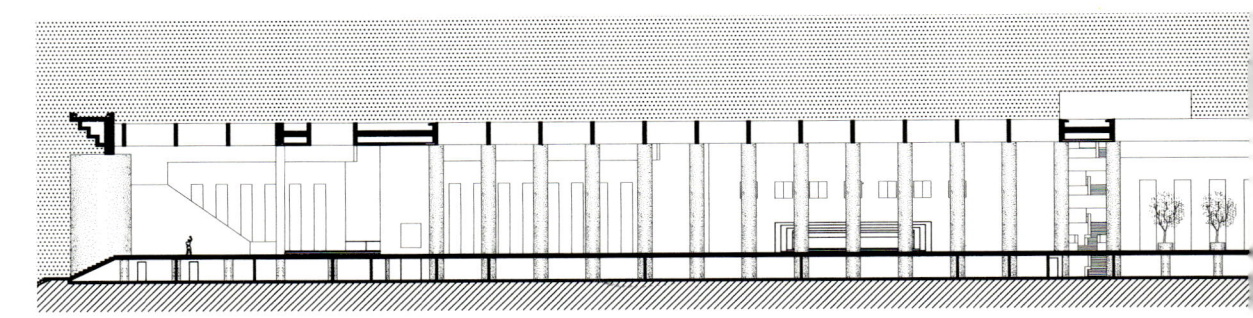

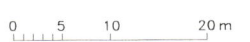

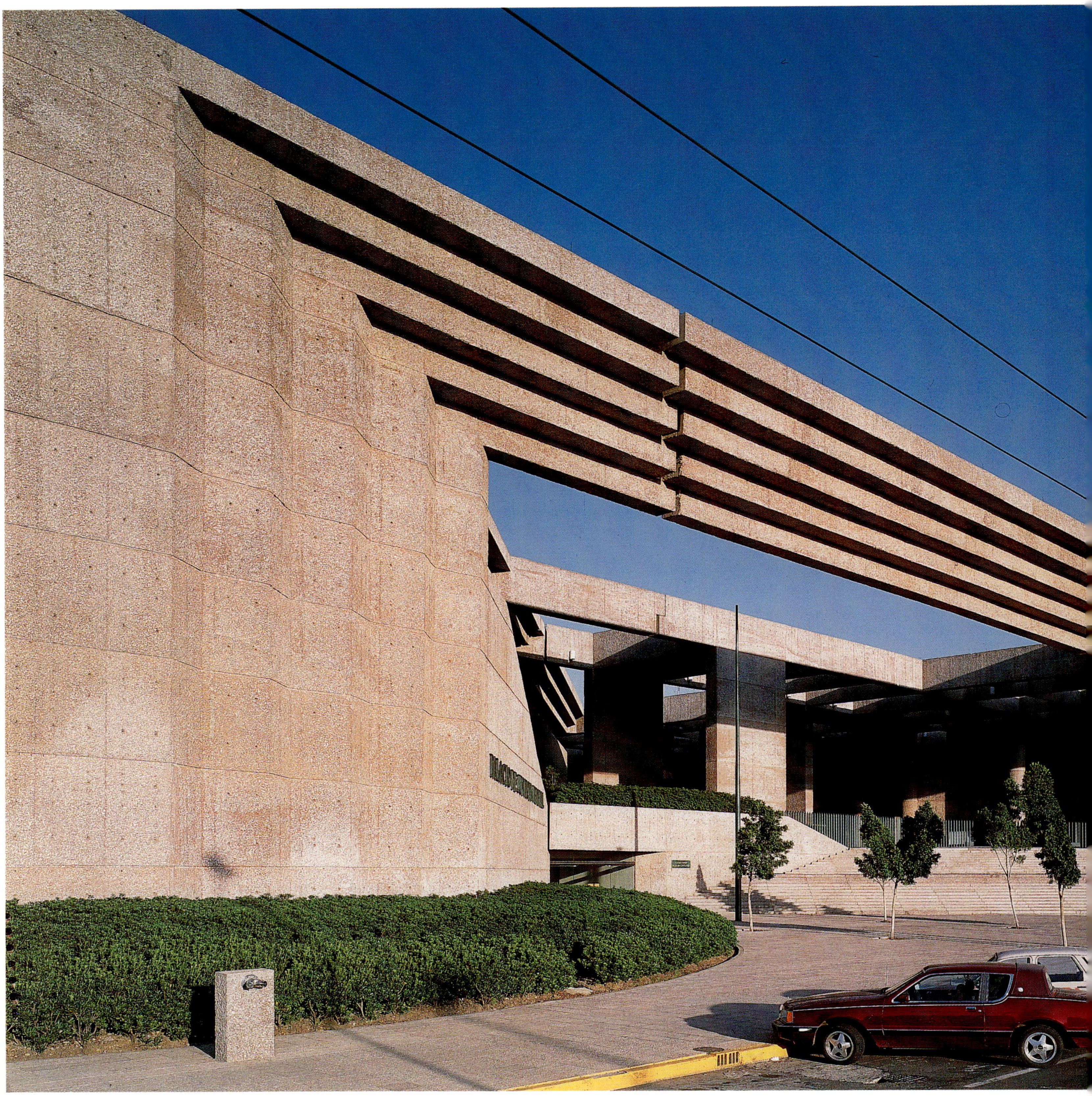

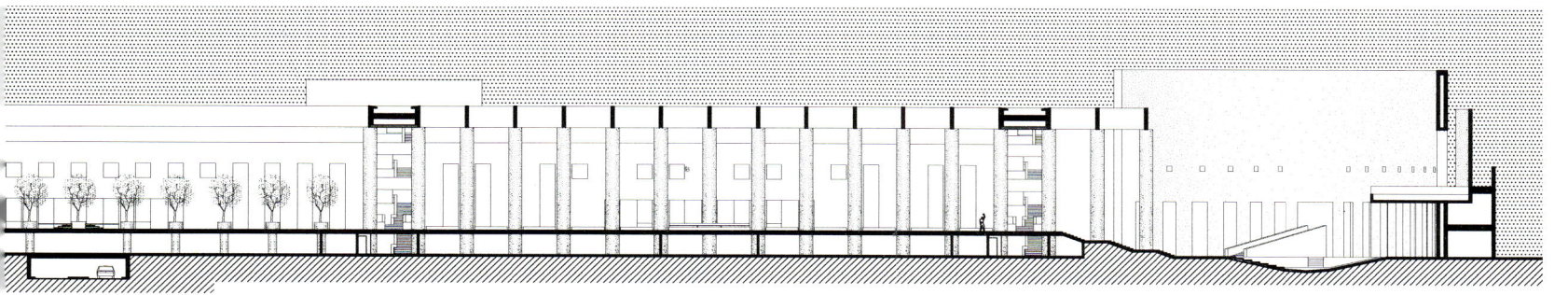

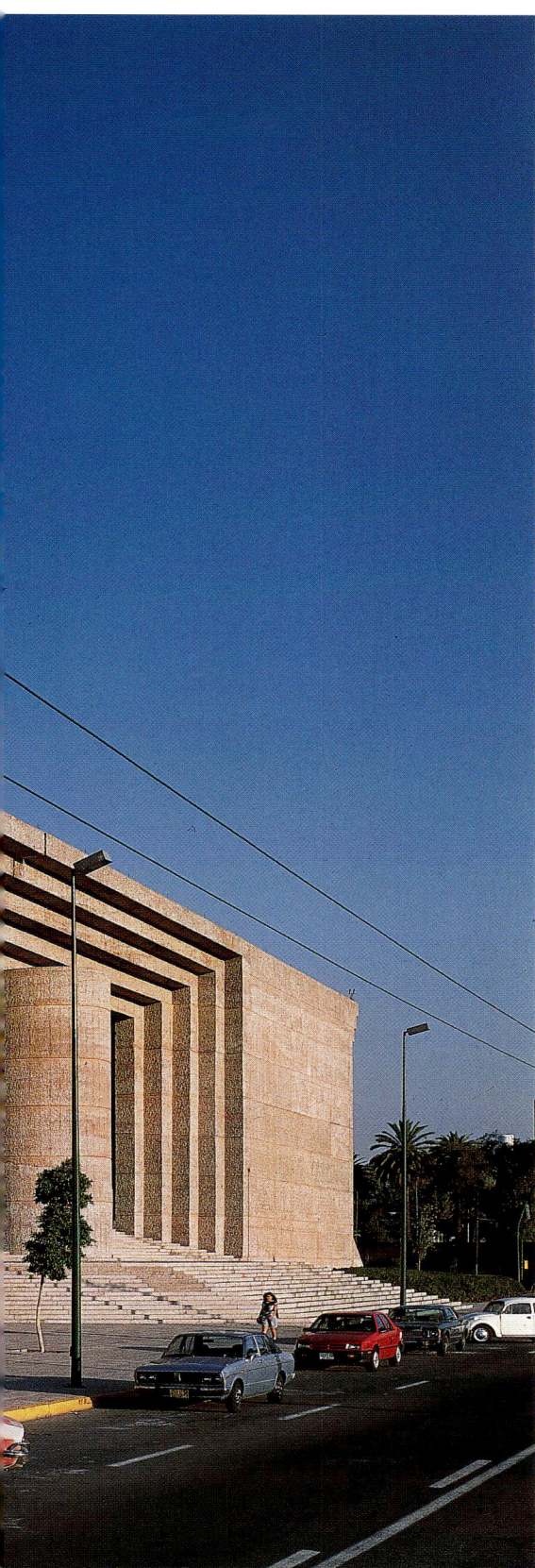

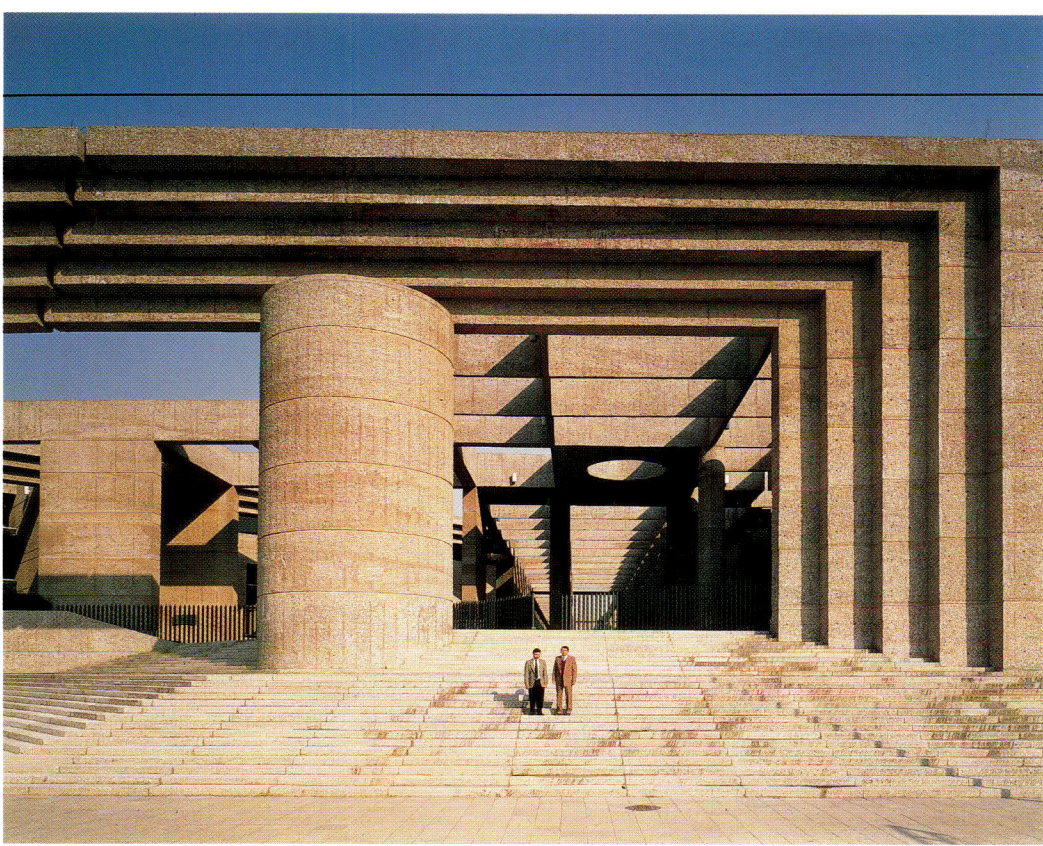

Detail of the entrance steps.

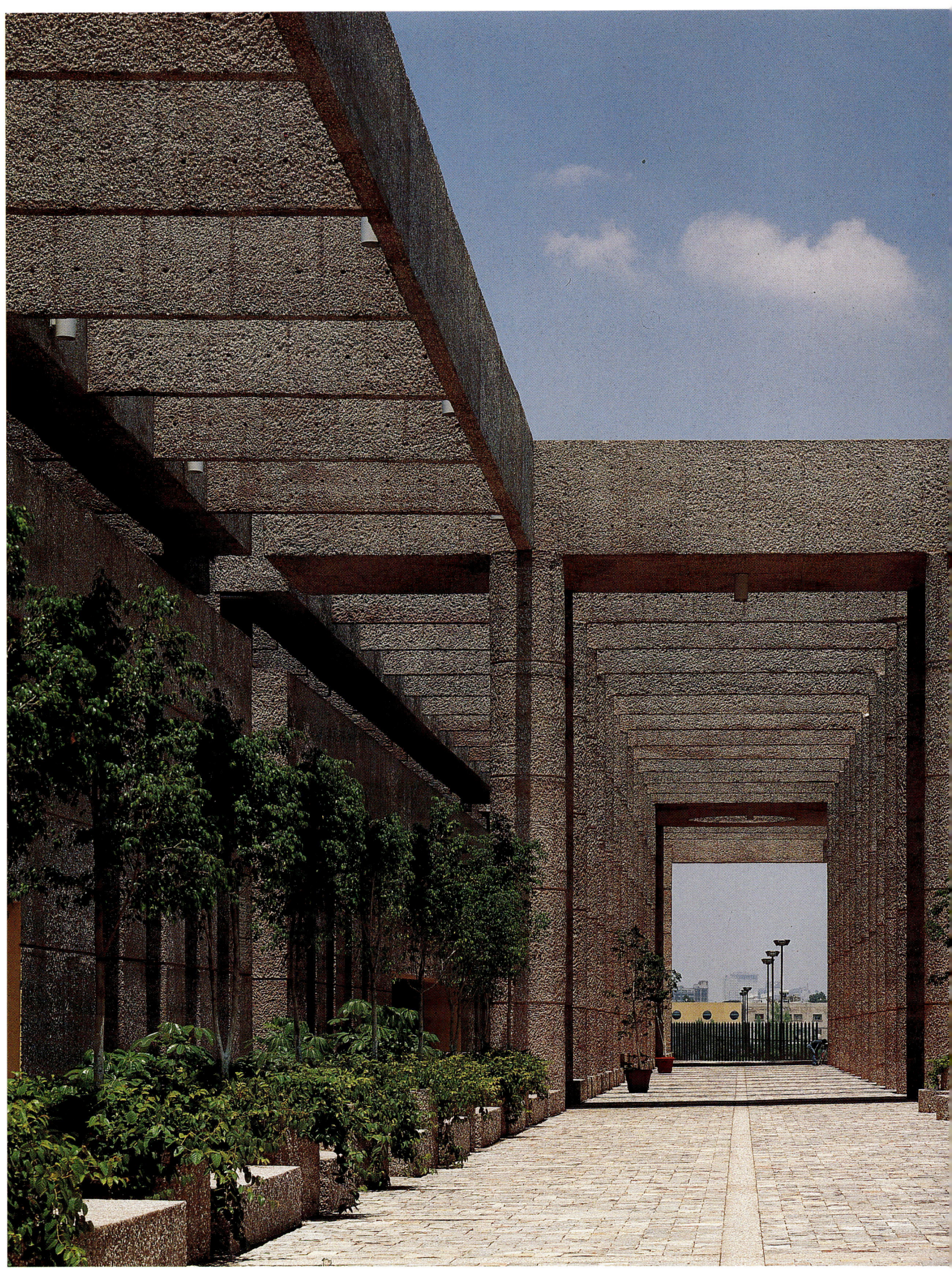

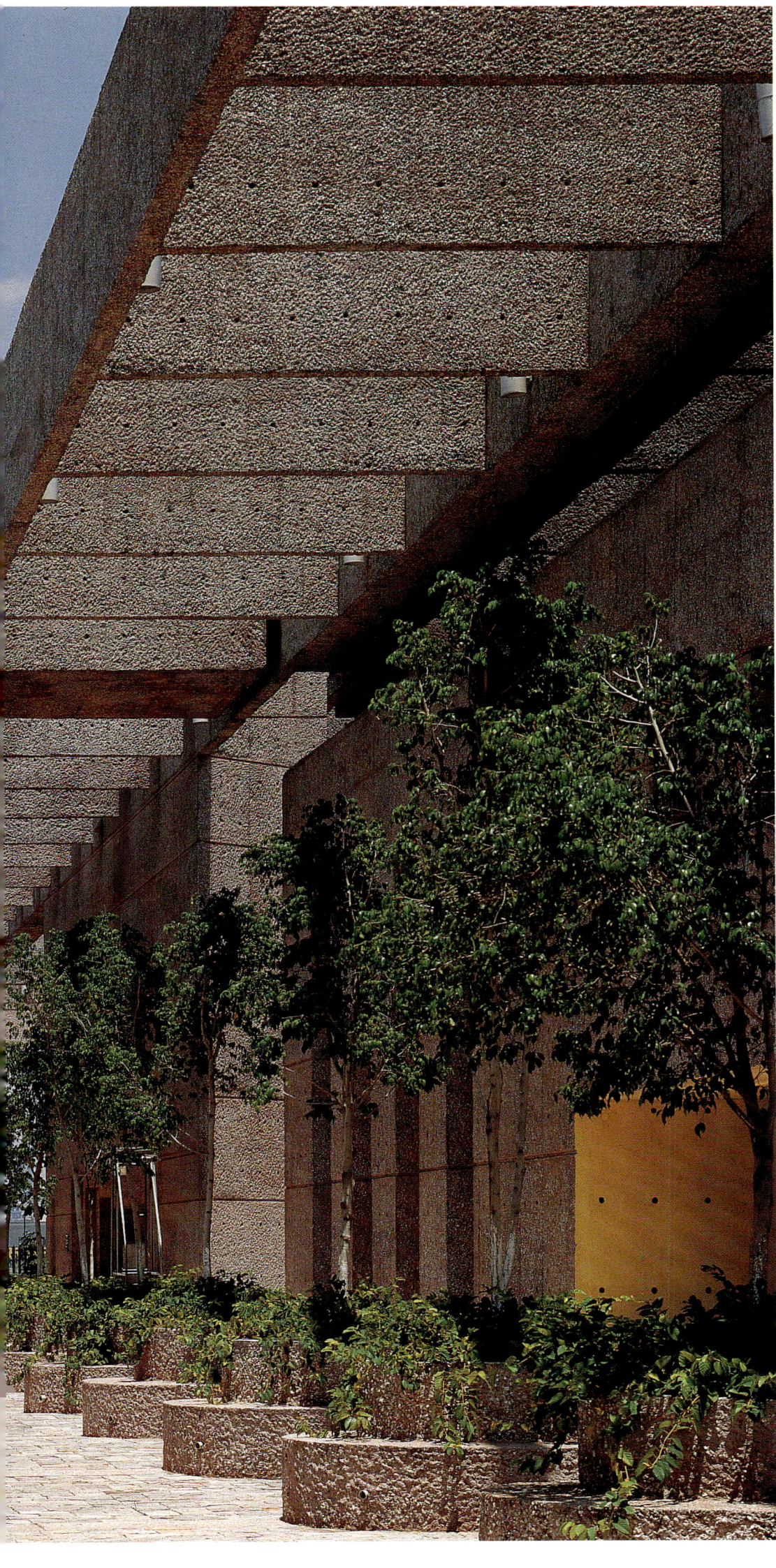

The central path, marked by approximately 12-metre-tall columns, is the main distributional hub of the entire complex. There are 24 courtrooms and 32 legal offices at the sides, while the auditorium and social services are located at either end. Following spreads, details of the main front and side facade.

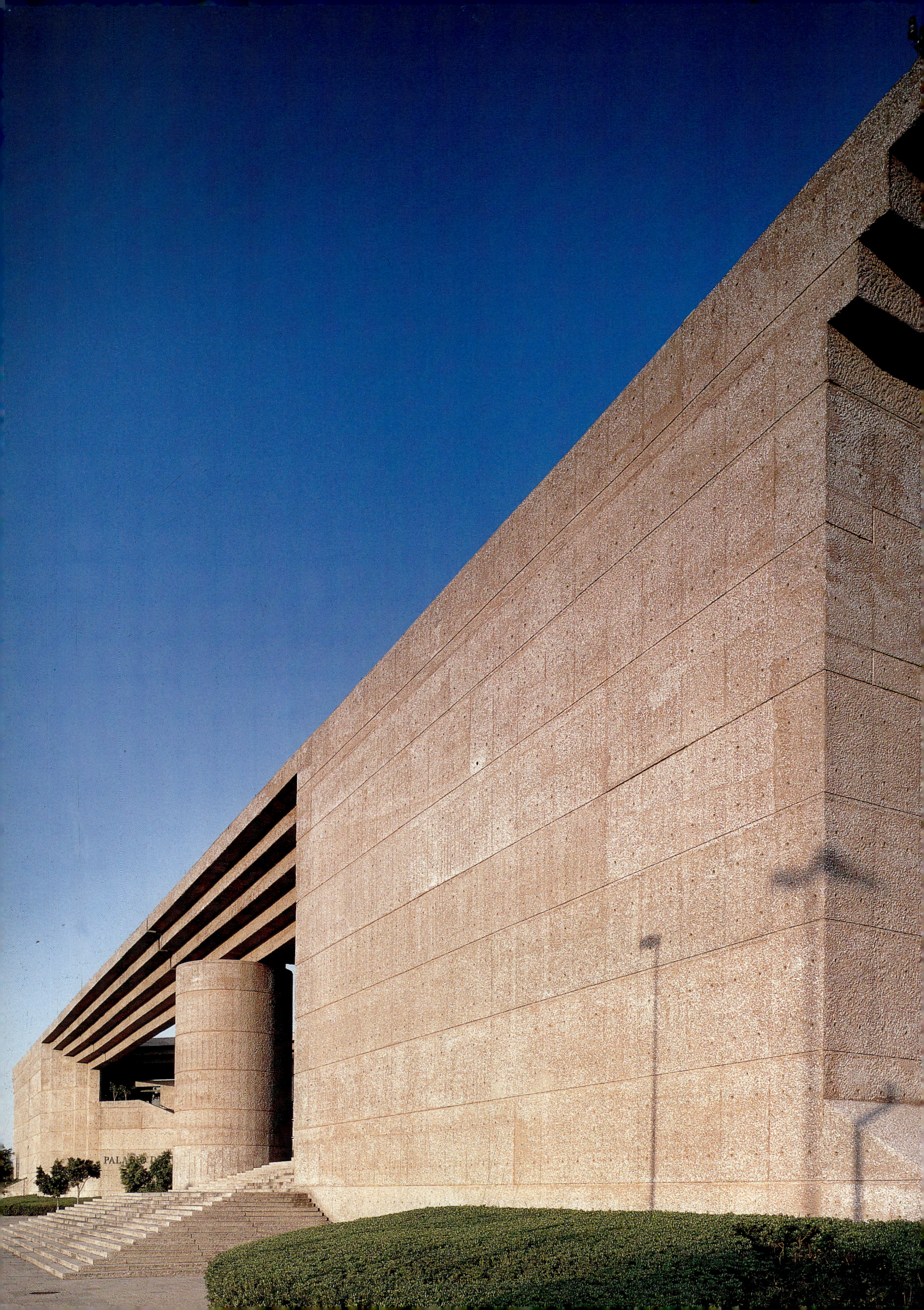

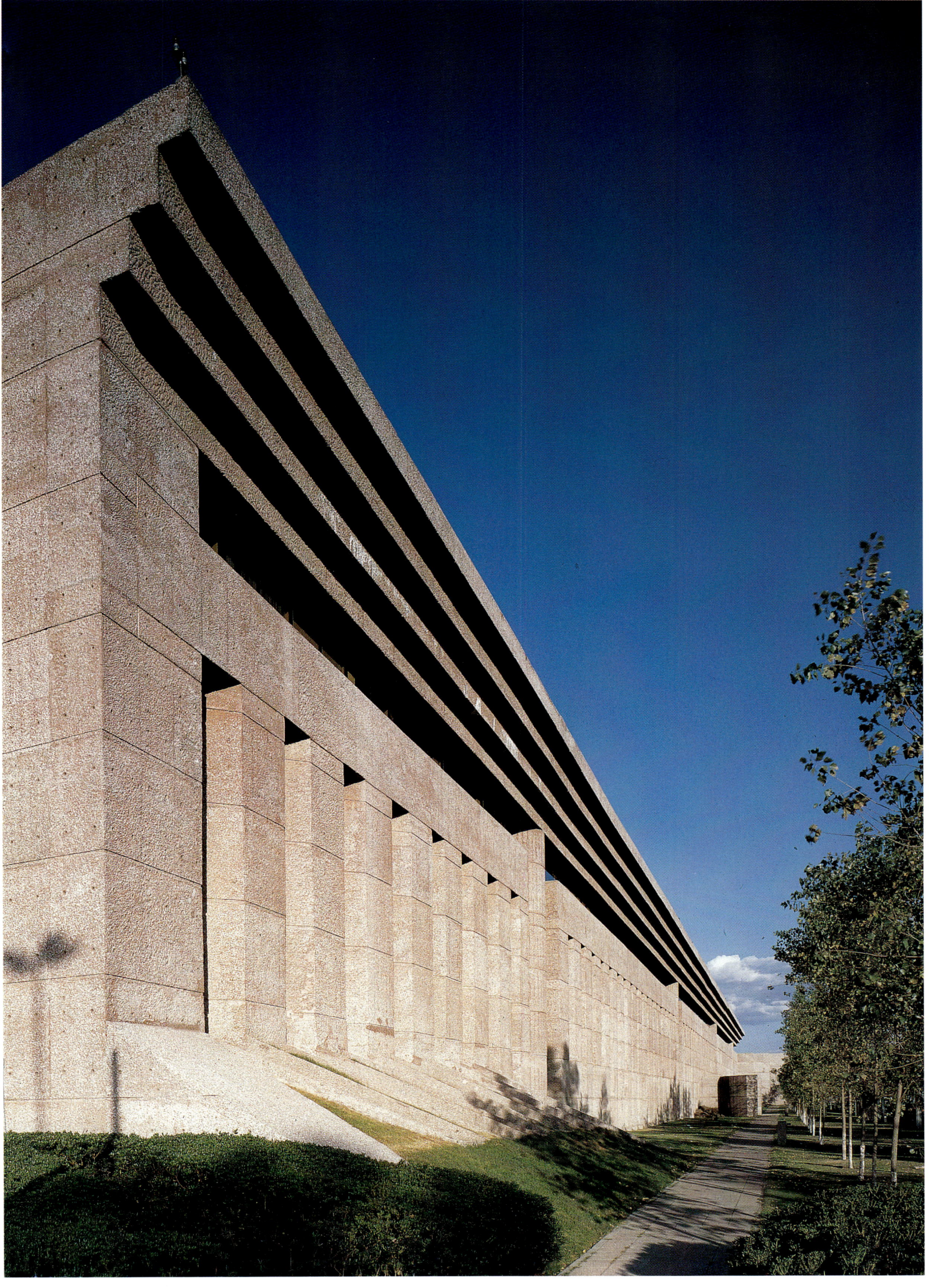

Mexico City, 1989-1991

Renewal of the National Auditorium

Owner
Instituto Nacional de Bellas Artes
Departamento del Distrito Federal

Architects
Teodoro González de León
Abraham Zabludovsky

Collaborator
José Arce Gargollo

Acoustics and sound
Jaffe Acoustics Inc.

Structural design
Colinas de Buen, S.A. de C.V.

Lighting
Jules Fisher & Paul Marantz

Lighting and theater mechanics
Jules Fisher Associates

Air conditioning design
Calefacción y Ventilación, S.A.

Electric design
Cid Instalaciones, S.A.

Hydraulics and sanitary design
GHA y Asociados, S.A. de C.V.

Areas
12,000 sq.m. renewal
11,750 sq.m. construction
18, 400 sq.m. parkings
30,150 sq.m. total

Mexico City's National Auditorium was originally built in 1946 with a seating capacity of approximately 14,000. Over the following ten years it fell into such a state of decay that it urgently needed to be modernised, at the same time bringing its seating capacity up to the purposes for which it was first built. Teodoro González de León was commissioned to carry out the modernisation work in 1989, first creating an entrance facing the city and an entrance/theatre dominating the street level to provide a privileged view across the cityscape. This instantly accessible entrance also evokes the colonnades of compartments found in nineteenth-century European theatres. The Auditorium hall is immediately surrounded by car parks. Part of the plaza/lobby is located beneath the entrance hall (which partly covers it), while nearby there are ramps and staircases to facilitate internal circulation for the general public.

The hall ceiling is held up by triangular girders creating a strangely plastic image and also forming a curious entrance way.

The Auditorium's architecture hinges around a huge archway acting simultaneously as a doorway, triumphant arc and monument commemorating the art of music; in other words a sort of landmark clearly embodying the spectacular nature of this public entertainment centre. The entrance door is the real key feature of the building front, acting as a facade and providing decoration designed in the same sloping fashion as the road it follows to create a triangular plot of land in Paseo de la Reforma almost appearing to line up the rest of the buildings along the road. The slope is also designed to inject greater force into the design through the kind of plastic experimentation that González de León was to draw on again in later projects.

It is worth pointing out that the renovation work on the Auditorium has increased the seating capacity by 9,980, guaranteeing good views and perfect acoustics everywhere.

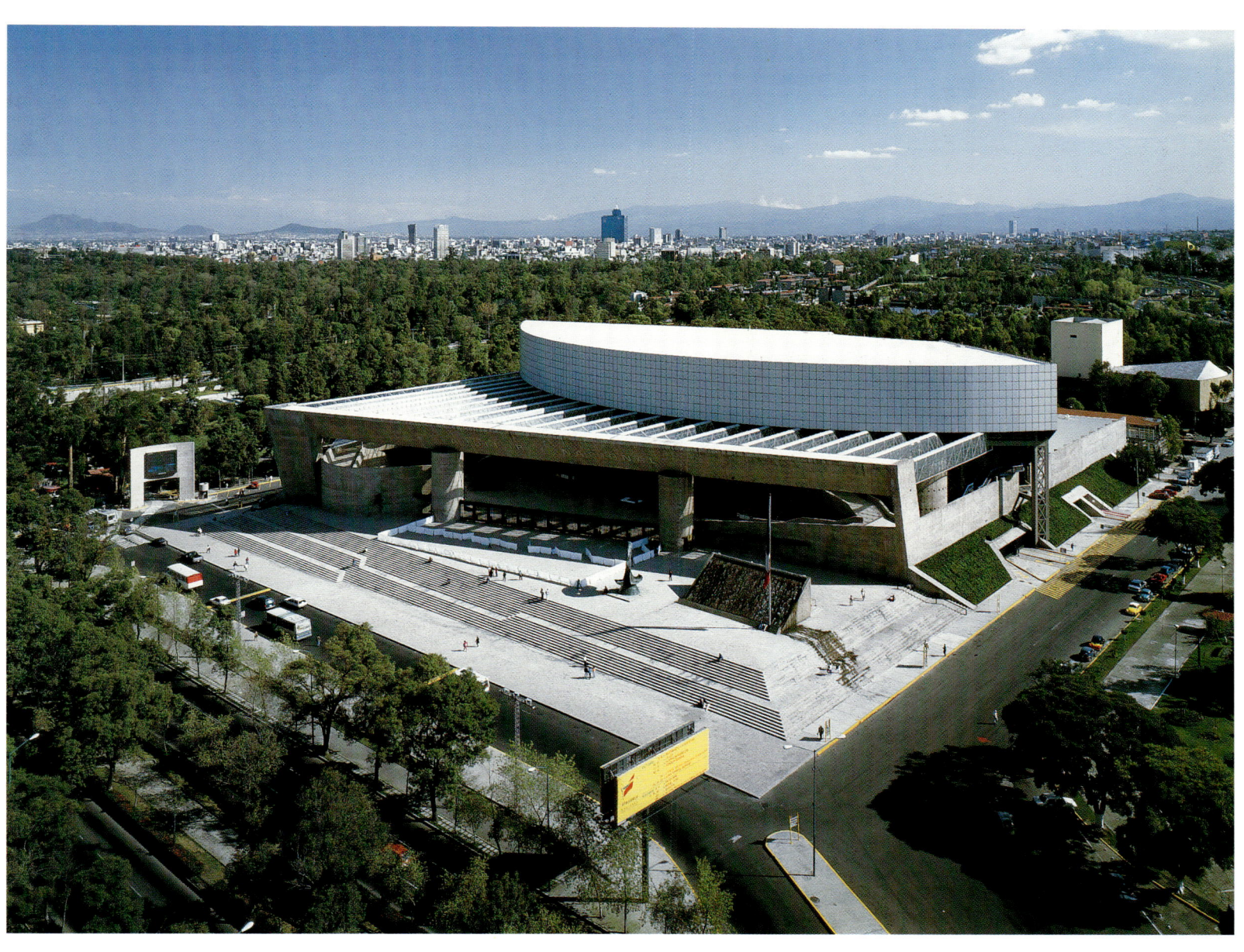

General view of the modernised National Auditorium, originally built in 1946.

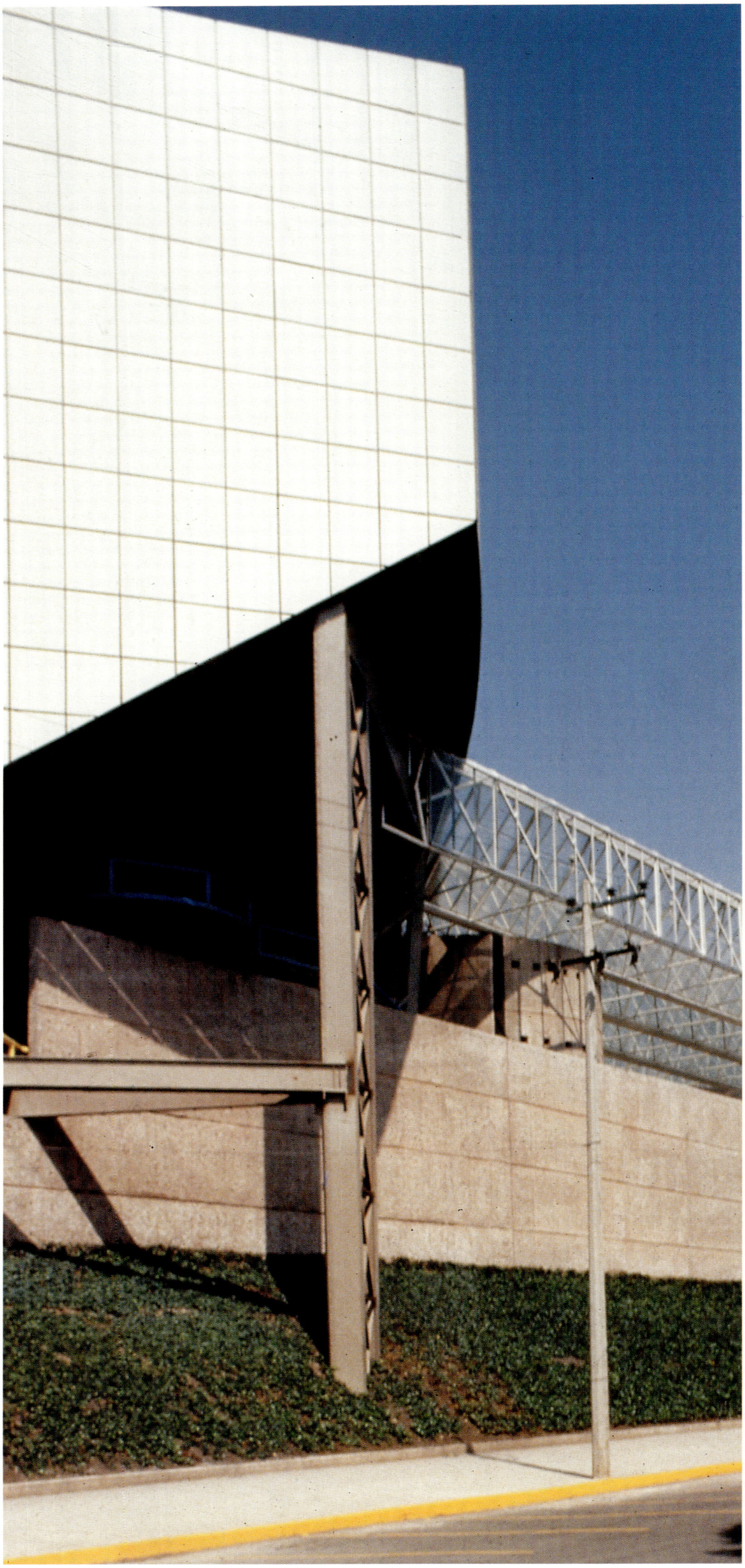

Details of the large raised platform providing a carefully staged entrance to the theatre.

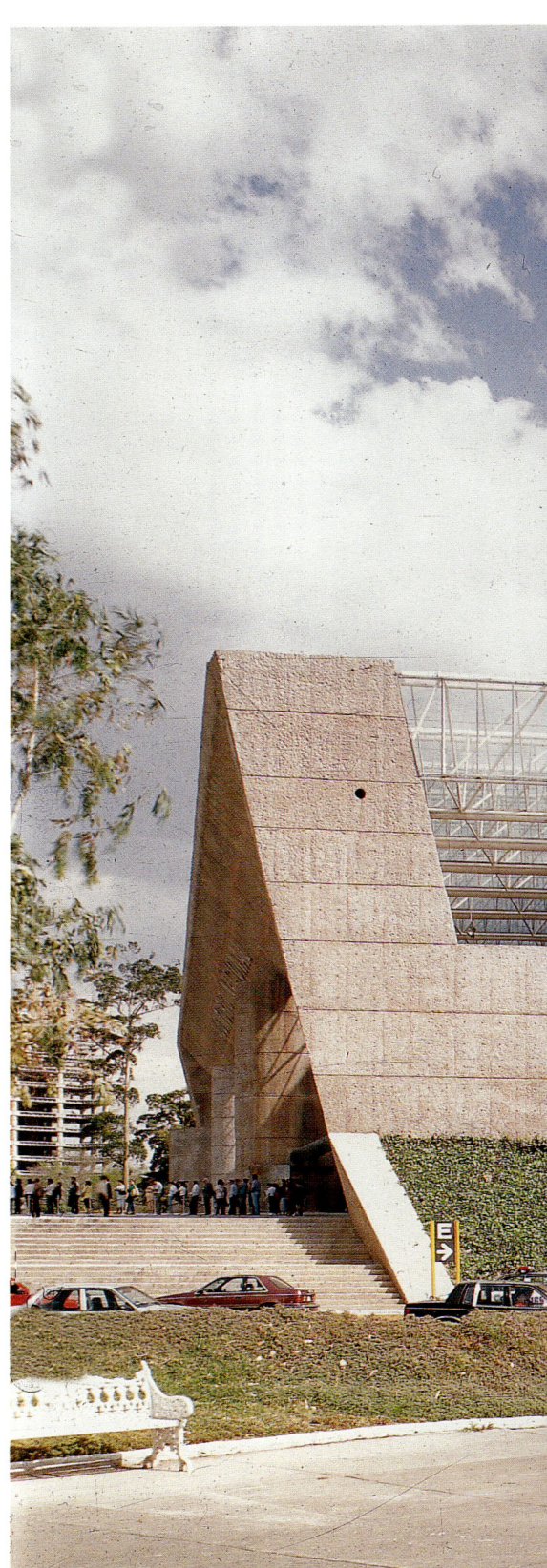

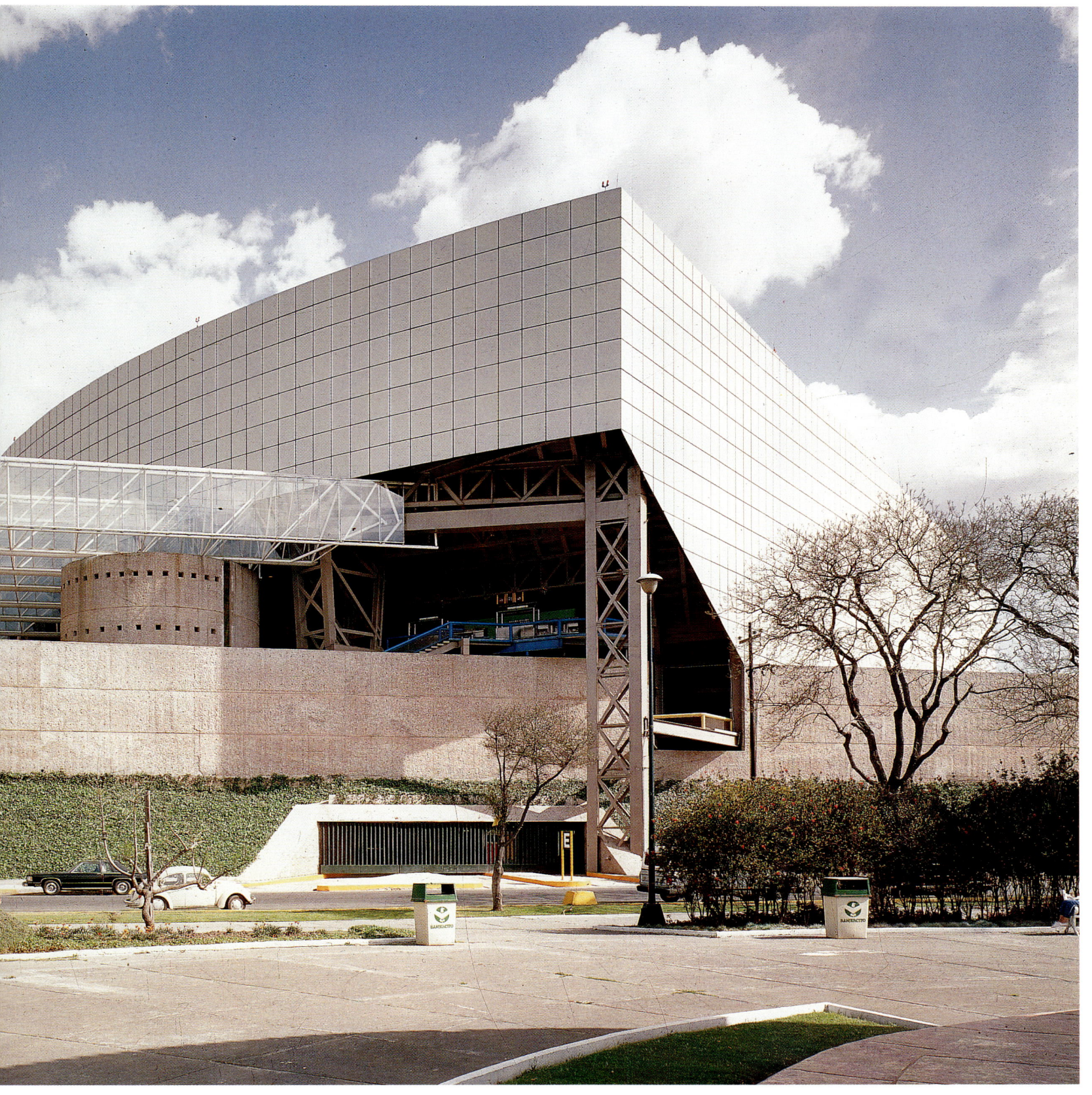

Below, plan of the first floor and, bottom, plan of the entrance plaza level. Right, the 14,000-seat auditorium hall whose capacity has been increased by a further 9,980.

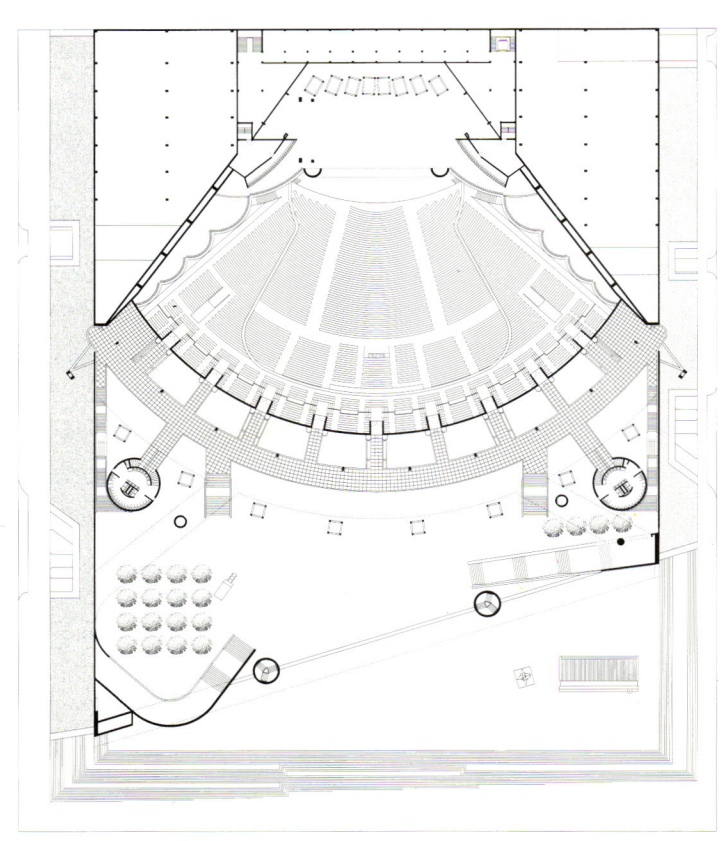

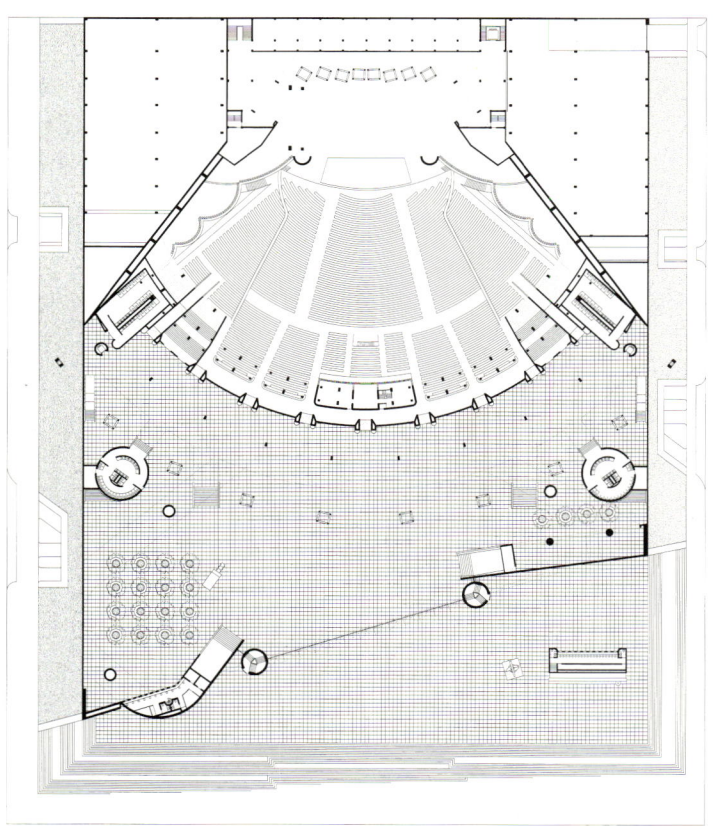

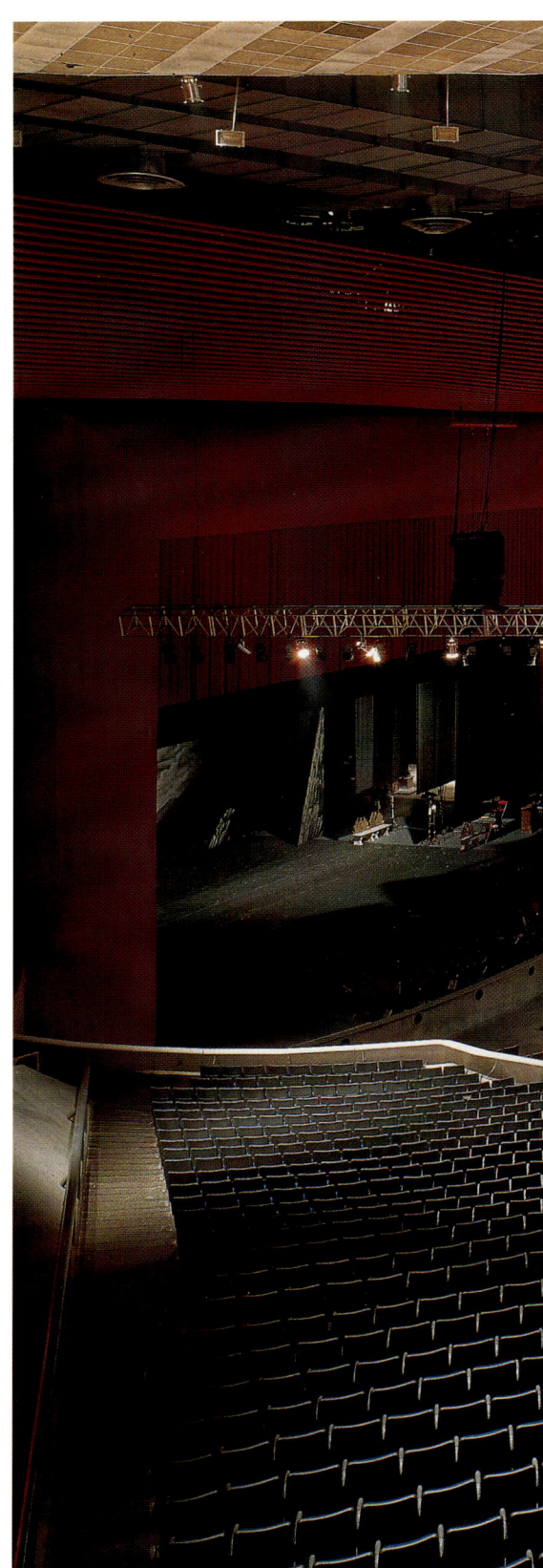

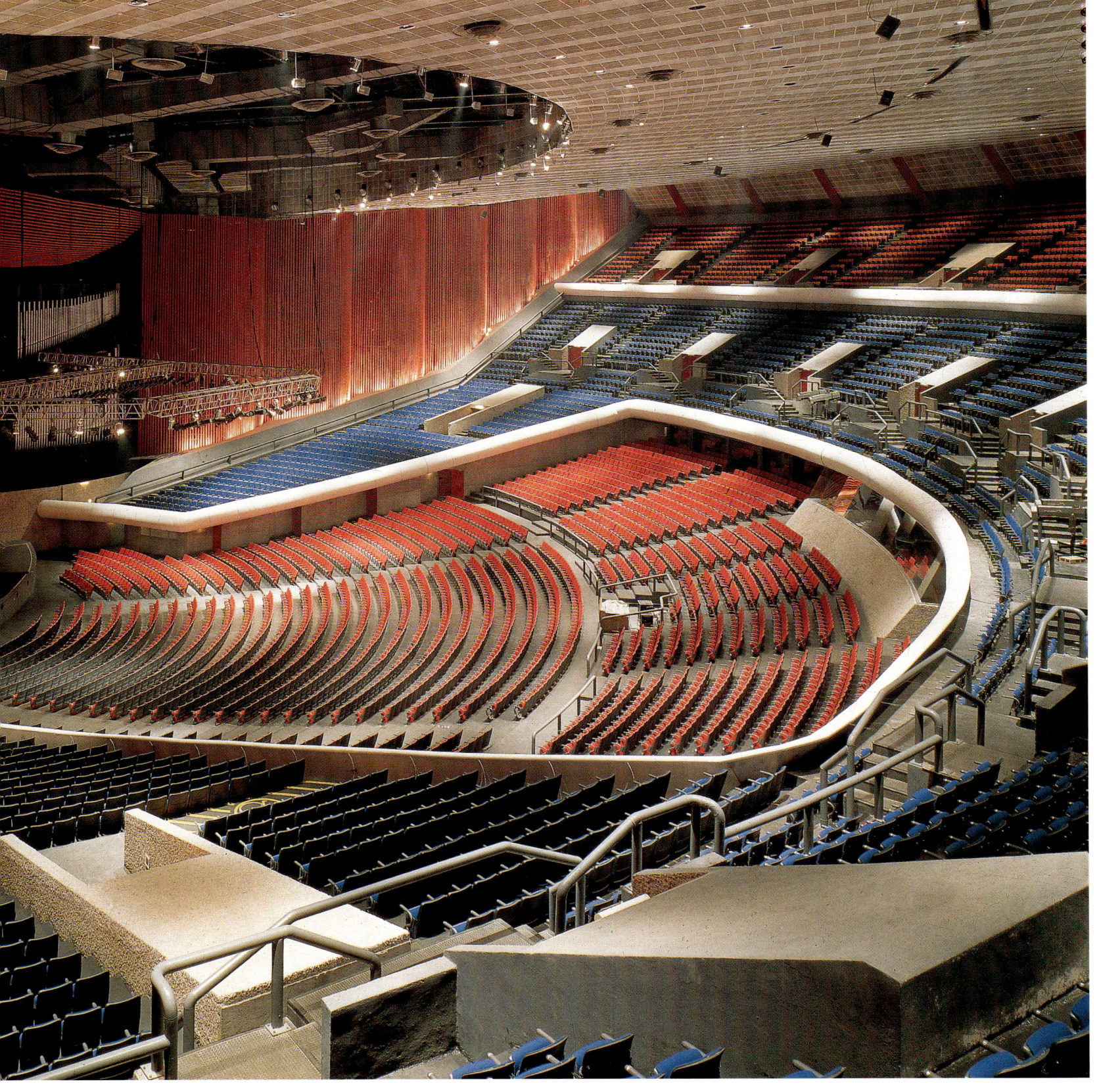

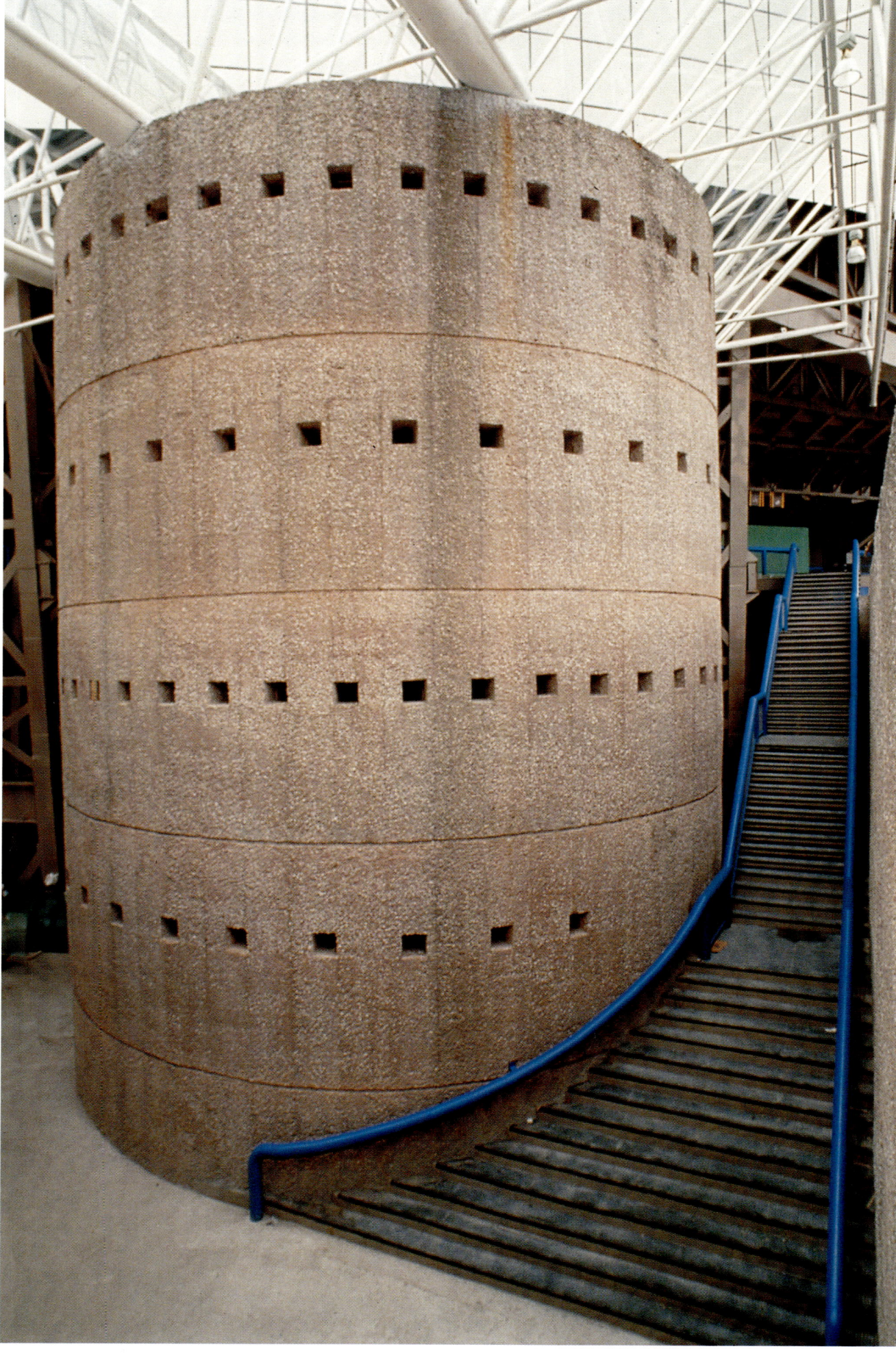

Detail of the stairway and service shaft.

42

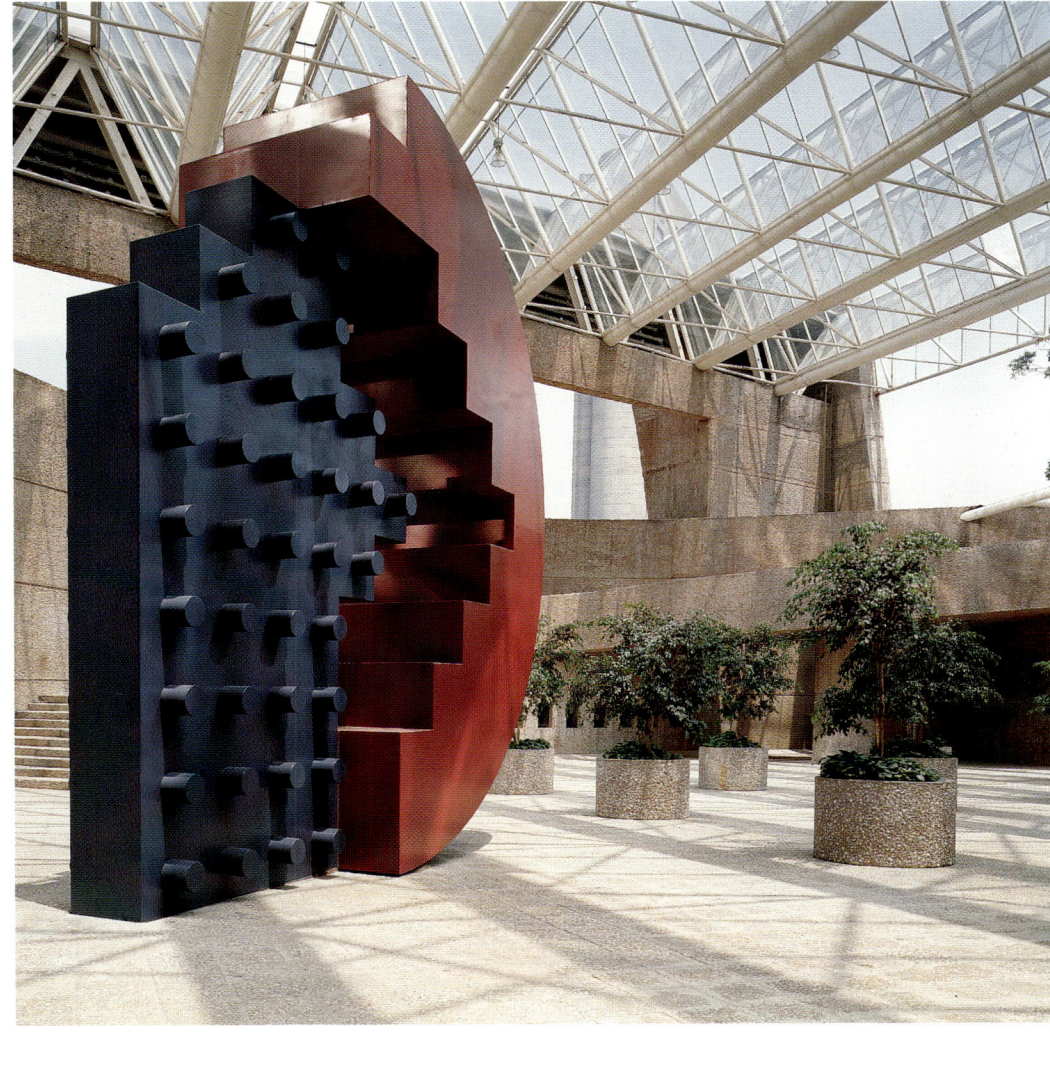

Details of the covered public plaza showing the sculpture by Vicente Rojo.

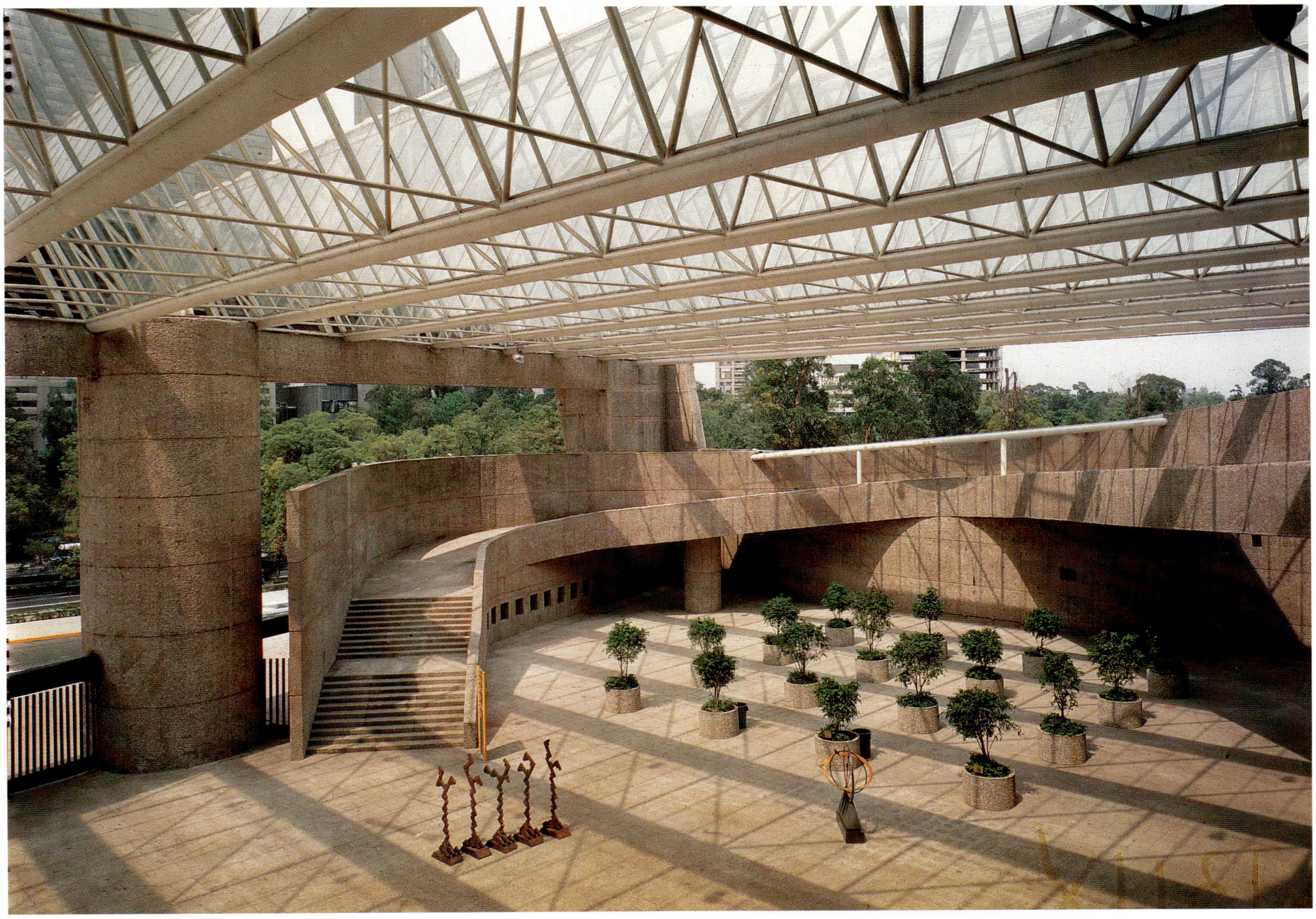

Mexico City, 1990-1992

Fondo de Cultura Económica

Owner
Fondo de Cultura Económica

Architect
Teodoro González de León

Collaborator
Ernesto Betancourt

Interior design
Luis A. de Regil

Structural design
Héctor Margain Ancira

Air-conditioning design
Calefacción y Ventilación, S.A.

Electric design
COESA Ingenieria, S.A.

Hydraulics and sanitary design
GHA y Asociados

Construction area
8,400 sq.m.

In 1992 Teodoro González de León managed to complete a building complex he actually began twenty years earlier. This project for the Fondo de Cultura Económica mainly is basically designed out of three self-contained blocks serving separate specific purposes. In 1995 González de León also constructed the connecting bridge built in the front section of the main building.

It must immediately be pointed out that González de León decided to design a triangular-based metal structure at the top of the building to inject a sense of lightness into the imposing overall building design.

The central staircase constructed around a circular design clearly evokes Bramante's design for the steps in the Vatican Gardens in Rome. Nevertheless, the key feature of this new project is its determined attempt to give the main facade a flexible, plastic image as viewed by onlookers. The strange thing is that the designer has chosen to hide this key feature inside a curved sculptural form designed, as usual, with great artistry. It almost seem as if this imposing building is trying to take off and fly away. Its plastic forms are light, monumental, powerful, and highly inventive. The whole construction creates a great sense of architectural elegance as concave and convex forms come together at both the front plaza and in the overall building elevation.

One final important feature of this project is the great respect González de León shows for nature. The area at the back of the Conference Building contains a natural deposit of volcanic rocks, which the design carefully encompasses as if to take hold and actually embrace them.

González de León has put into practice his beliefs regarding the interaction between form and nature, well aware as he is that this is one of the most important issues in contemporary debate on architectural design.

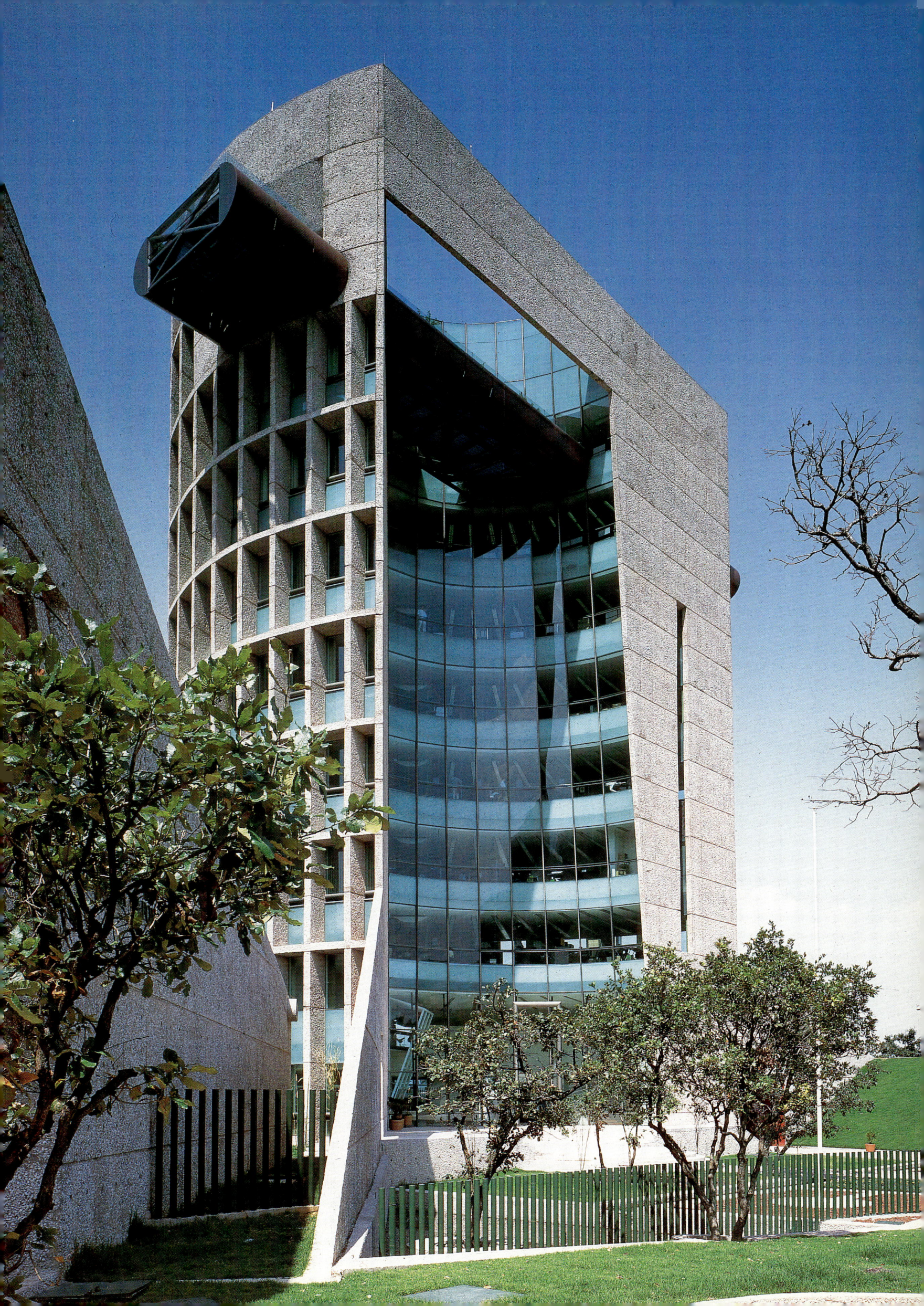

Plan of the ground floor and view of the main facade of the tower housing the offices of the Fondo de Cultura Económica complex.

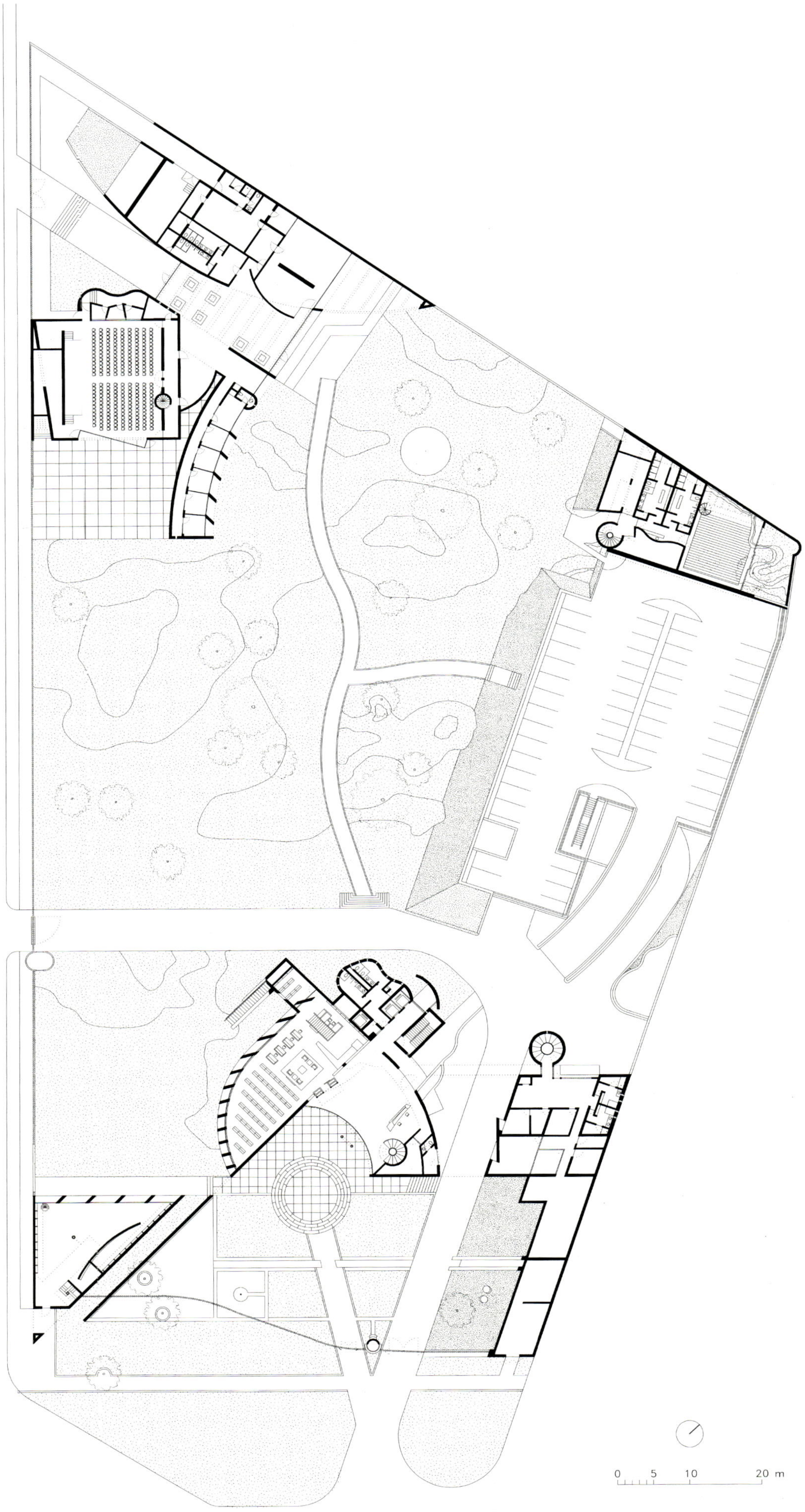

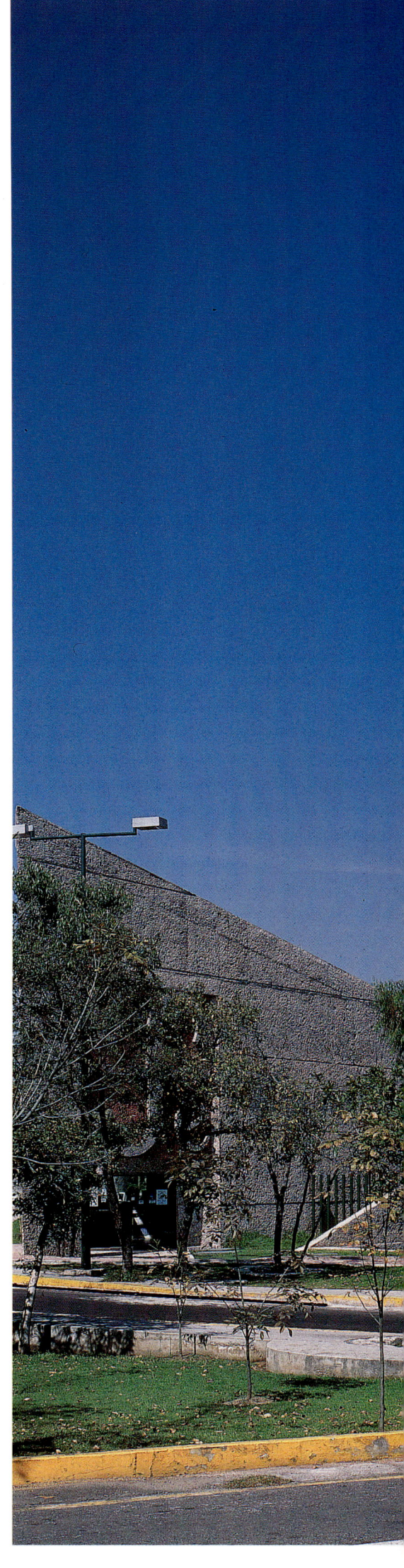

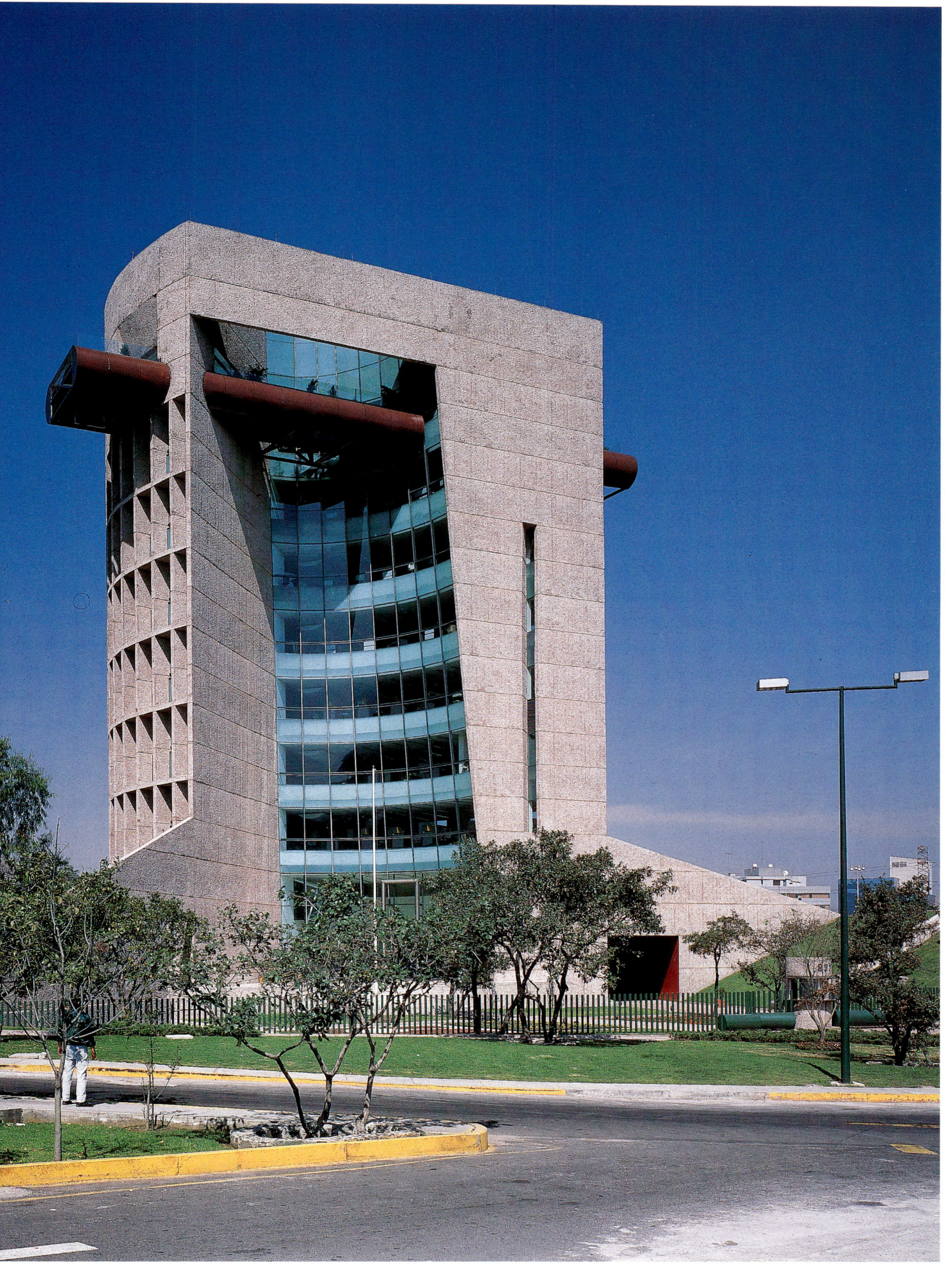

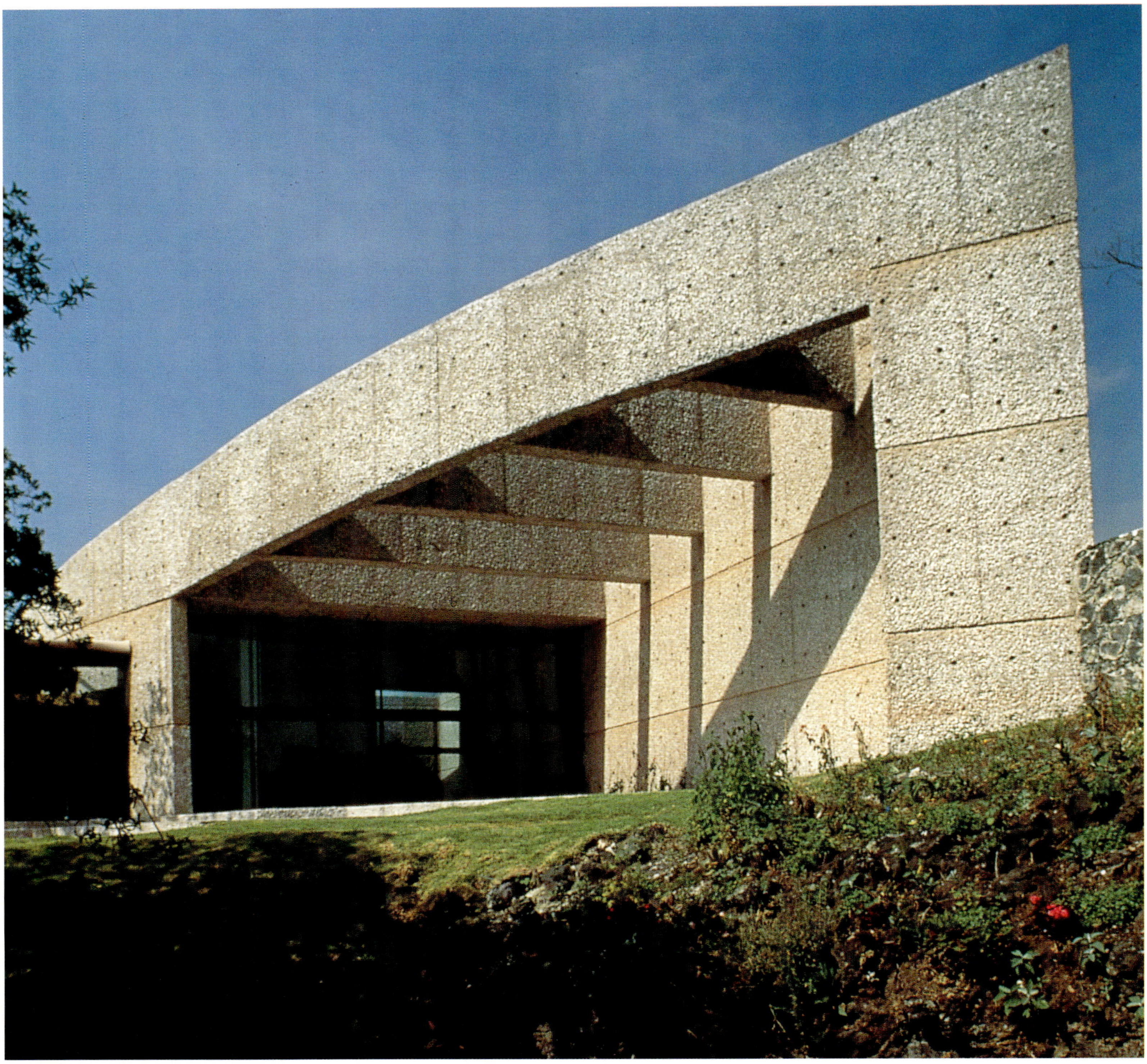

Above and opposite page, details of the porticoed area in front of the complex's canteen.
Right, plans of the seventh floor and a standard floor.

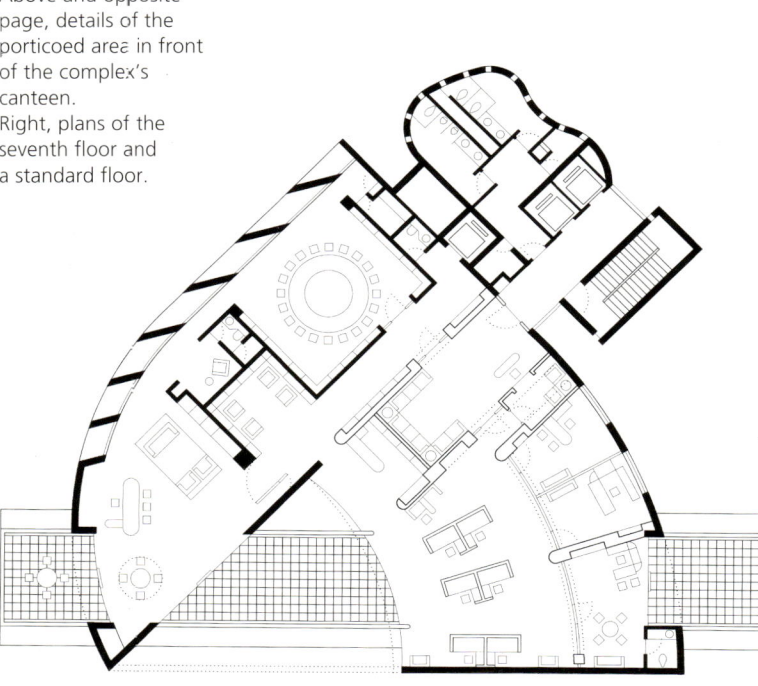
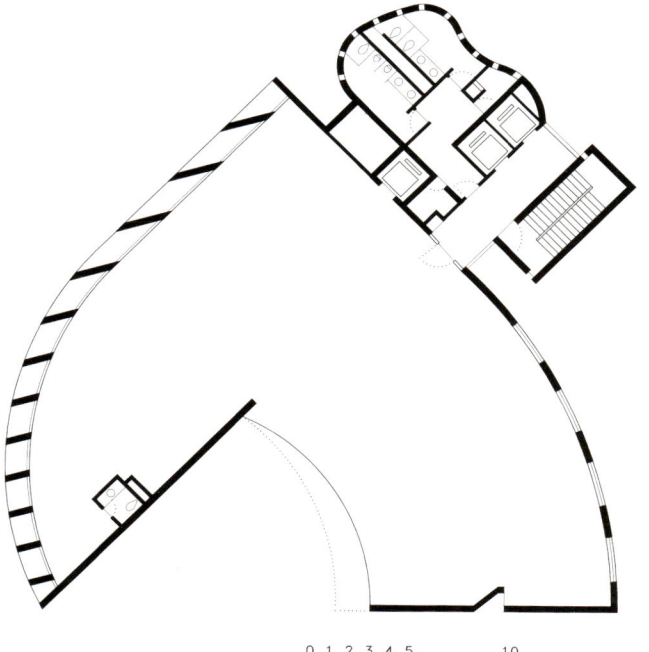

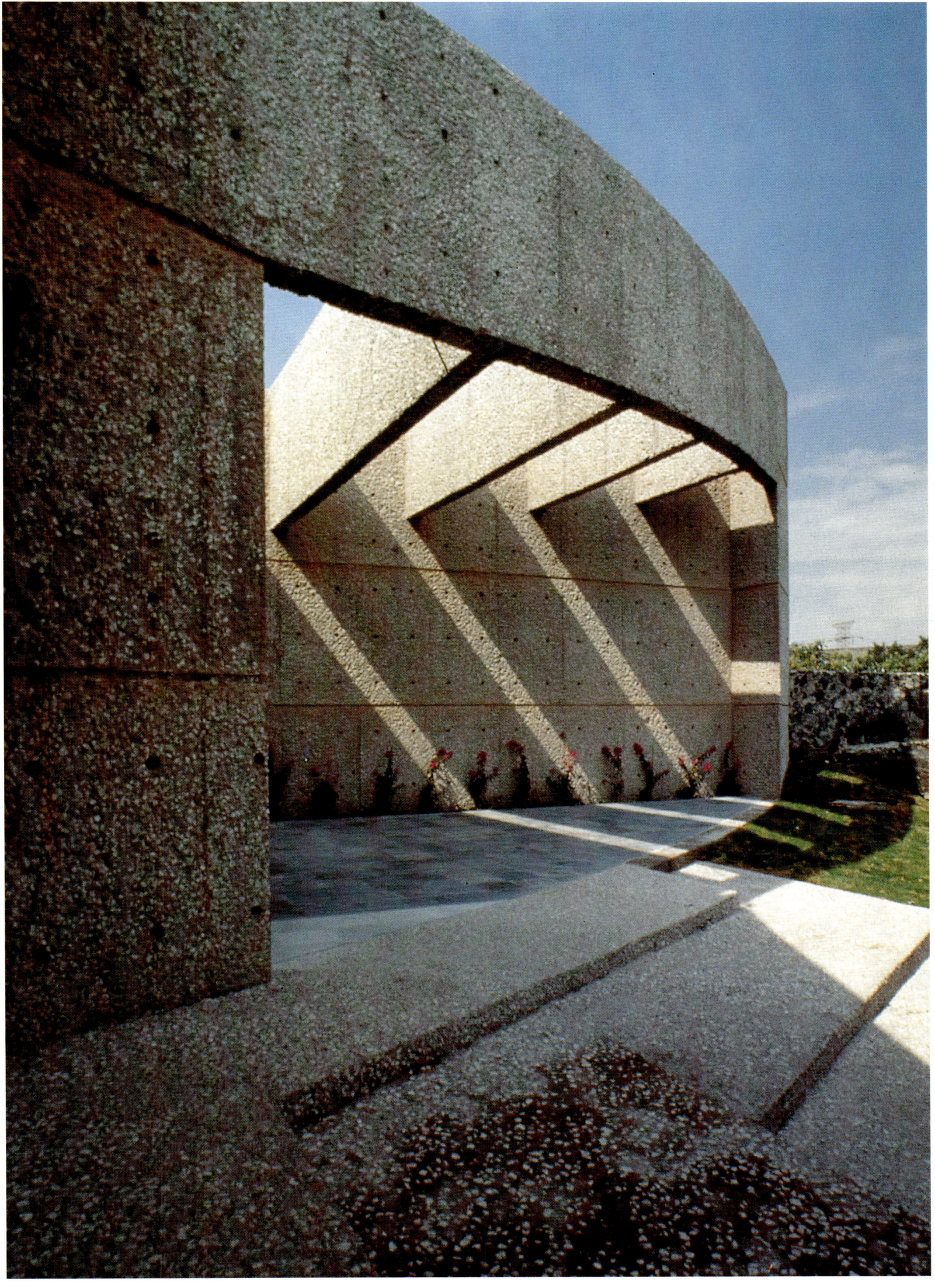

Section of the office block.
Right and opposite page, perspective views of the complex whose light, transparent metal and glass structure combines with the monumental proportions of the parts filled with concrete.

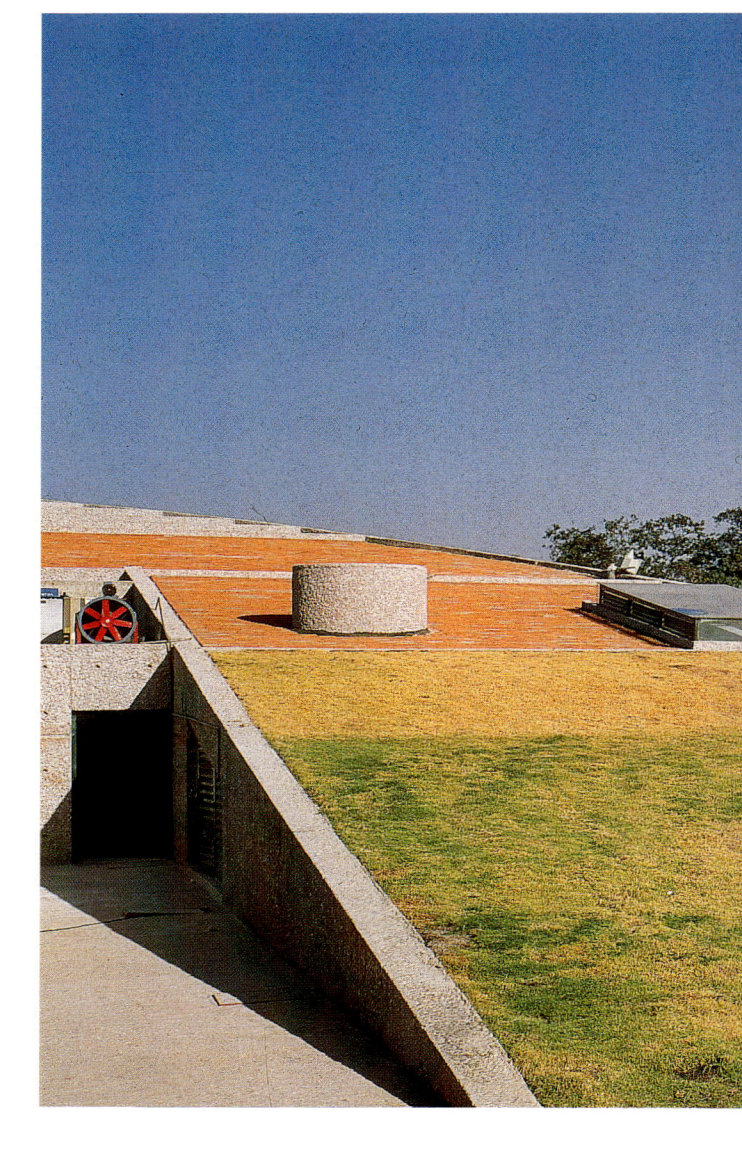

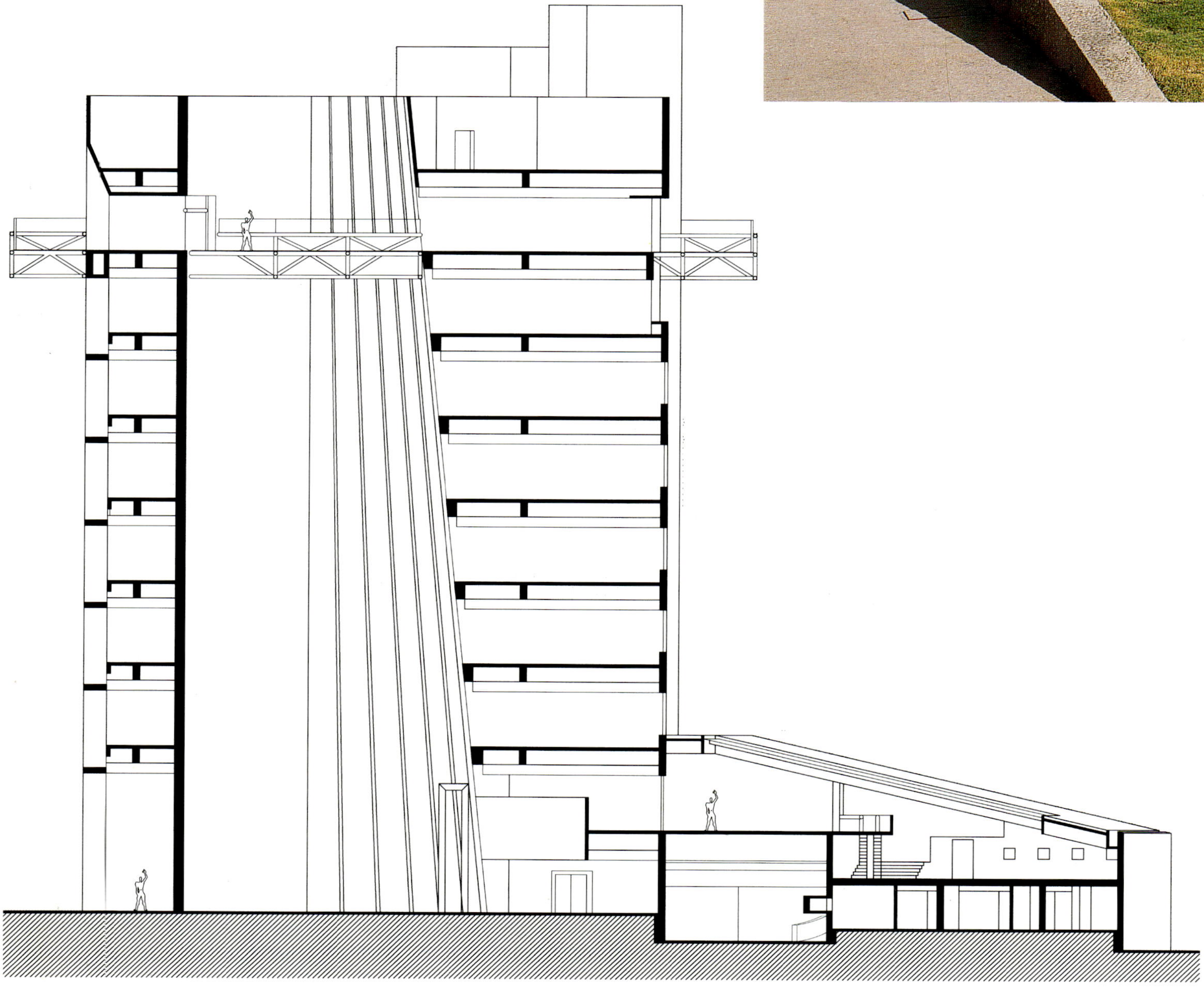

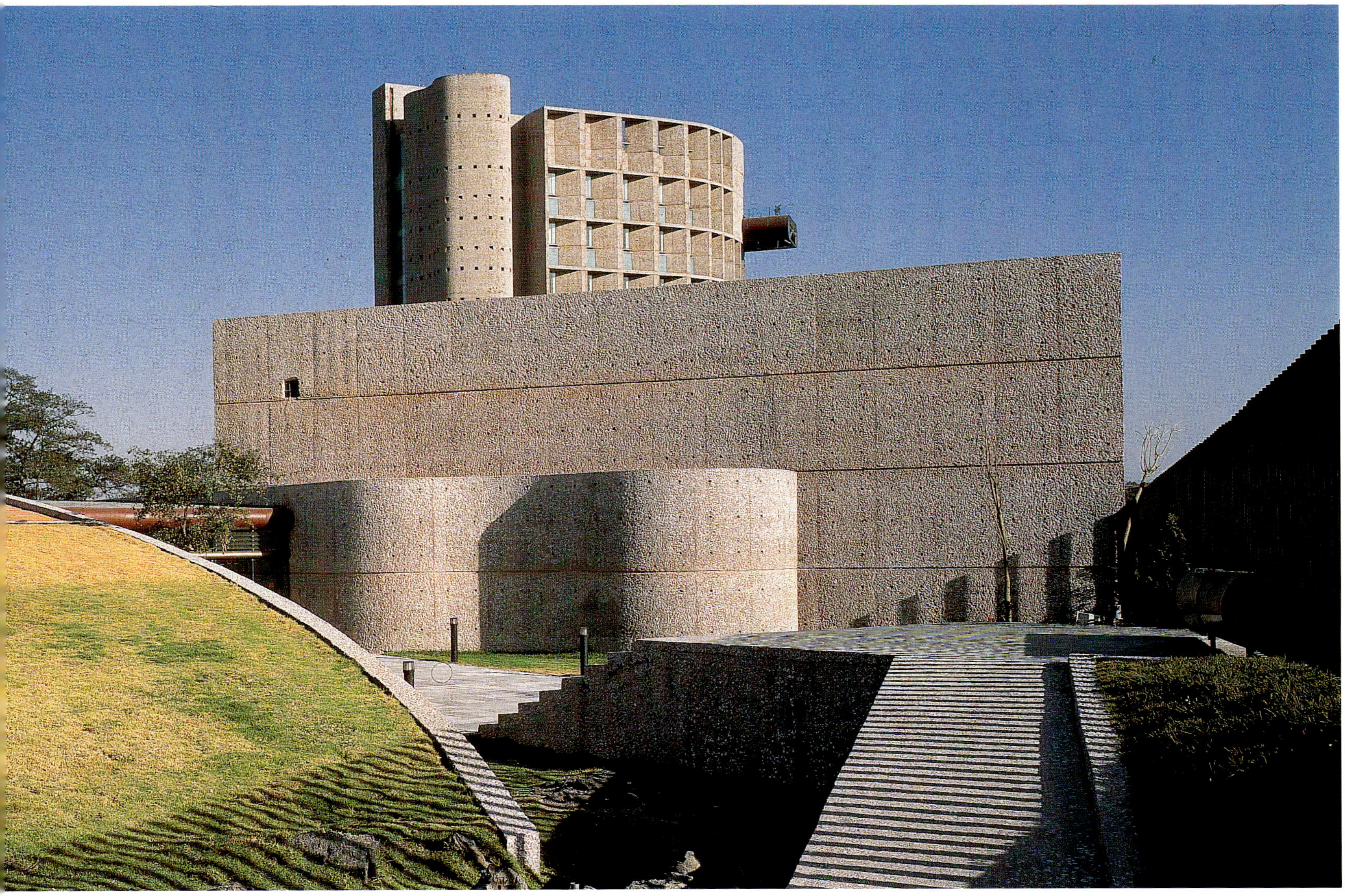

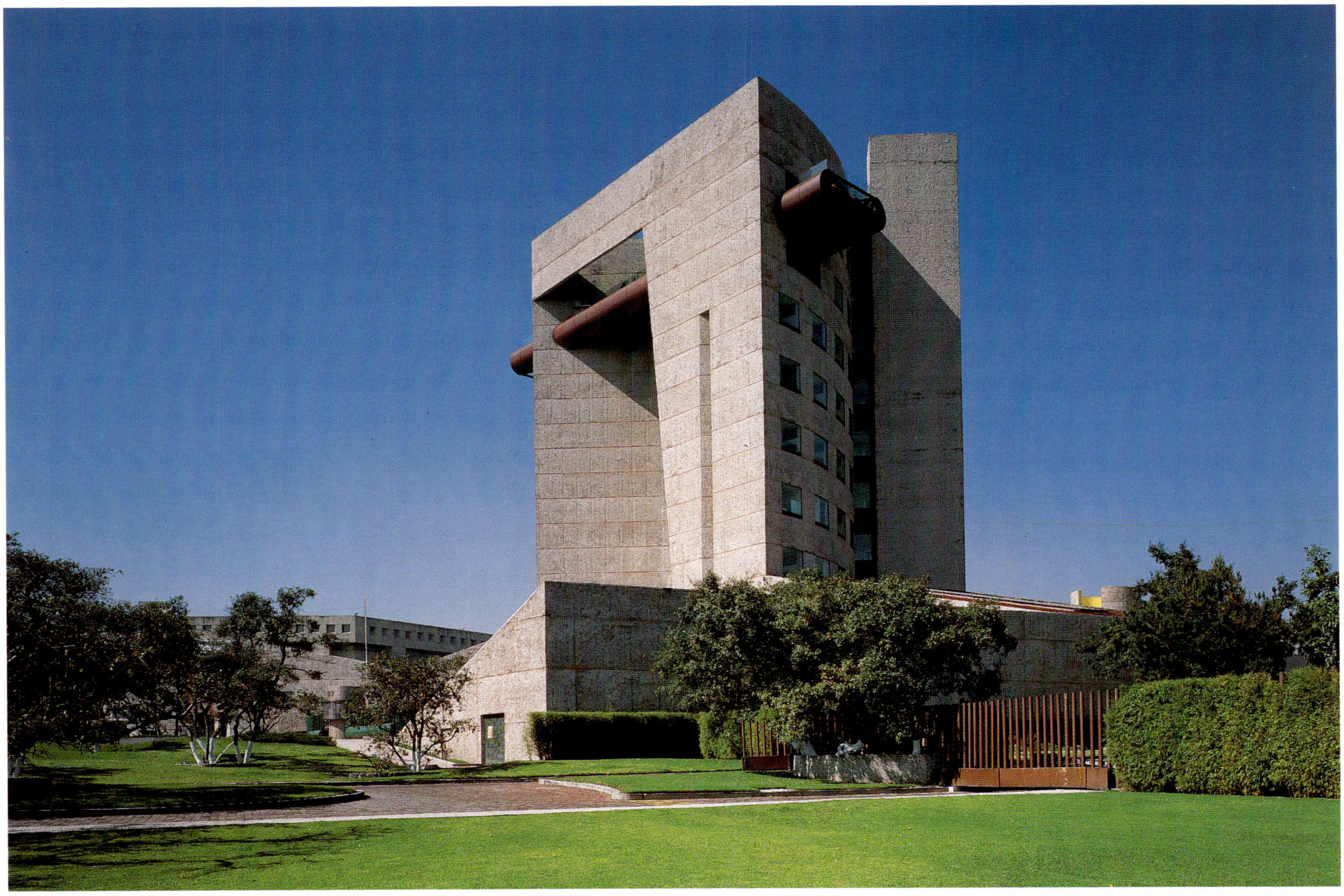

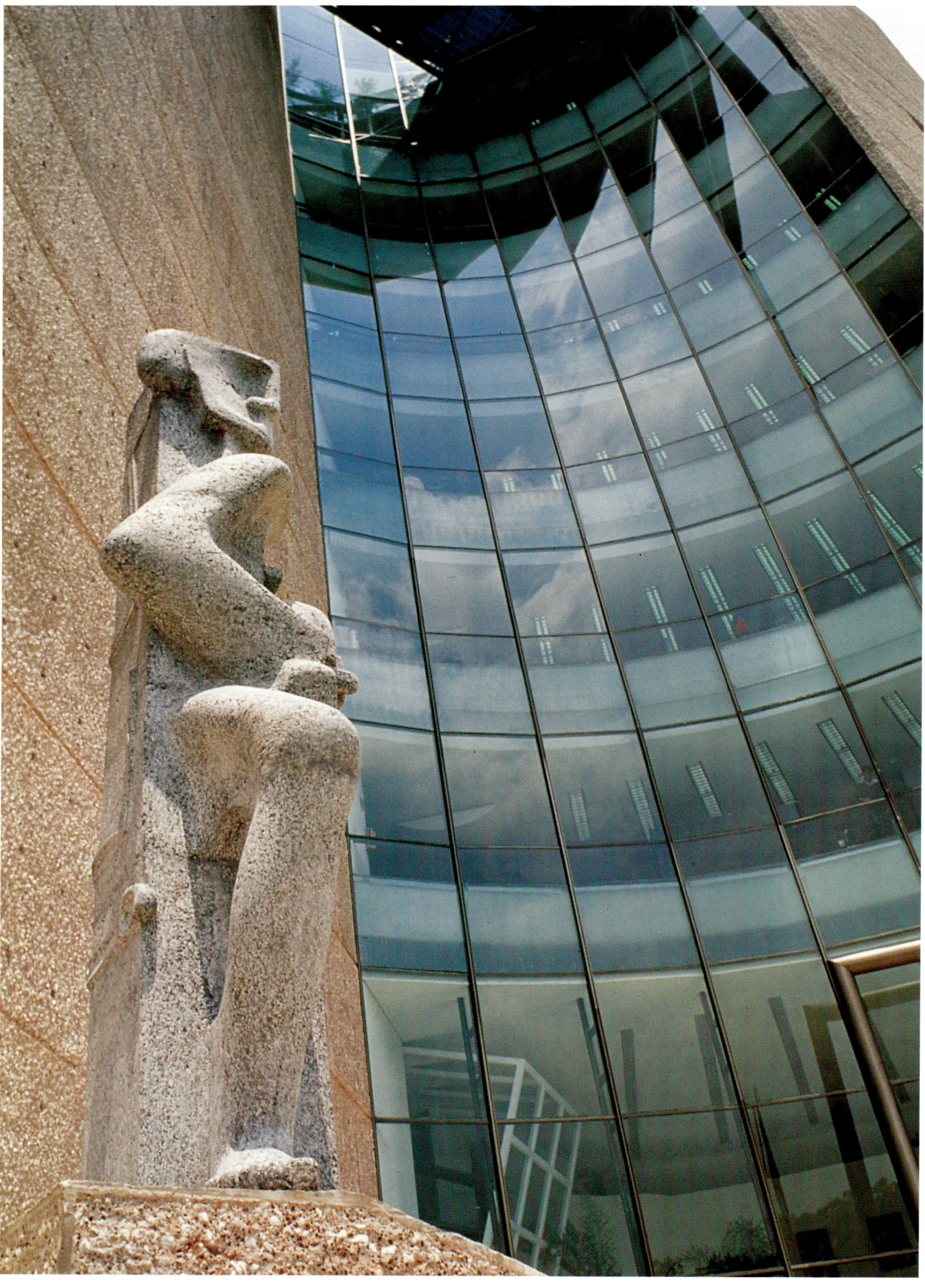

Opposite page, detail of the curved glass facade. Below, the entrance steps underlining the design of the facade behind them.
Sculpture: *Minerva*, by Herbert Hofmann-Ysenburg
Right, plan of the entrance floor of the Unidad de Seminarios in the rear part of the Fondo de Cultura Economica.

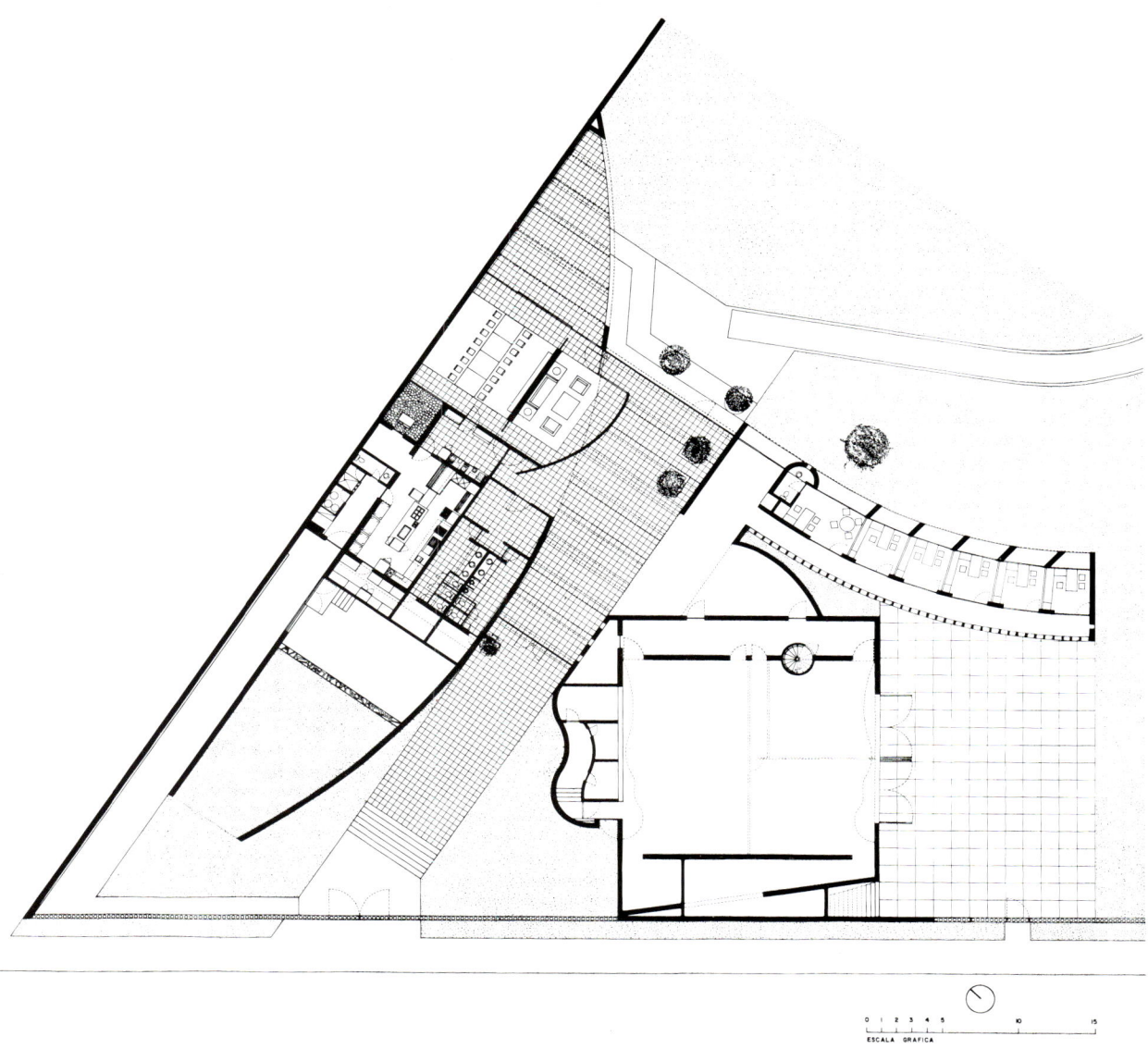

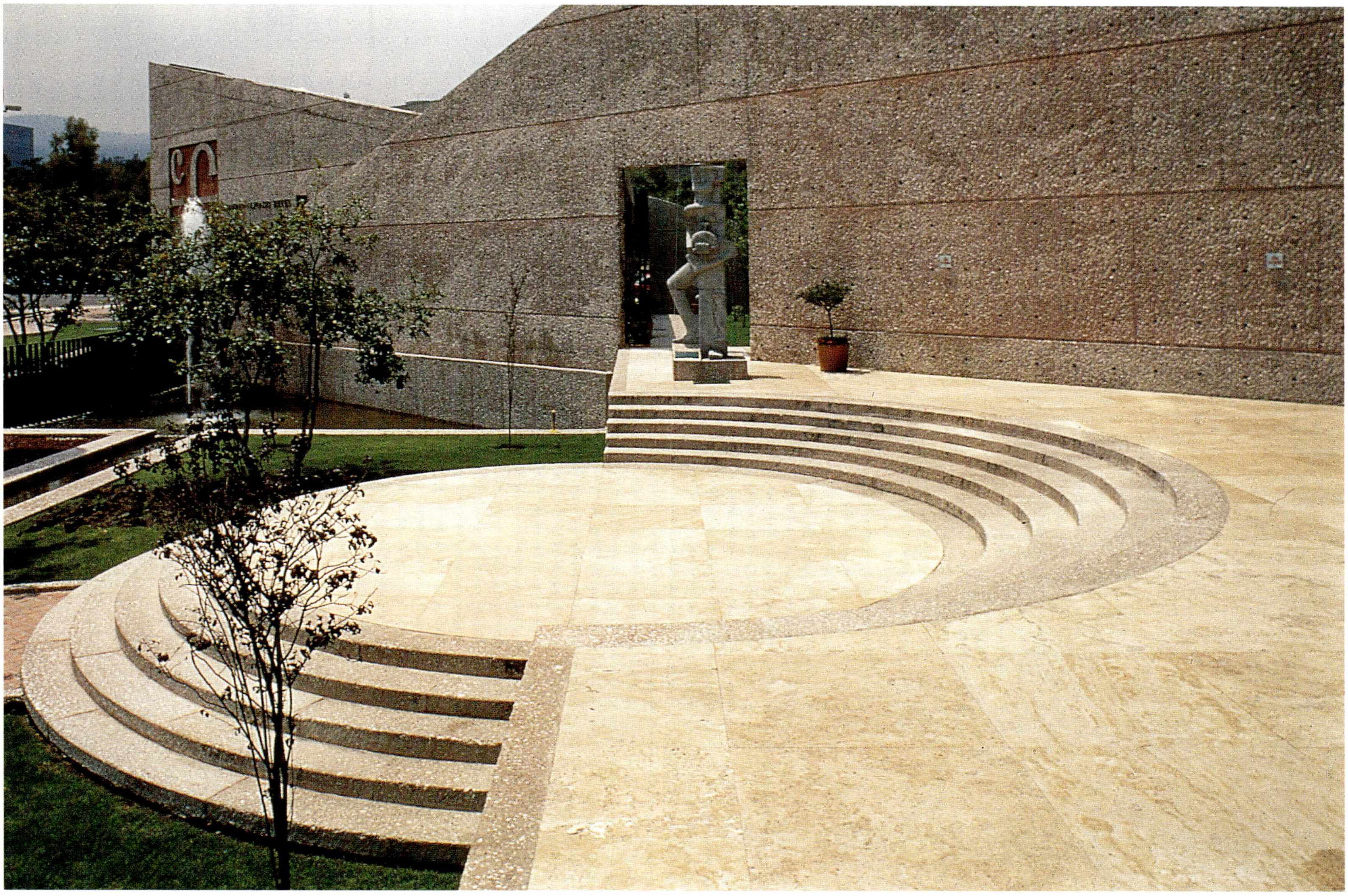

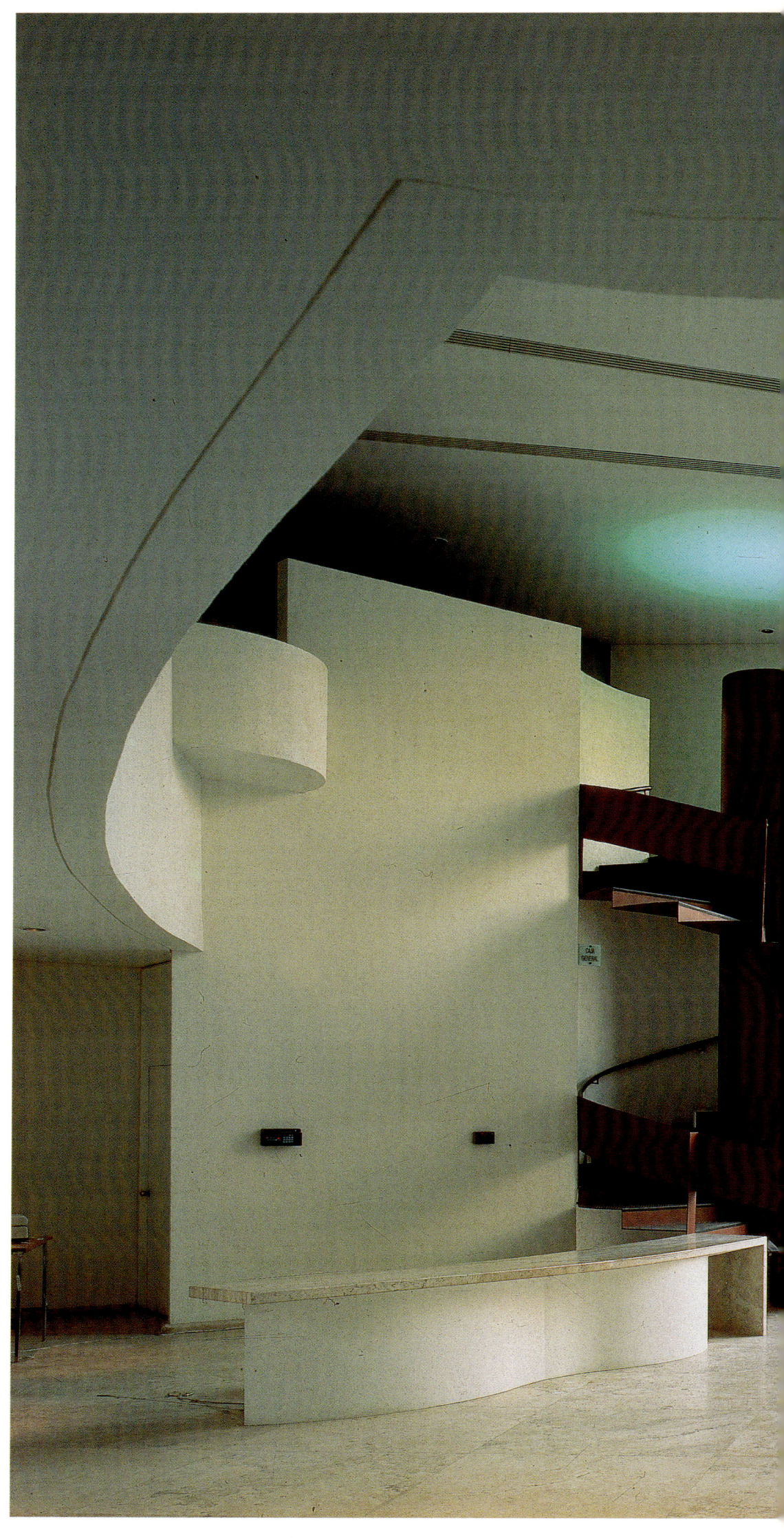

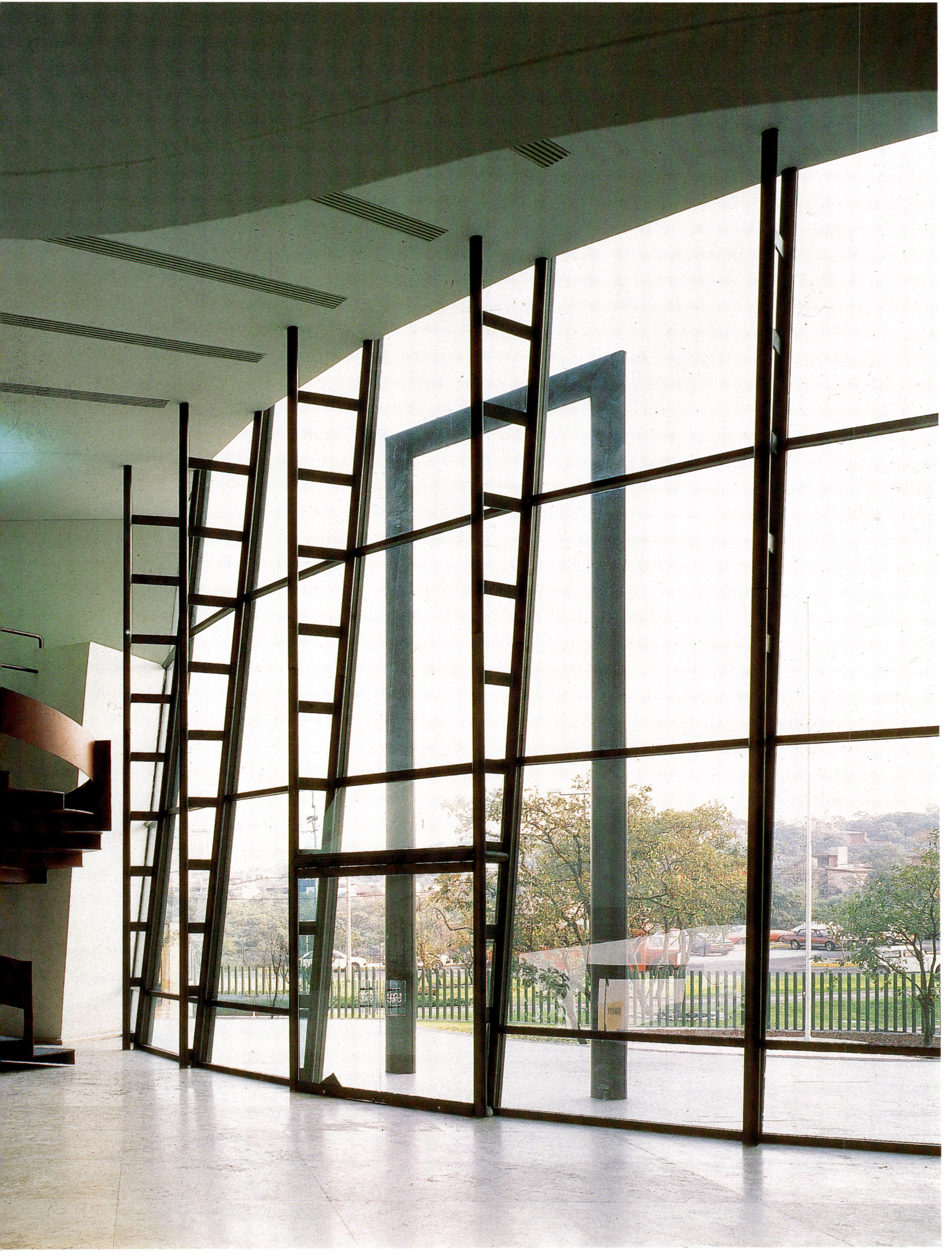

Mexico City, 1990

Children's Museum

Competition

Architect
Teodoro González de León

Collaborator
Ernesto Betancourt

Project area
1600 sq.m.

In 1990 Teodoro González de León took part in a competition to design a Children's Museum in Mexico City with the help of Ernesto Betancourt. González de Leon used this project to experiment with his own peculiar "style". In other words, he experimented with new approaches to stylistic design on a building planned to be built in his own home city. A city whose characteristics and connotations, underlying the architecture itself, are perfectly familiar to González de León.

His intentions are clearly outlined in the project brief, in which he spends more time over his stylistic intentions and design approach than construction details.

"El museo es un juego de volúmenes a escala urbana. Desde el Periférico, la composición será un acontecimiento urbano con cuatro sólidos que simularán estar depositados al azar". A careful analysis of the ground floor of the museum shows what González de León means by "placing the structures so that they rise up" (... estar depositados al alzar).

This calls for a profound knowledge of architectural design, working first from mental representations to eventually create real projects down on paper.

This is the "erudite" way of creating architecture and, as the great masters usually say, it is the only authentic way of "feeling" architecture.

Perhaps the most intriguing part of the entire design is the large cube buried in the ground at an angle of approximately 12.5 degrees.

This method of structural decomposition precedes computer assisted design and opens up the doors to a subtle form of deconstructivism that González de León is quite comfortable with and which he himself experiments on with great precision. As we will see, his later projects bear further evidence of this great intuition of a real master of architecture.

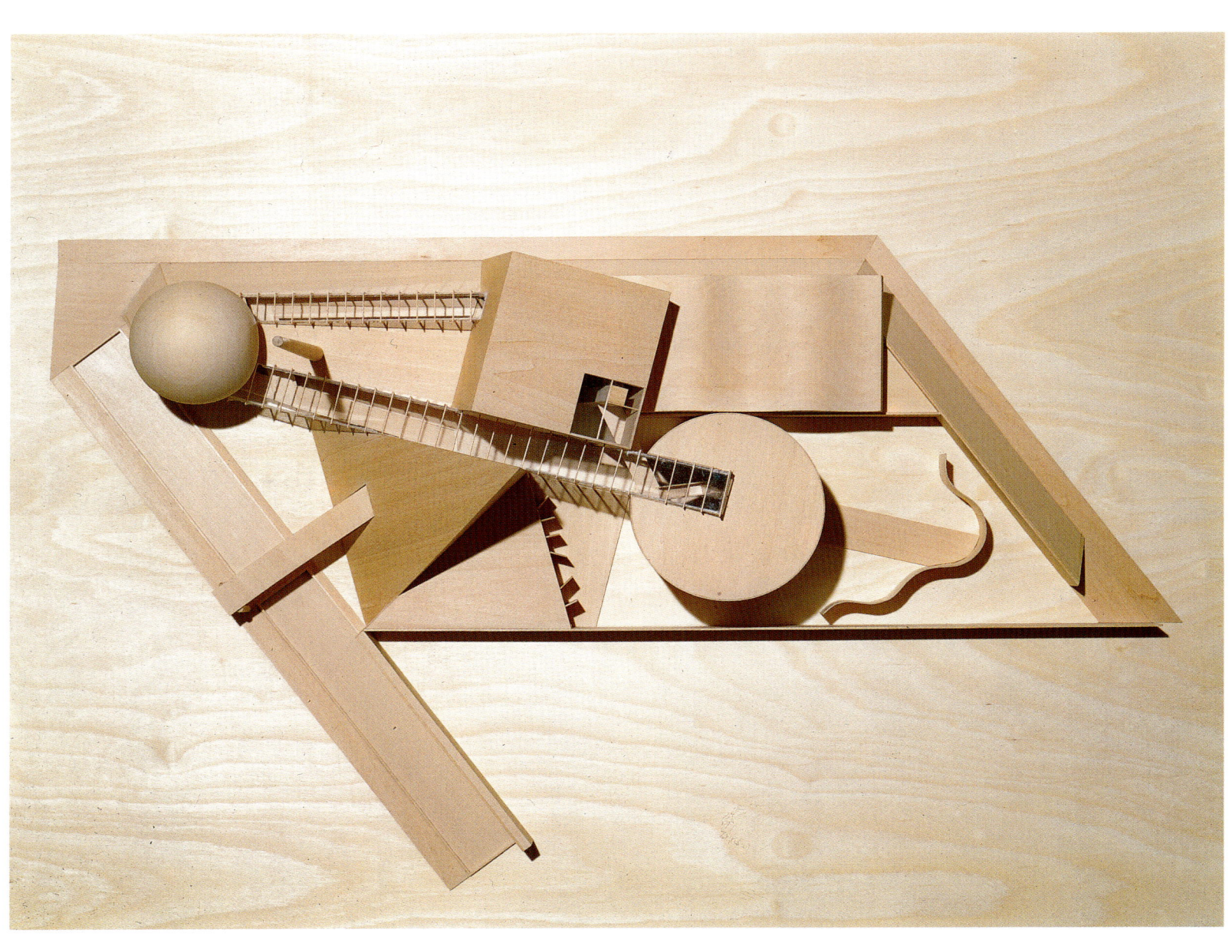

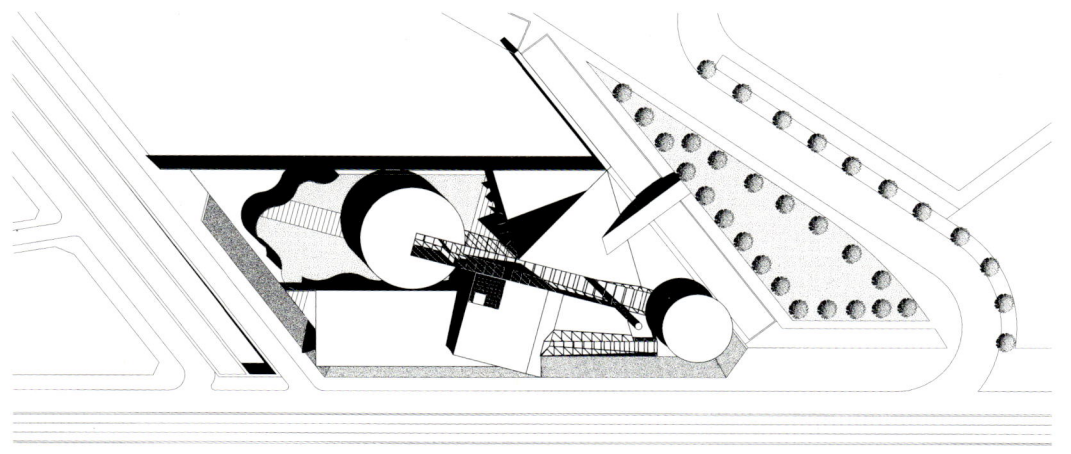

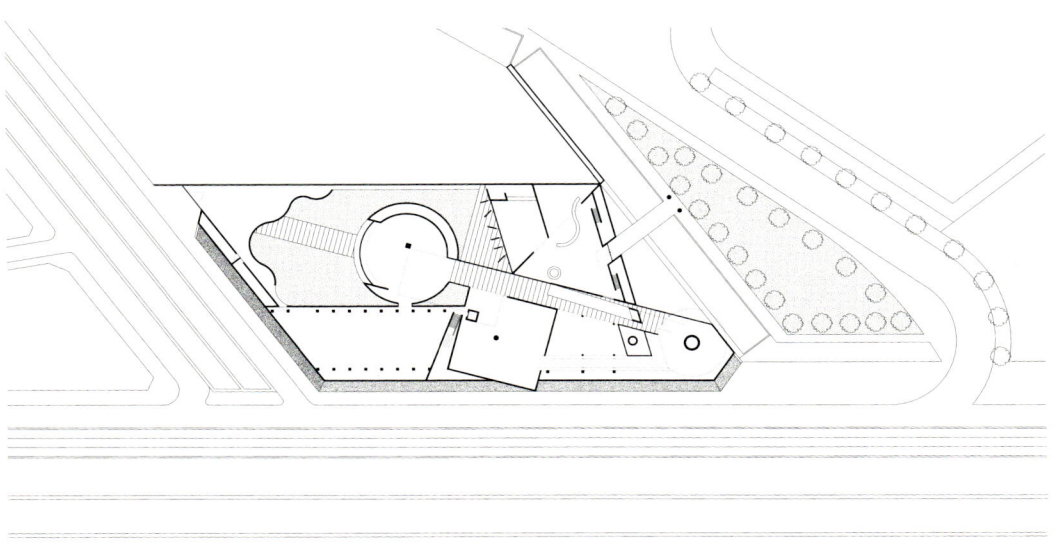

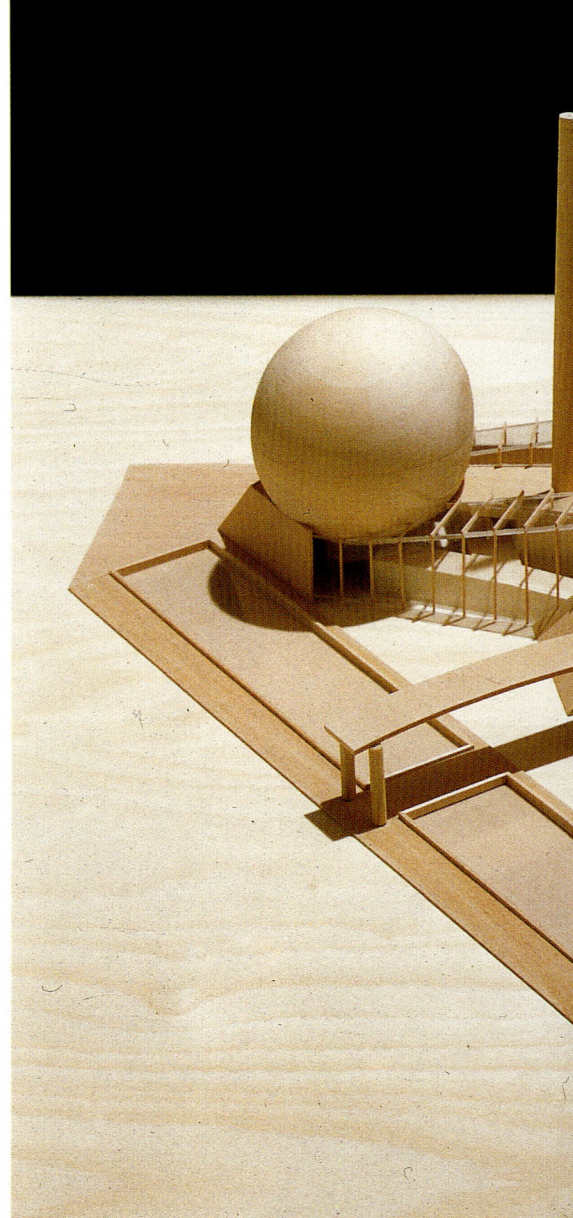

Site plan and plan of the complex. Opposite page, section and model of the museum designed like an interplay of urban-scale volumes.

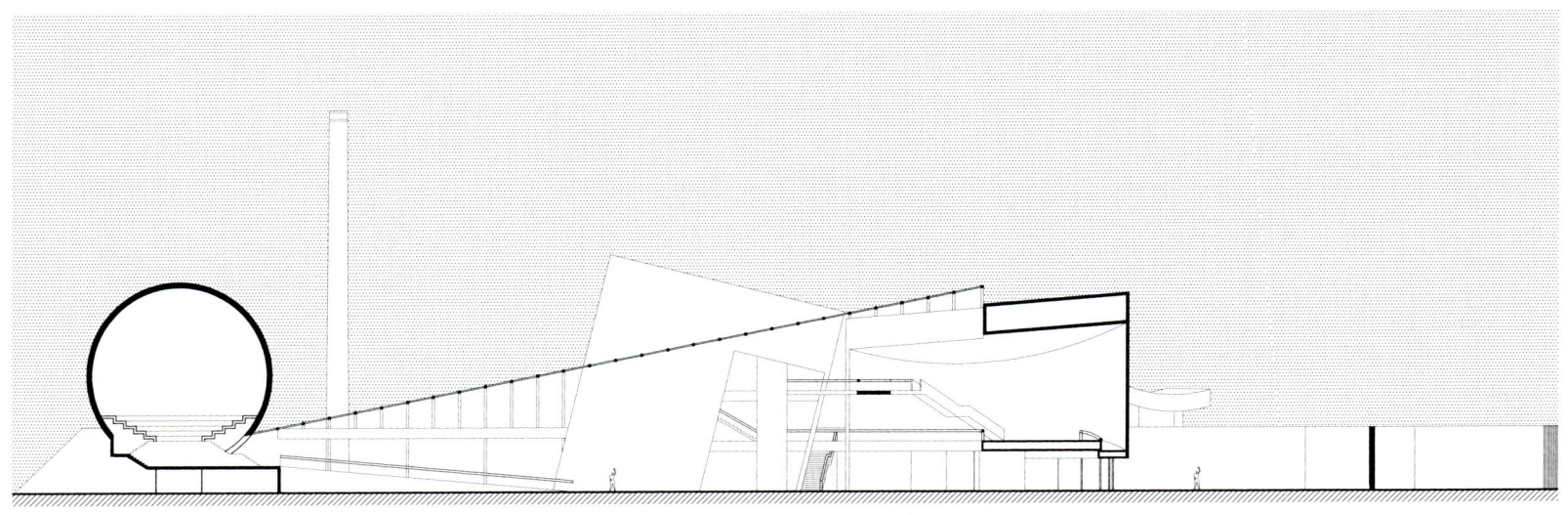

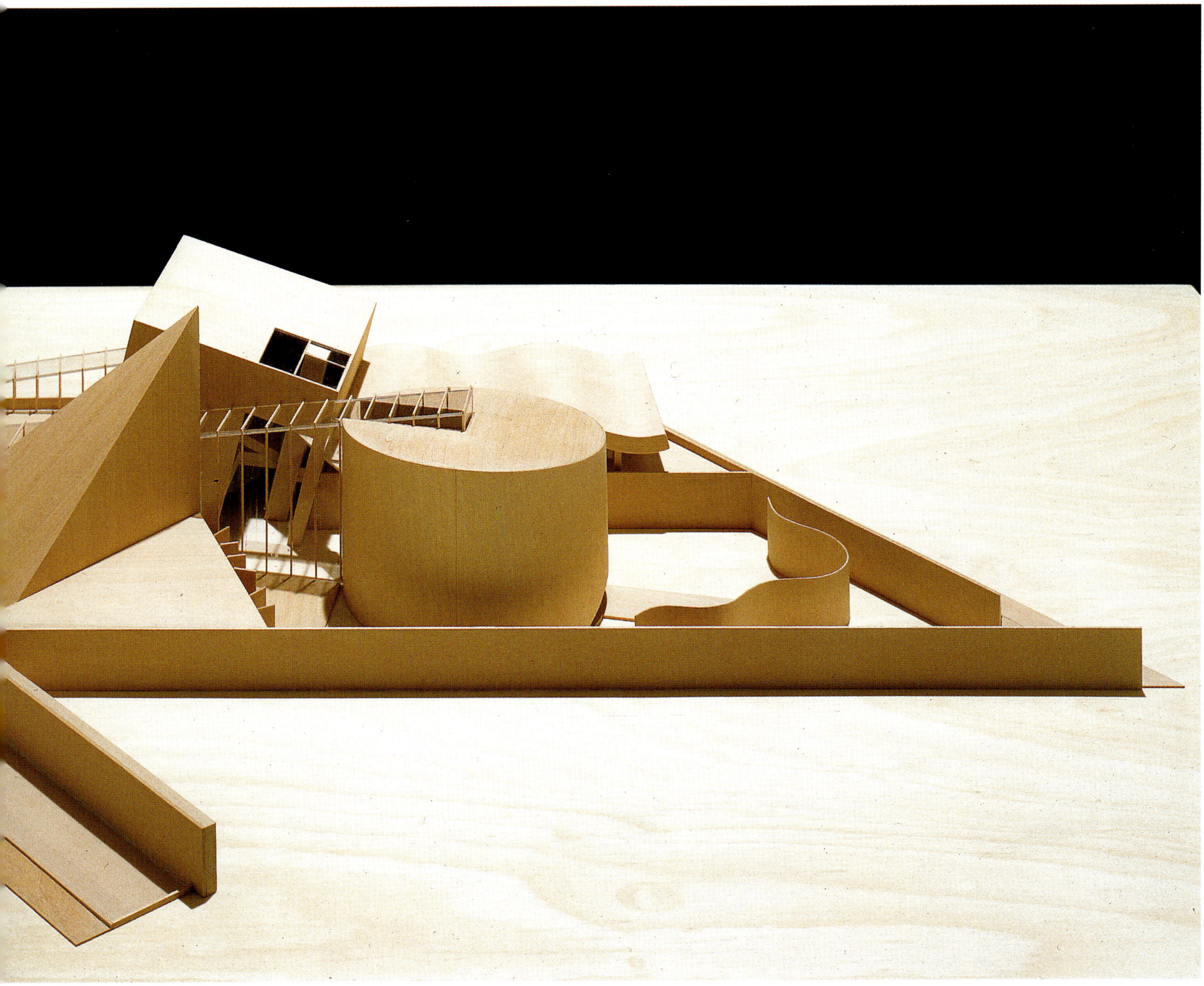

Veracruz, Mexico, 1991-1992

Site Museum at El Tajín

Owner
Gobierno del Estado de Veracruz

Architect
Teodoro González de León

Collaborator
Miguel Barbachano Osorio

Structural design
Héctor Margain

Museography
Rodolfo Rivera

Air-conditioning, electric, hydraulics and sanitaiy design
Tecnoproyectos, S.C.

Construction area
2,760 sq. m.

This Museum is situated 150 metres from El Tajín archeological site.

The entire complex is constructed around a covered circular space that both attracts the visitor's attention and, at the same time, provides an observation point over the archeological site and monuments.

The sheer complexity of the project makes it look like a rather random collection of forms, if analysed in haste. However, a more careful examination shows that the basic layout conceals a definite attempt to project the museum into close interaction with its surroundings, transforming this work of architecture into an event capable of triangulating the land and, at the same time, providing some vital points of view over both the urban surroundings and archeological site.

Here again the project hinges around a "diagonal" form. González de León is often capable of desecrating the forms he has designed to find the best way of forming his structures and the true functional sense of his projects; a diagonal line through the site plan adds strength and importance to this particular design. Here again we have that characteristic boldness, enterprise and ability to tackle every aspect of architecture, encompassing them all in a complex design symbol placed at the community's disposal.

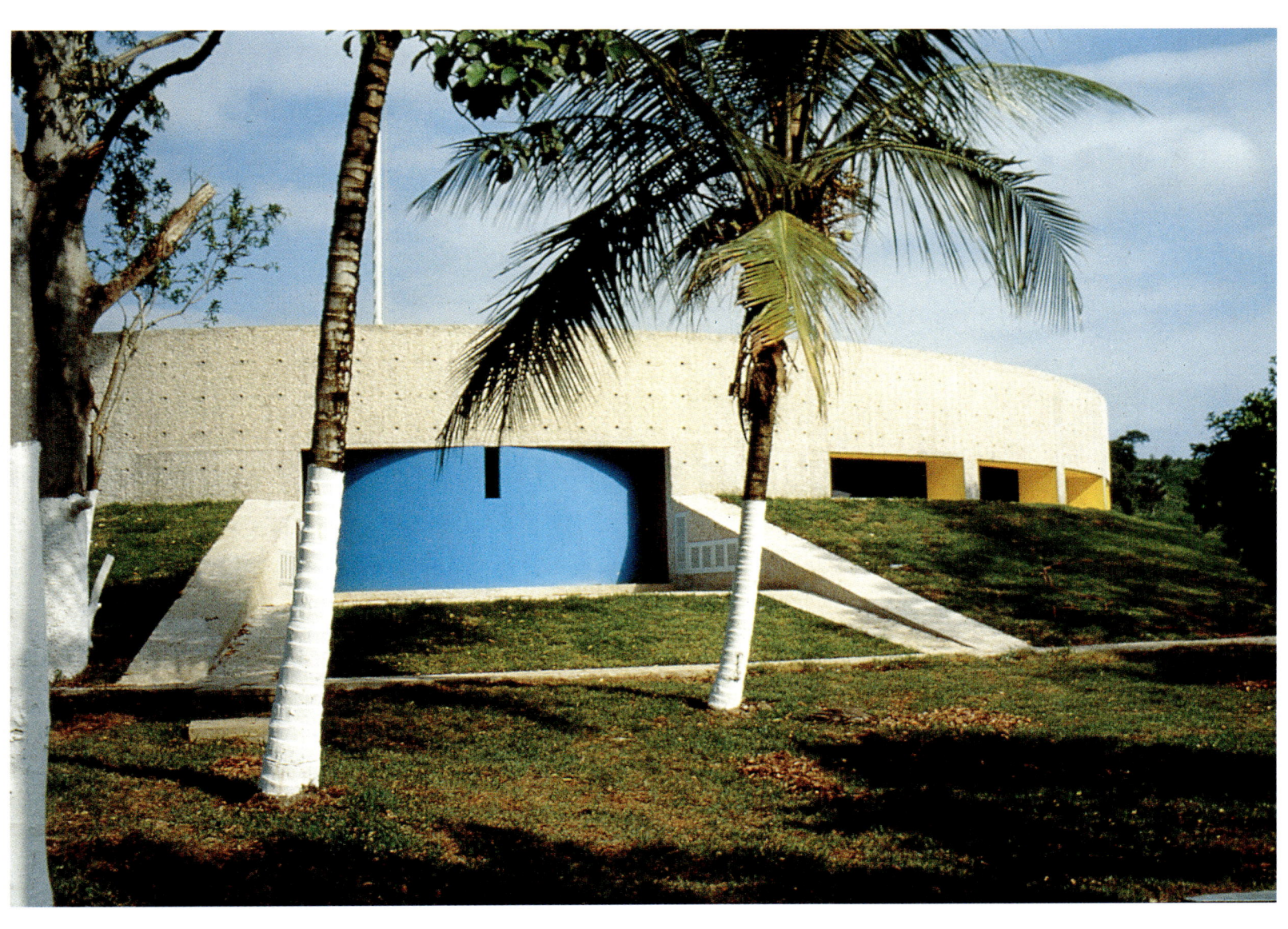

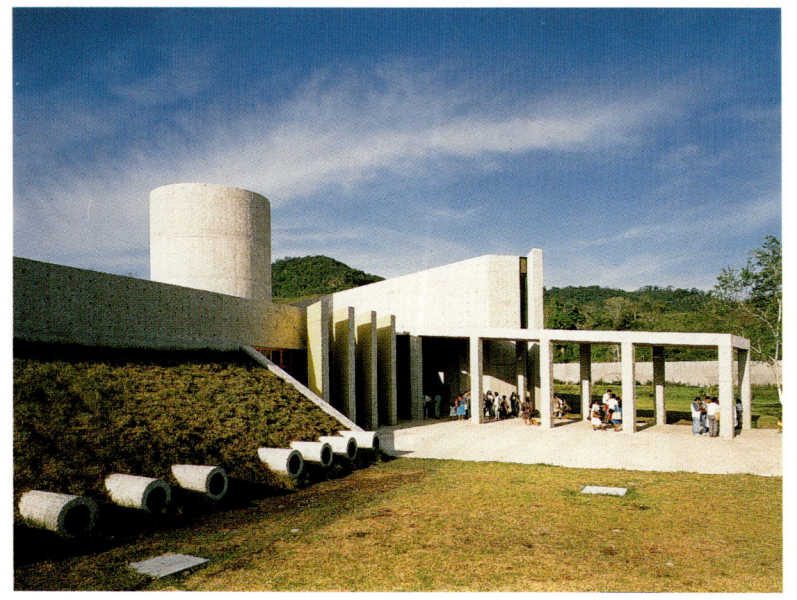
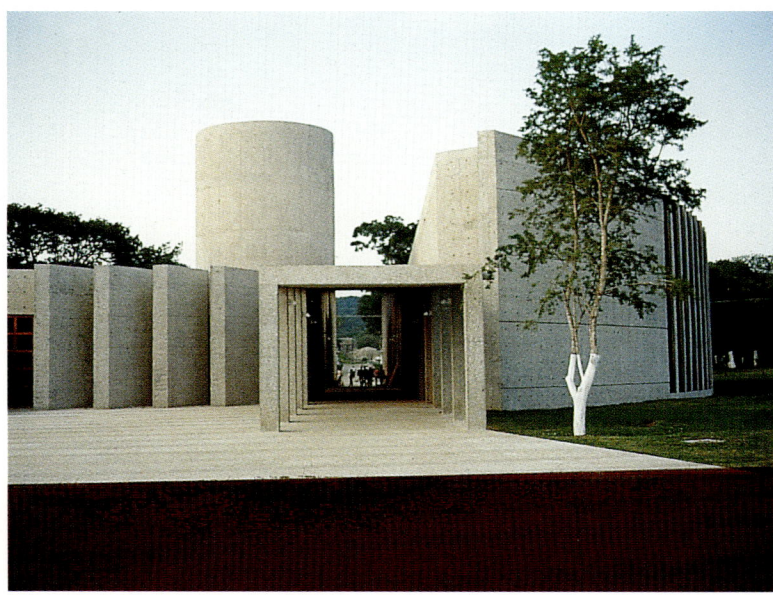

Details of the entrance to the museum designed to complete the archaeological site of El Tajín. Left, plan of the first floor and, below, site plan.

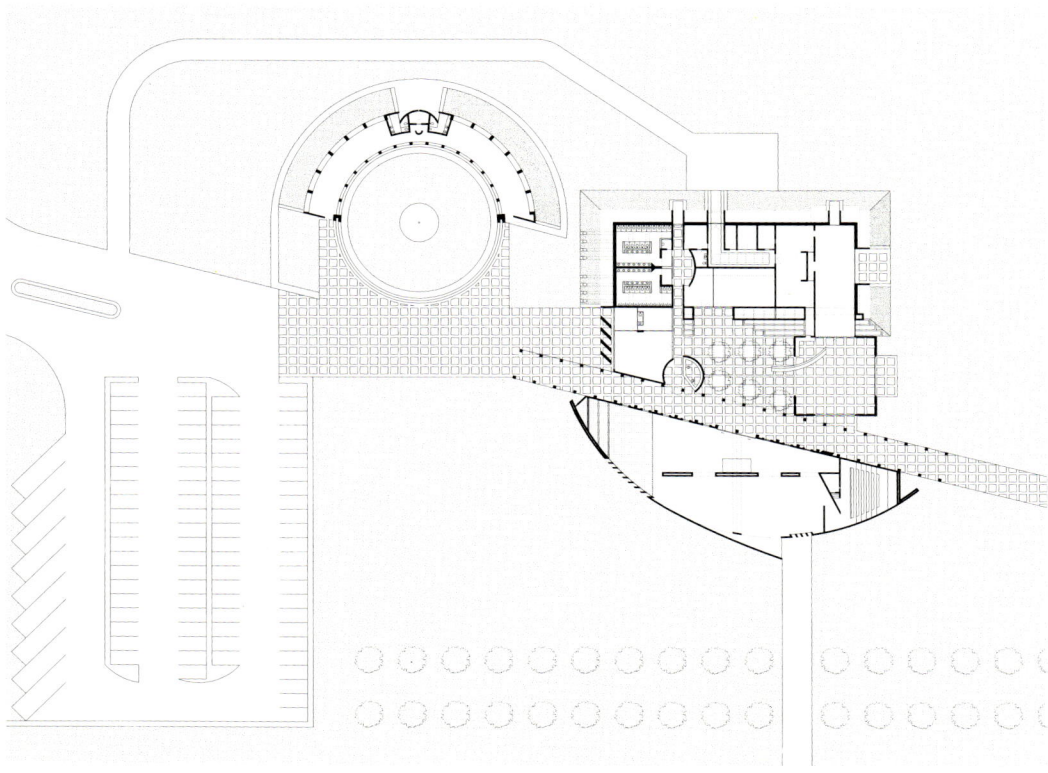
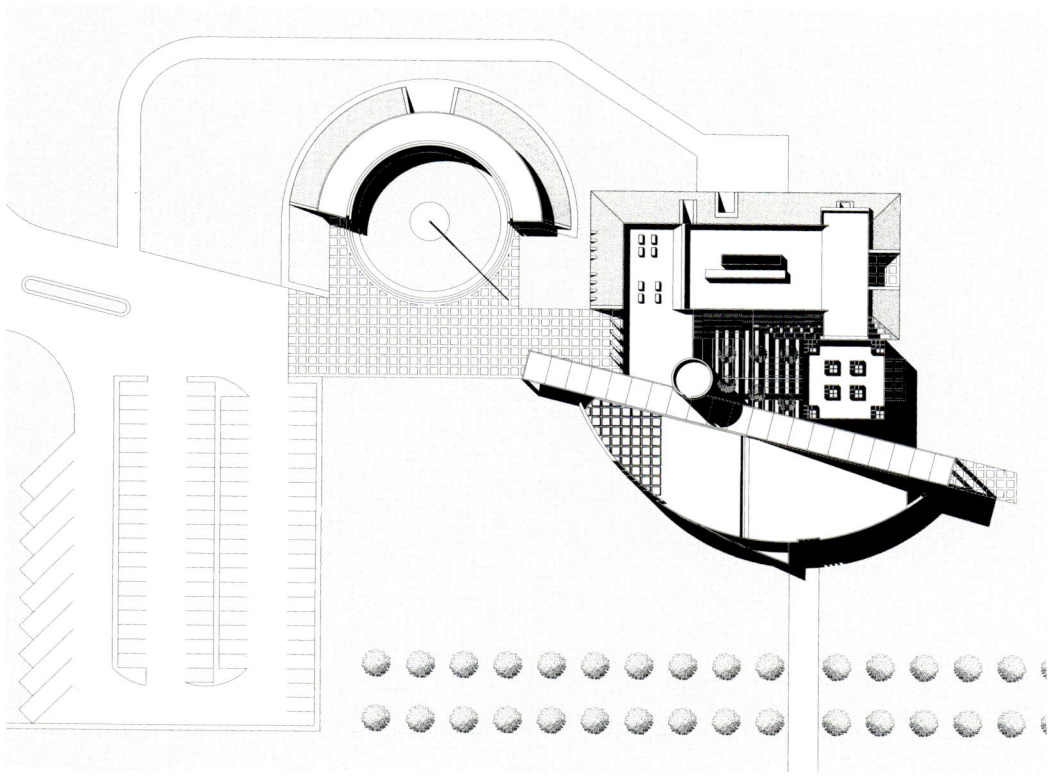

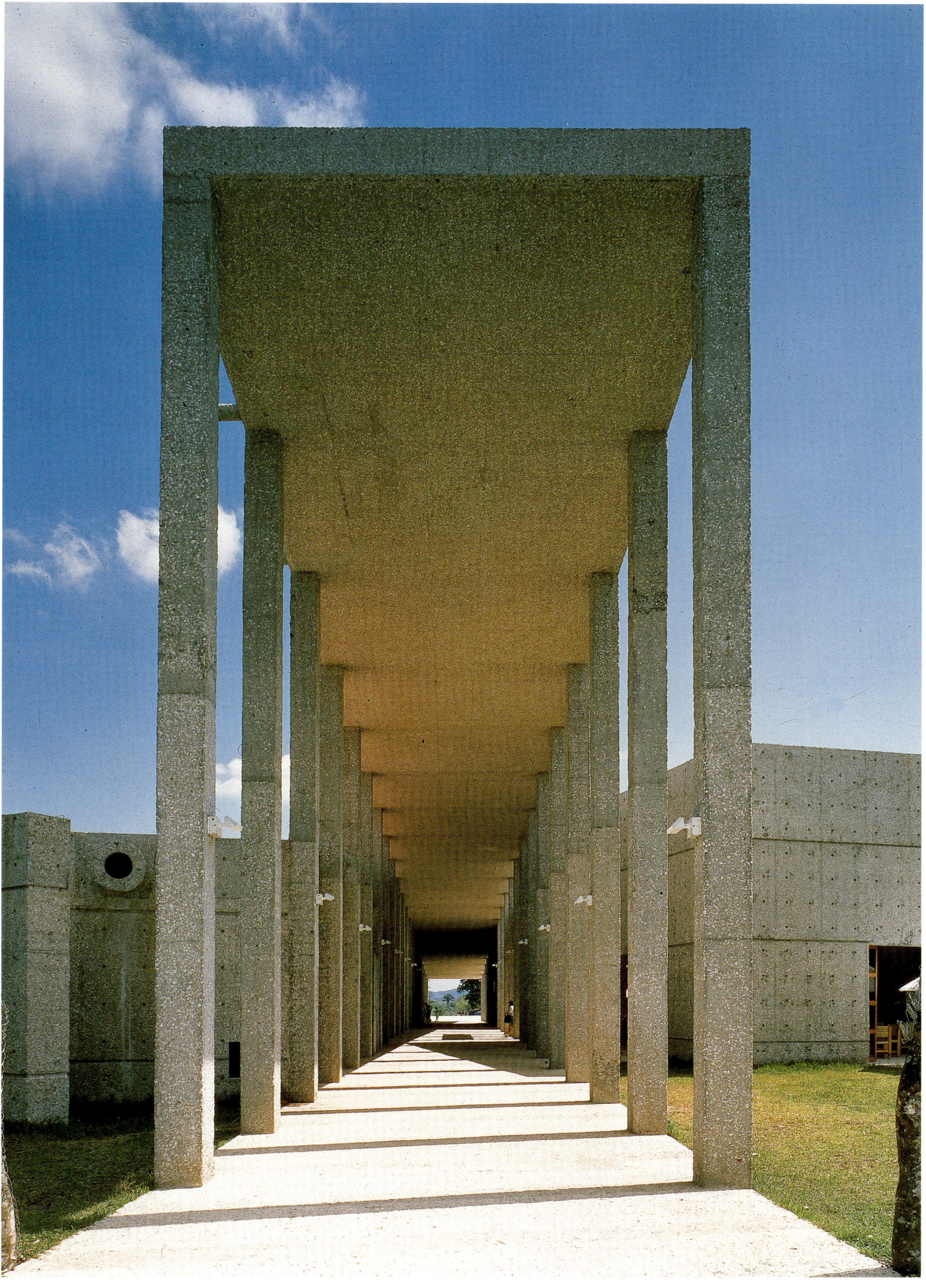

Mexico City, 1990-1996

Hewlett-Packard Offices

Owner
Arrendadora Hewlett-Packard

Architects
Teodoro González de León
J. Francisco Serrano

Collaborator
Antonio Rodriguez

Interior design
Luis A. de Regil

Structural design
Diseño y Supervisión, "DYS", S.C.

Air-conditioning design
DYPRO

Electric design
COESA Ingenieria, S.A.

Hydraulics and sanitary design
Sociedad Hidromecánica, S.A.,
Garza Maldonado y Asociados, S.C.

Construction area
18,180 sq.m. offices
33, 760 sq.m. parkings
51,940 sq.m. total

More than others, this project draws on González de Leon's experience as a painter. Hewlett-Packard's offices in Mexico City are based on a set of triangles which, even in the elevation design, determine the architectural form of the entire building.

The basic "L"-shaped building design is constructed around a central entrance, partly covered by a light-weight triangular metal structure. The entrance courtyard is also surrounded by a patio that creates that familiar sense of monumentality found in most of González de León's architecture.

This particular building exudes a greater desire to design a project which, more than others, strives towards the purity of basic geometric forms. A huge cylinder, cut through by a triangular plane, adds perceptual force to the entire architectural context and acts like a joint hinging together the surrounding architectural space.

González de León uses these absolutely pure forms, representing highly precise design functions, to show yet again just what a master of architecture he really is. This is the kind of architecture he is interested in exploring in a quest for gradual stylistic progression.

For González de León, details are the key to all the experimentation he carries out in search of new ideas for future designs. The project for Hewlett-Packard's new offices is further proof that González de León is now one of the leading figures on the contemporary international architectural scene.

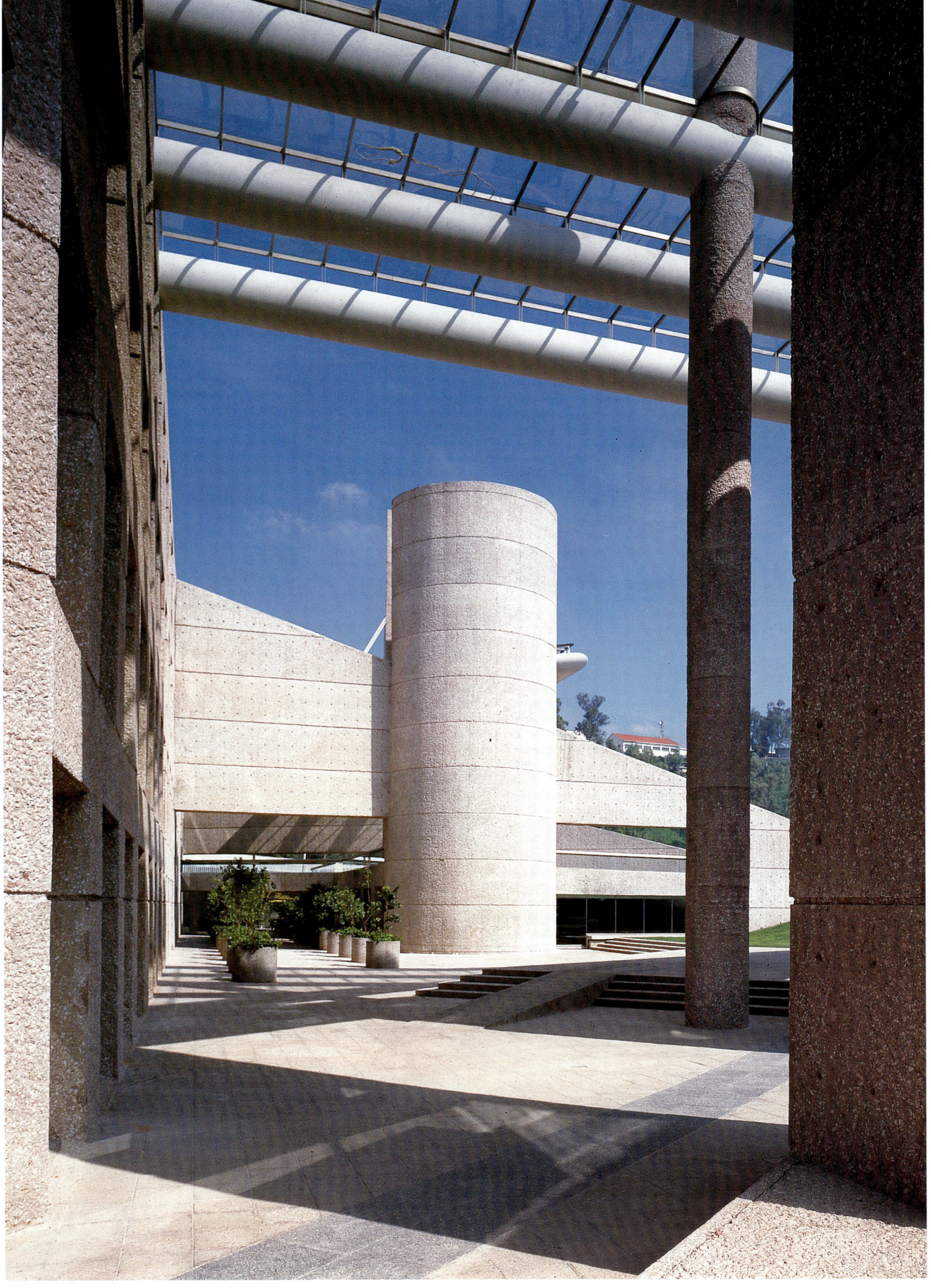

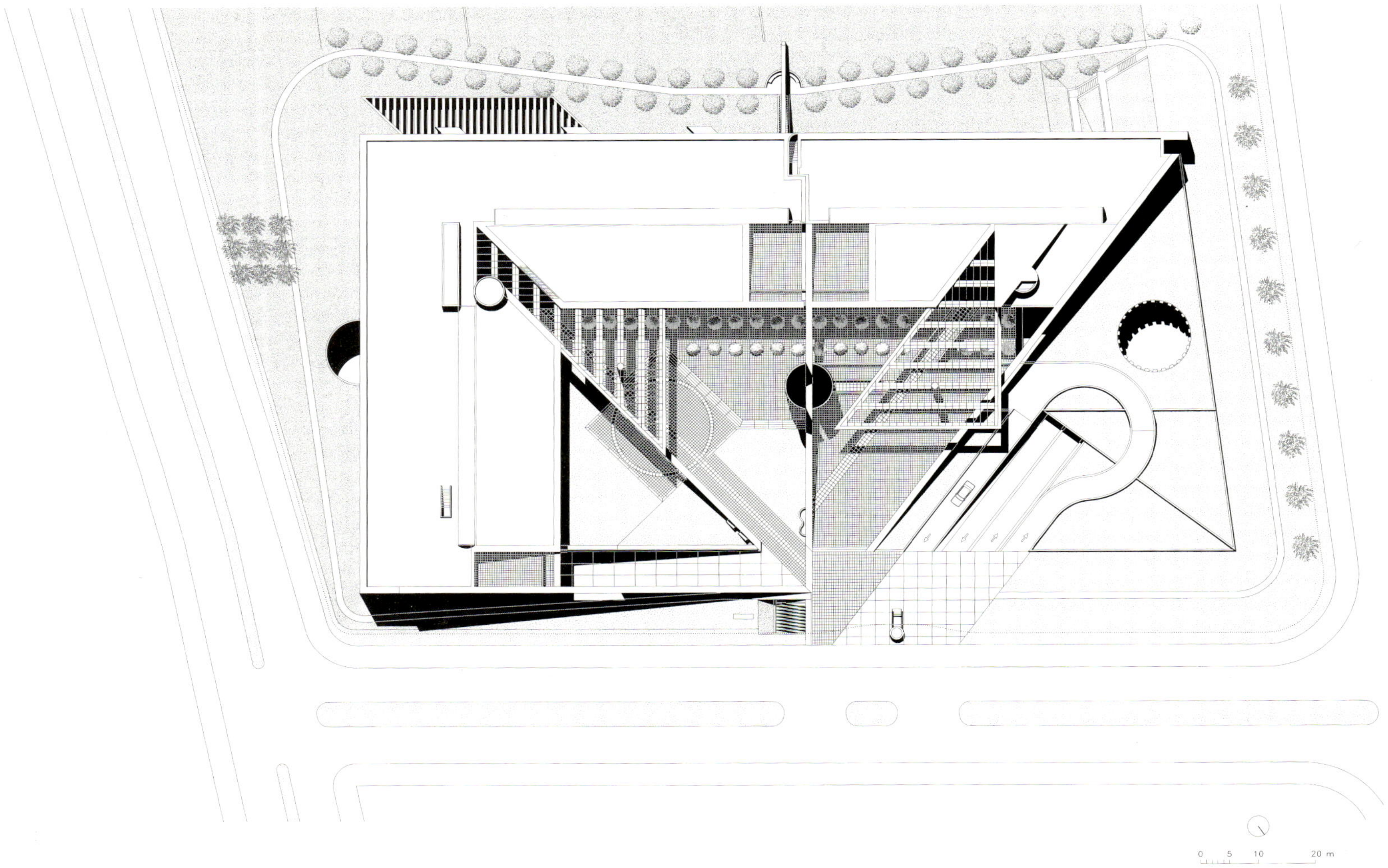

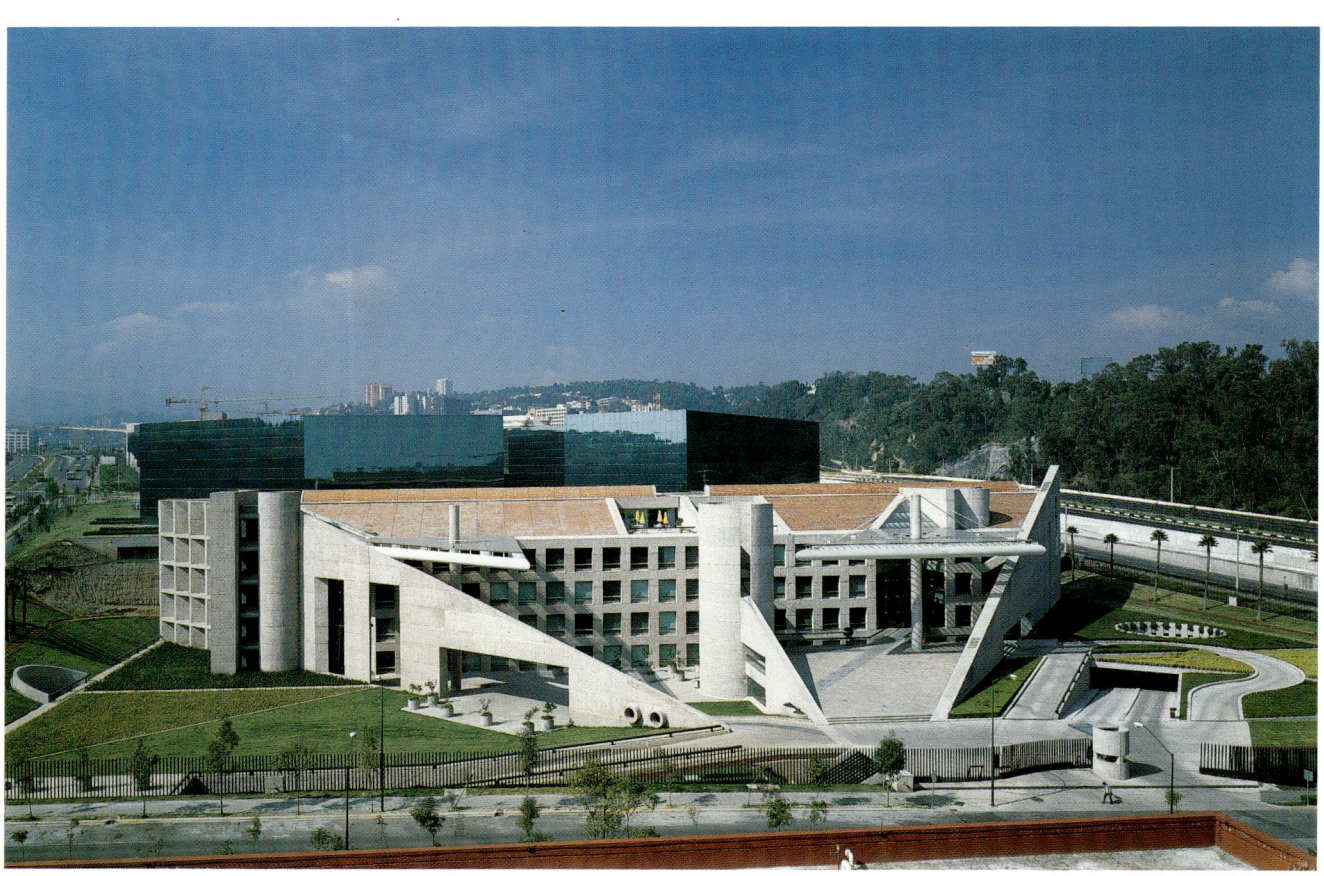

Above, site plan, left, general view and, opposite page, detail of the entrance to Hewlett-Packard's offices, whose design, hinging around the intersection of a group of triangles, alludes to Mexico's own painting tradition.

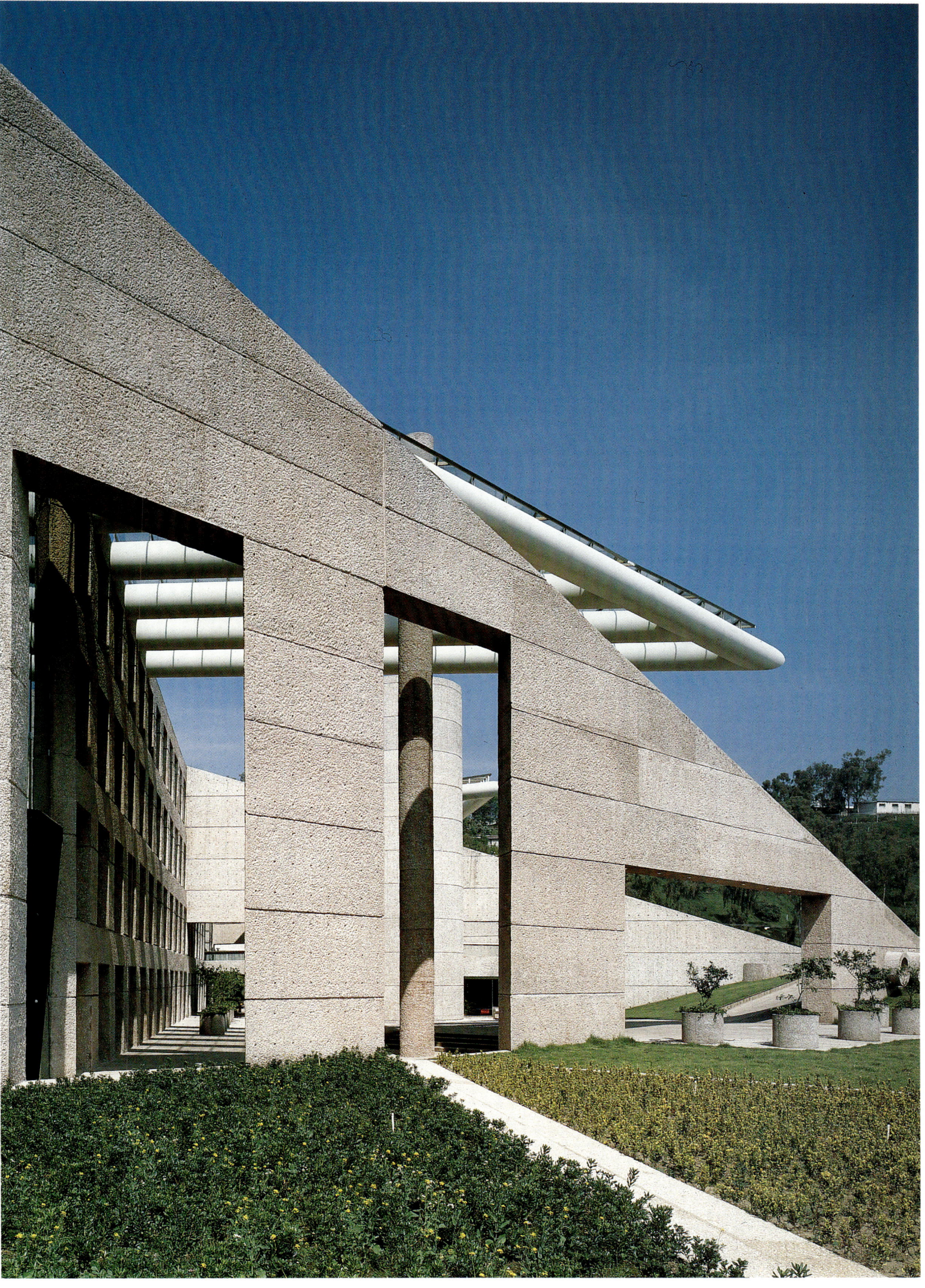

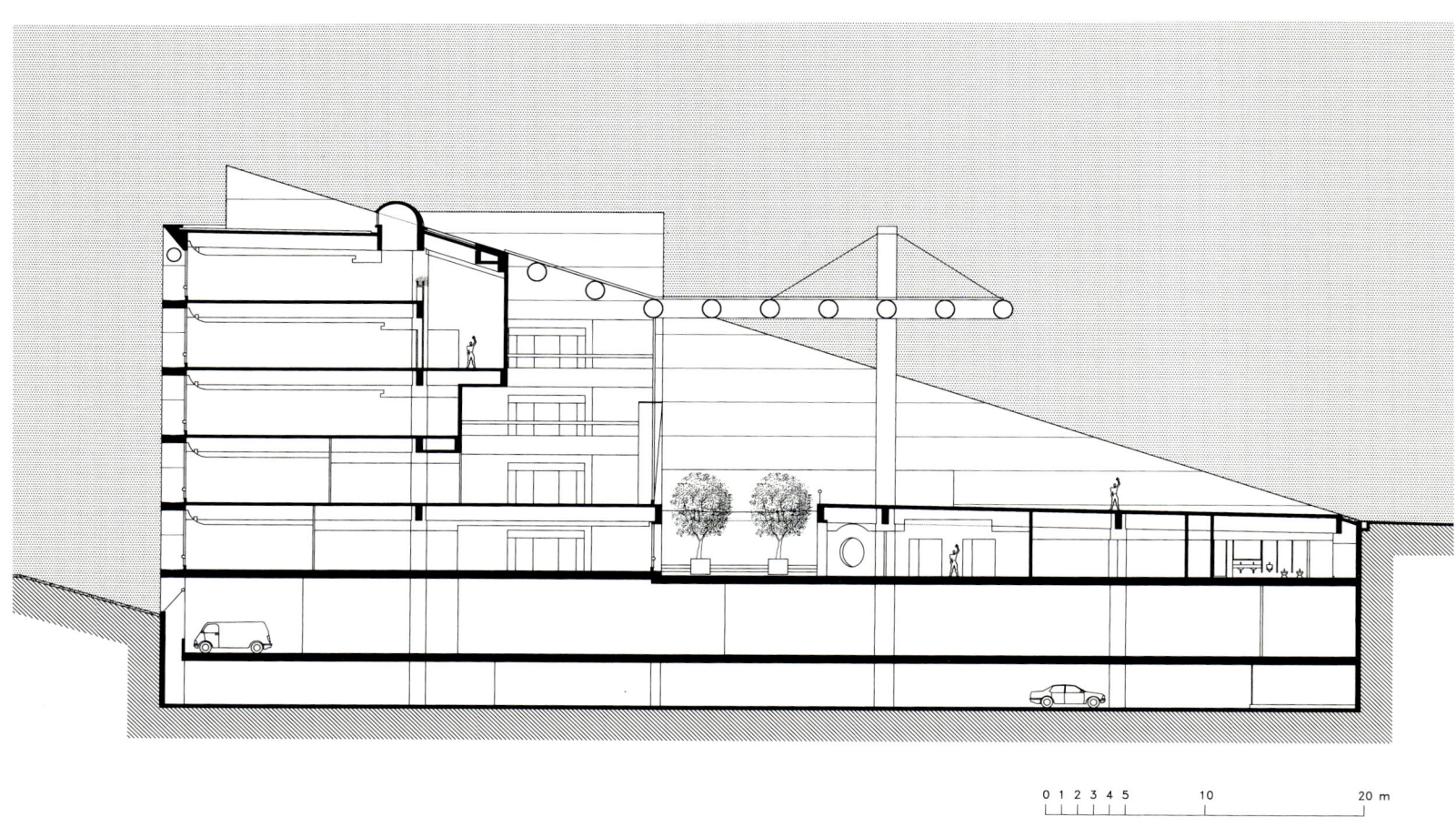

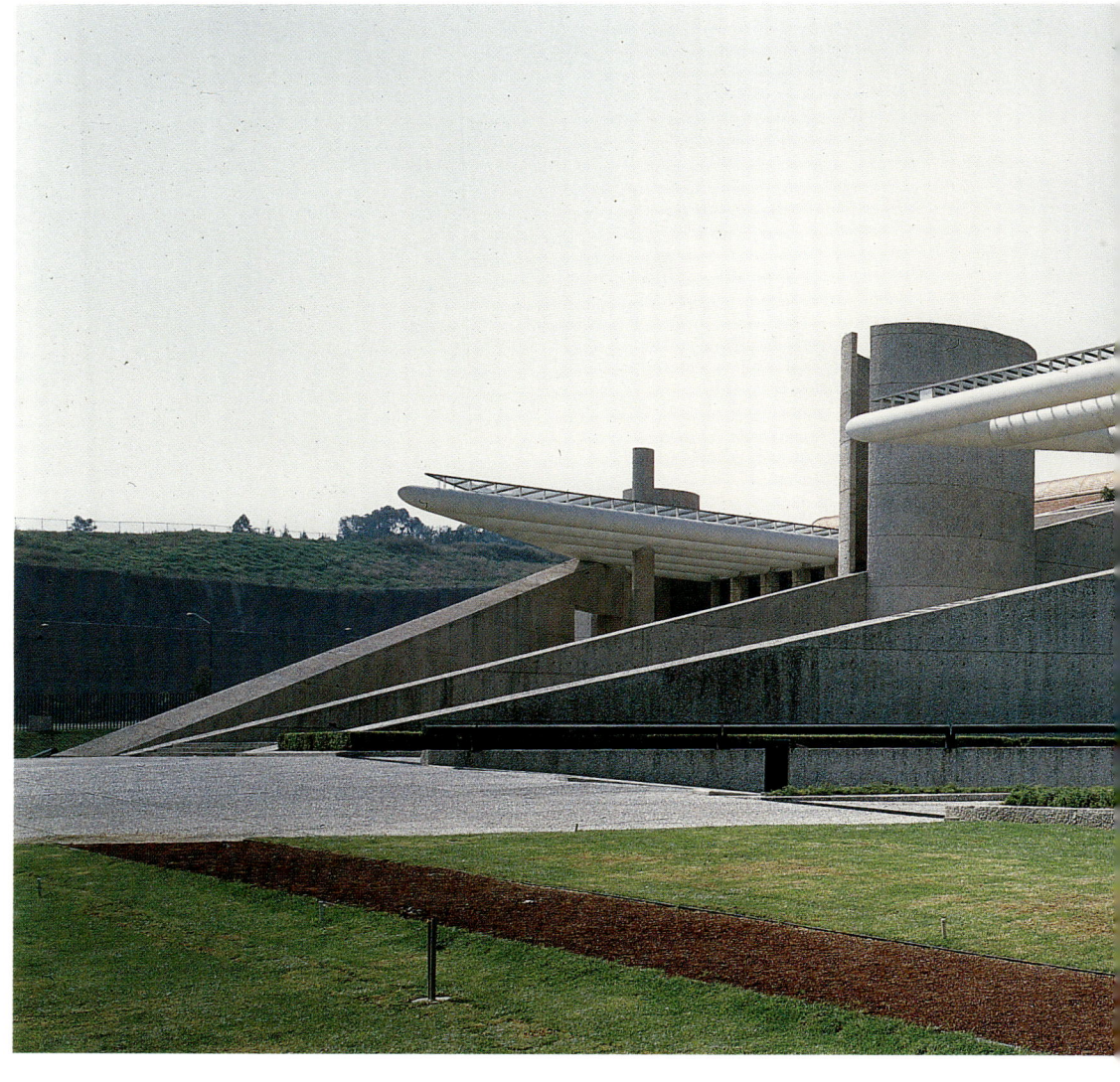

Above, cross section. Right and opposite page, perspective views of the building which features large triangular canopies sheltering the entrance courtyards.

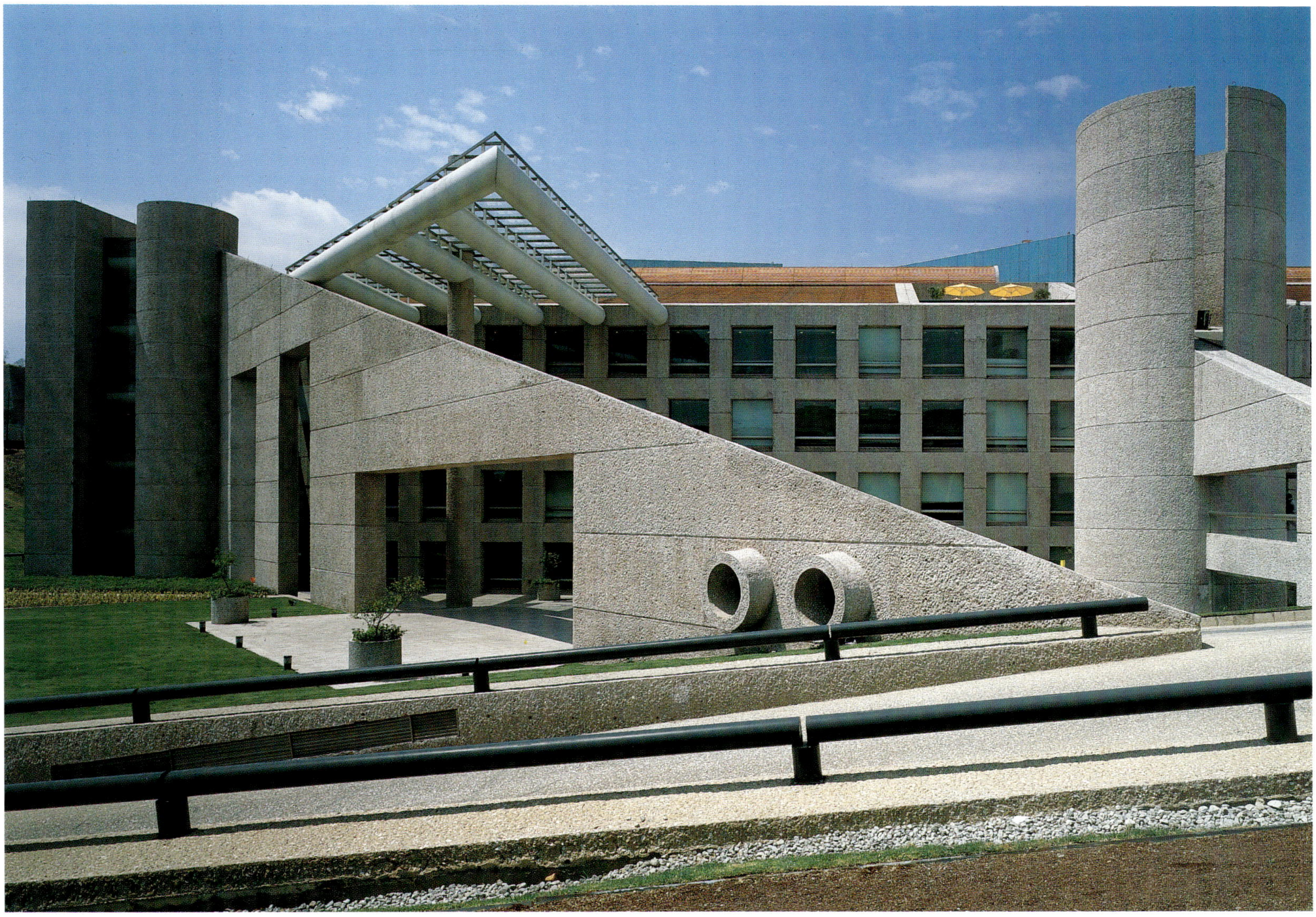

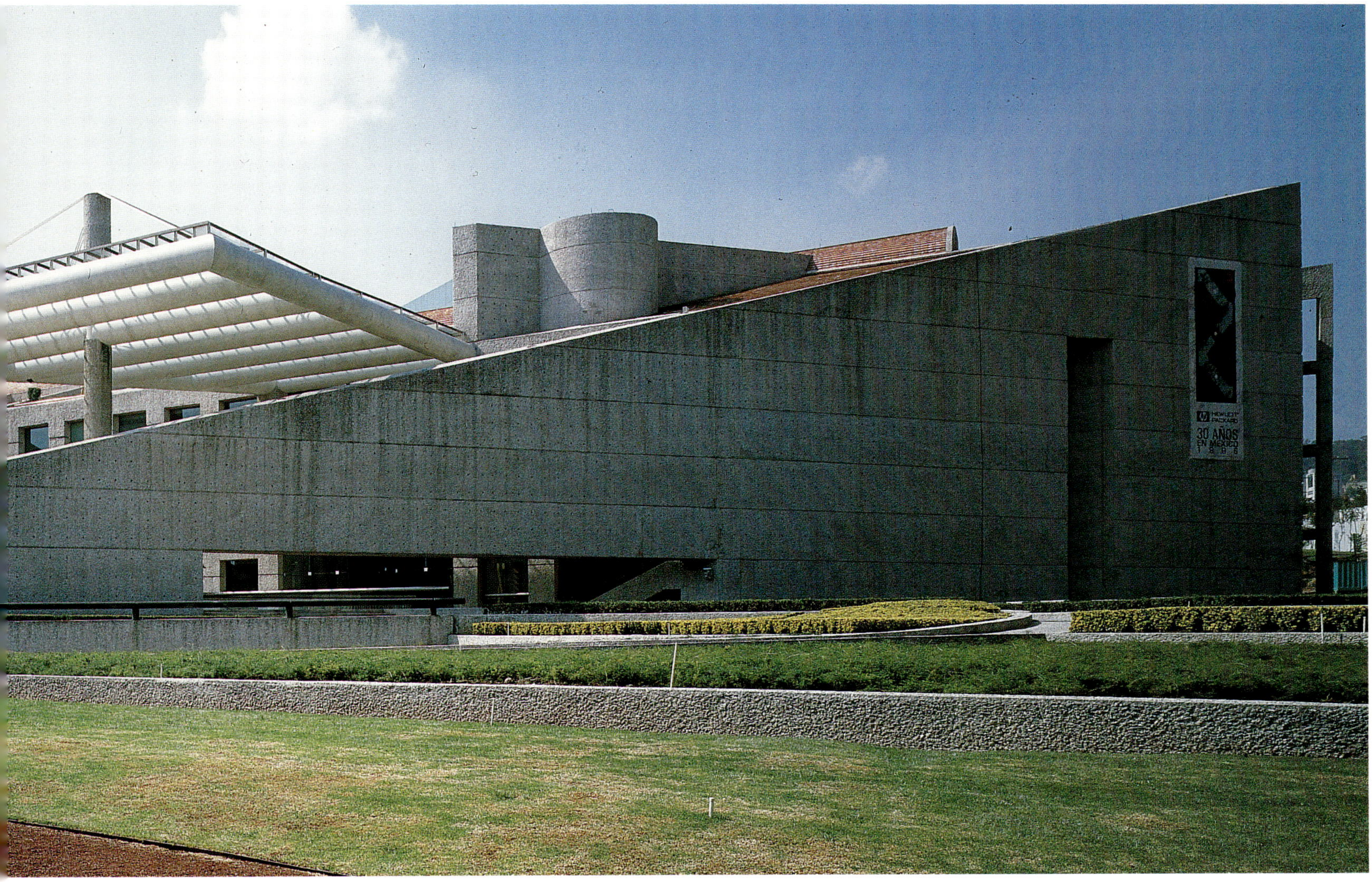

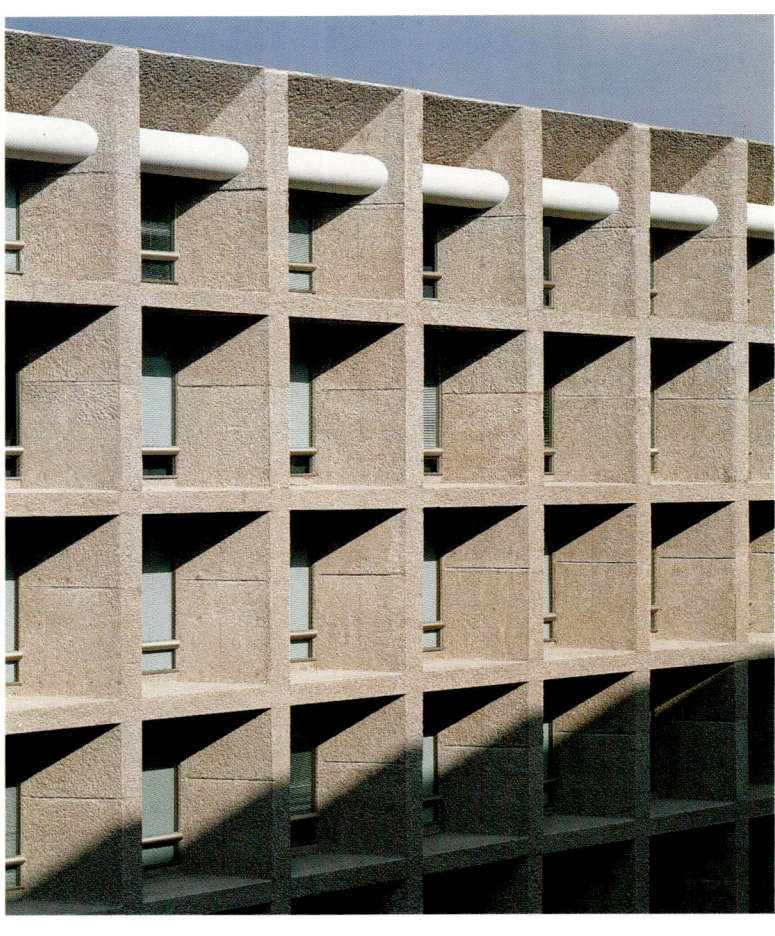

Detail of the south facade, whose windows are set back from the facade to ensure even greater shelter from the sunshine. Below, detail of one of the triangular walls around the complex.

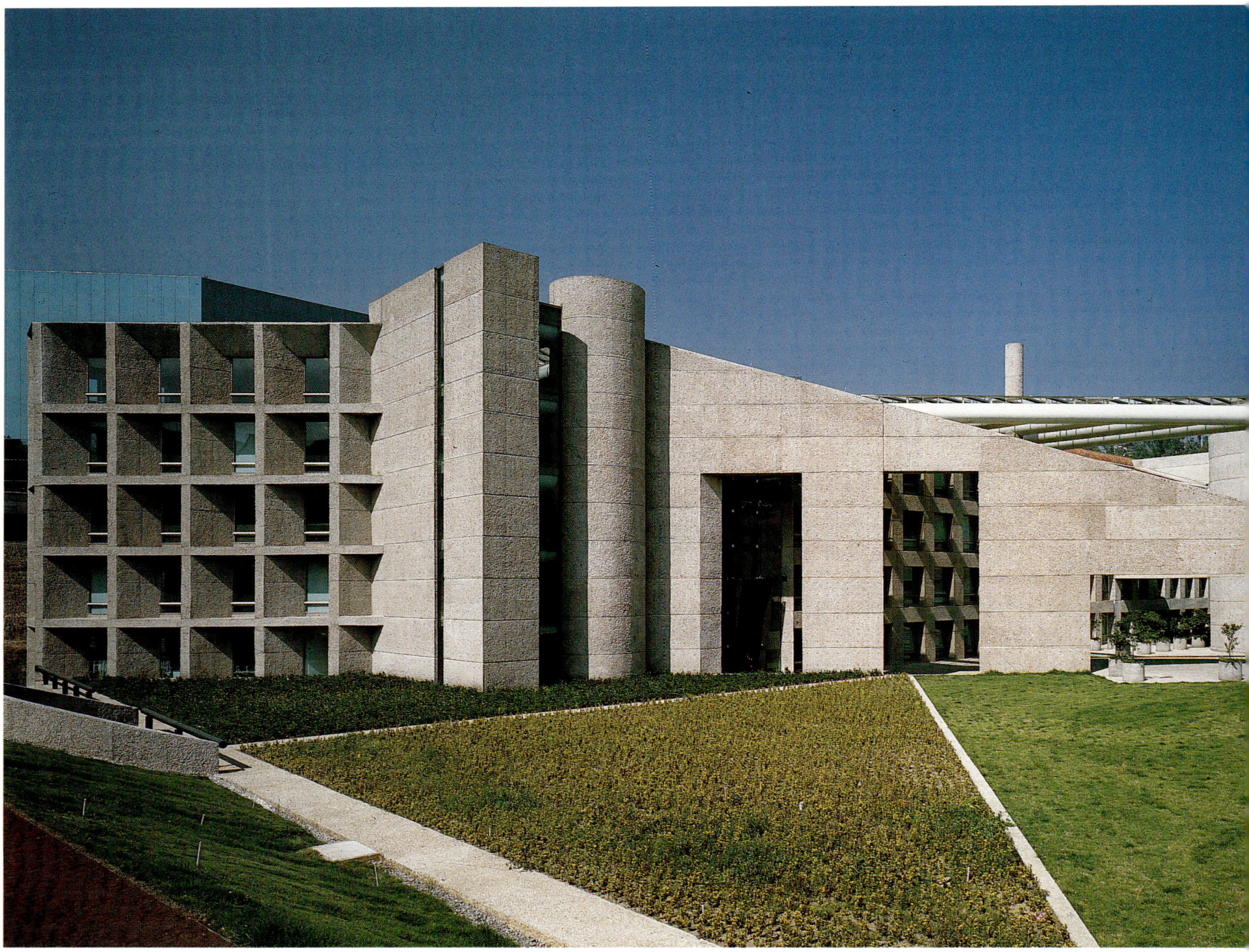

The cylinder containing one of the vertical lift shafts connected to the car park.

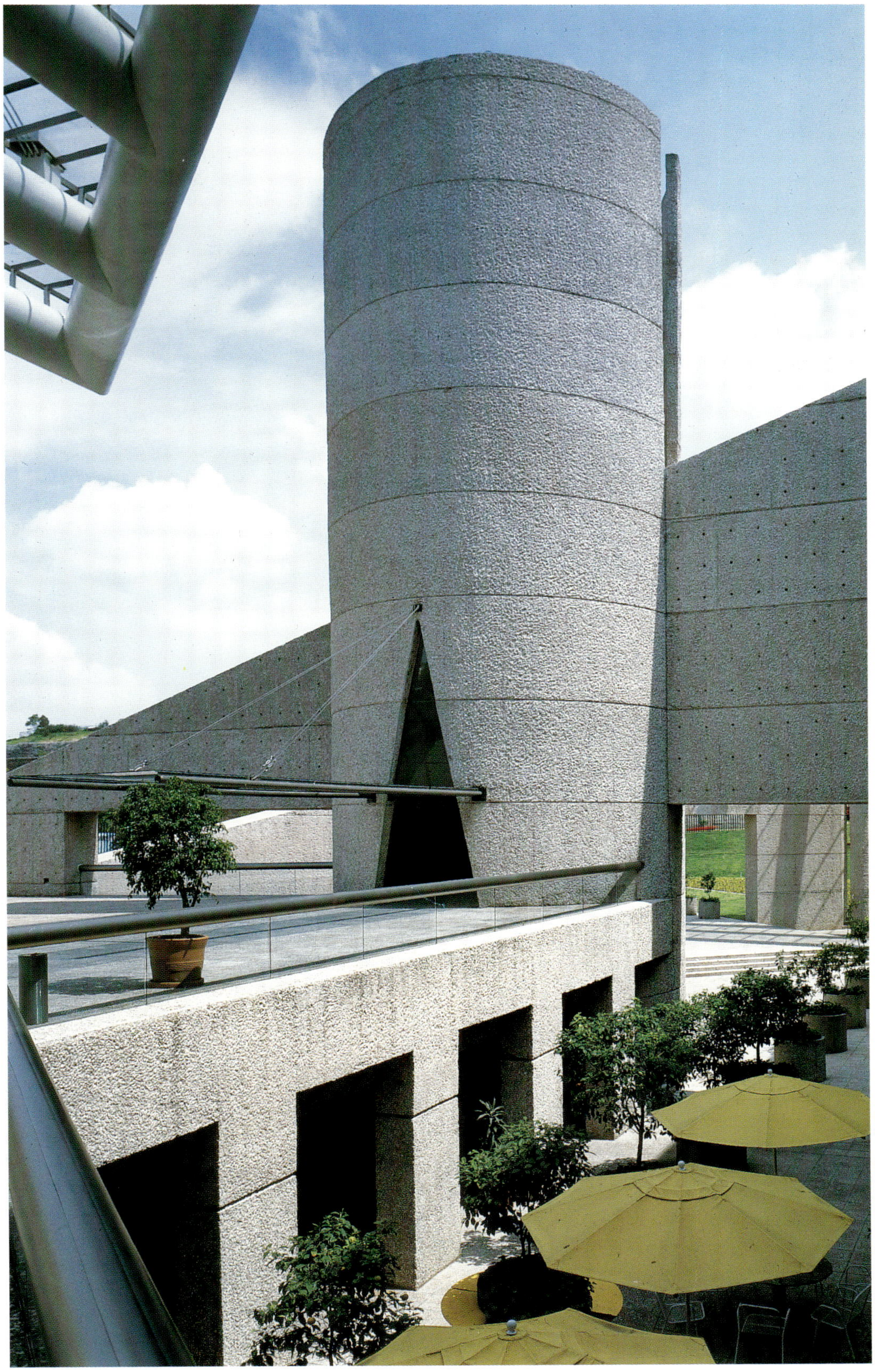

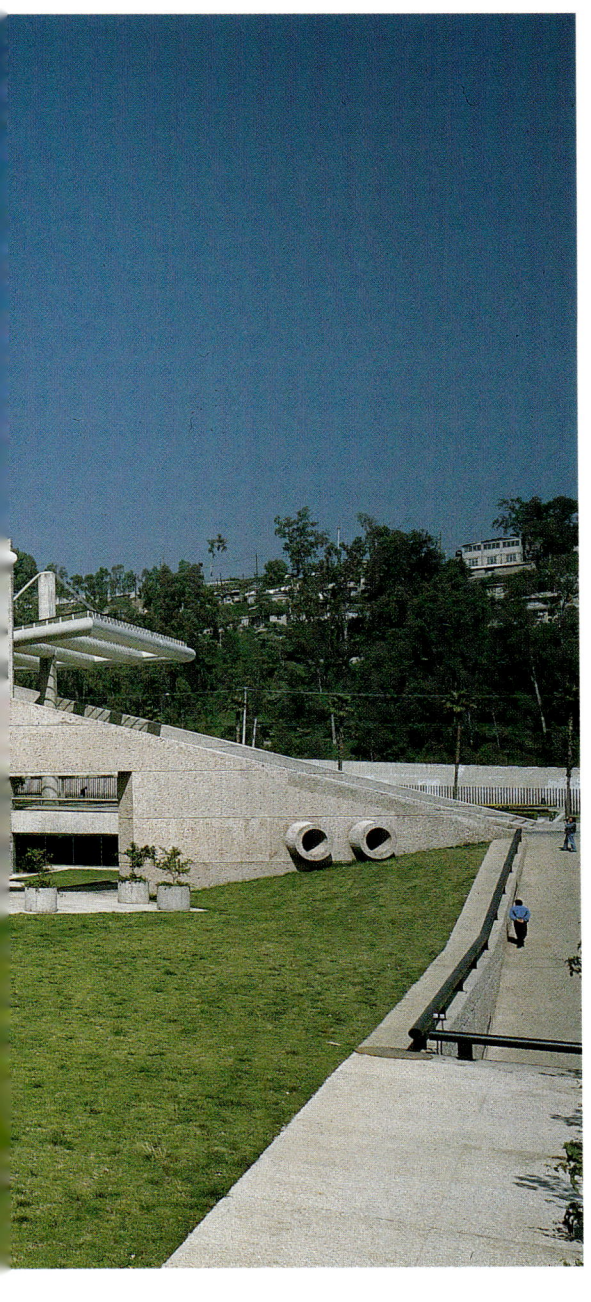

Mexico City, 1990-1991

Rufino Tamayo Square

Owner
Departamento del Distrito Federal

Architect
Teodoro González de León

Collaborator
Ernesto Betancourt

Gardening design
Eliseo Arredondo

Structural design
Héctor Margain Ancira

Electric design
COESA Ingenieria, S.A.

Hydraulics and sanitary design
GHA y Asociados

Construction area
5,100 sq.m.

This public garden named after Rufino Tamayo was designed and constructed by Teodoro González de León in 1990/91. It is composed of four main elements: the basic grounds, a tree-lined pathway, a carefully arranged layout of flower vases, and a series of water tanks along a wall decorated with a picture Rufino Tamayo painted in 1950 for a ballet set. González de León's project gives a highly scenographic reading of a series of natural features.

The perception of spatial perspectives creates the same sense of rhythm as Borromini's project for Piazza Spada in Rome, where geometric relations provide a means of dilating space in visual terms. González De León has interpreted the art of building in a distinctly scenographic-theatrical manner, using the same symbols the painter Tamayo was so fond of. He has handled the various project elements with great skill: epitomised, for instance, by the way he has divided the water tanks into a set of six rather insignificant square forms. He creates patterns and rhythms as if drawing on natural mirrors, speeding up our perception of the space in which the painting is framed. Vision is rendered three-dimensional by a pattern of portals.

This is the most important part of a project whose side sections also feature architectural touches of notable beauty. In this project González de León has used architecture in its purest form, as if he were probing into those same mysteries other great masters investigated in the past. This is how González de León tries to interact with the third dimension in which architectural design is actually grounded. His architectural structures draw force from both shadow and light, as is particularly evident in the use of concrete to strengthen his basic forms. Like the rest of his projects, this particular design is full of detail and brimming with creativity and style.

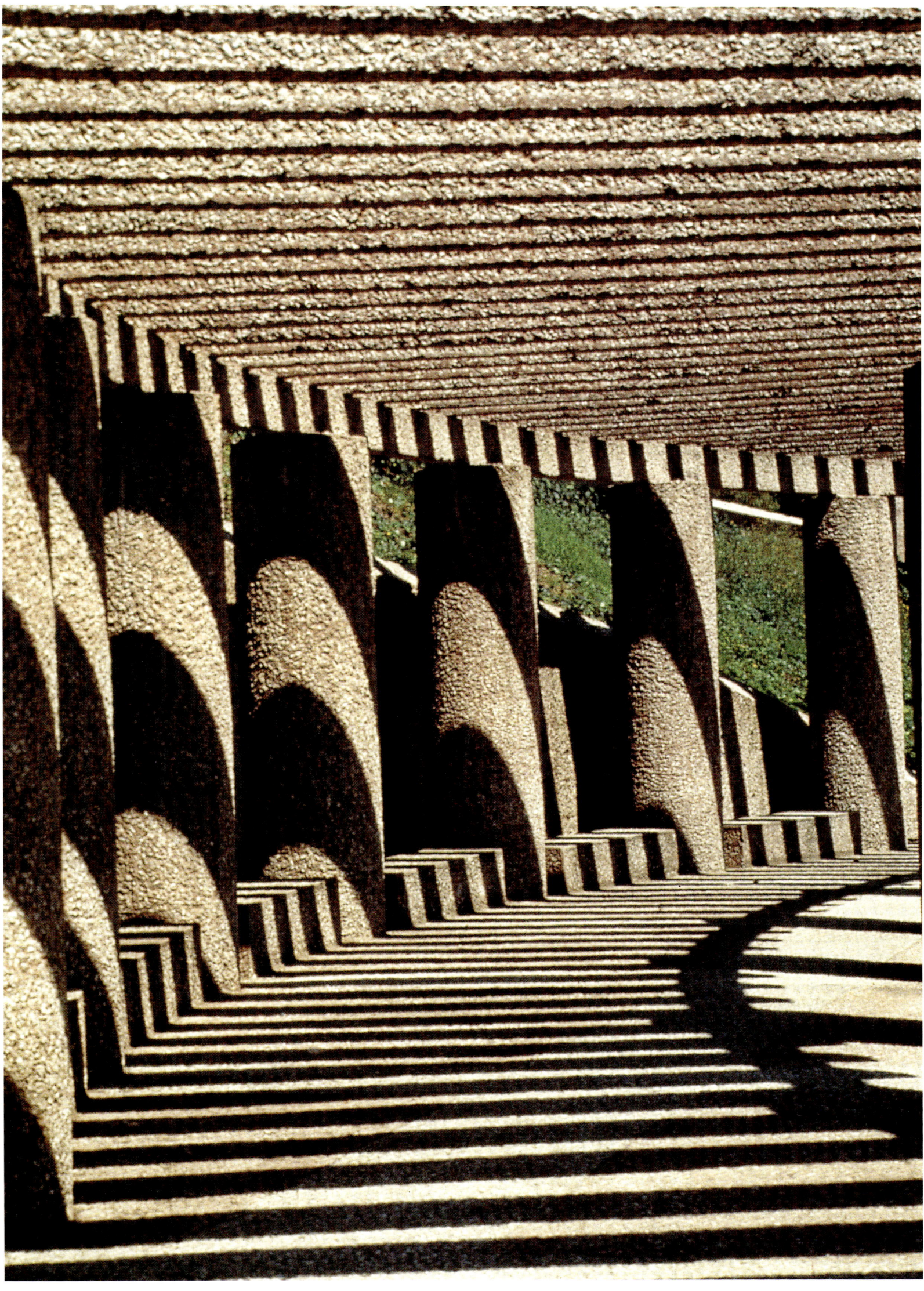

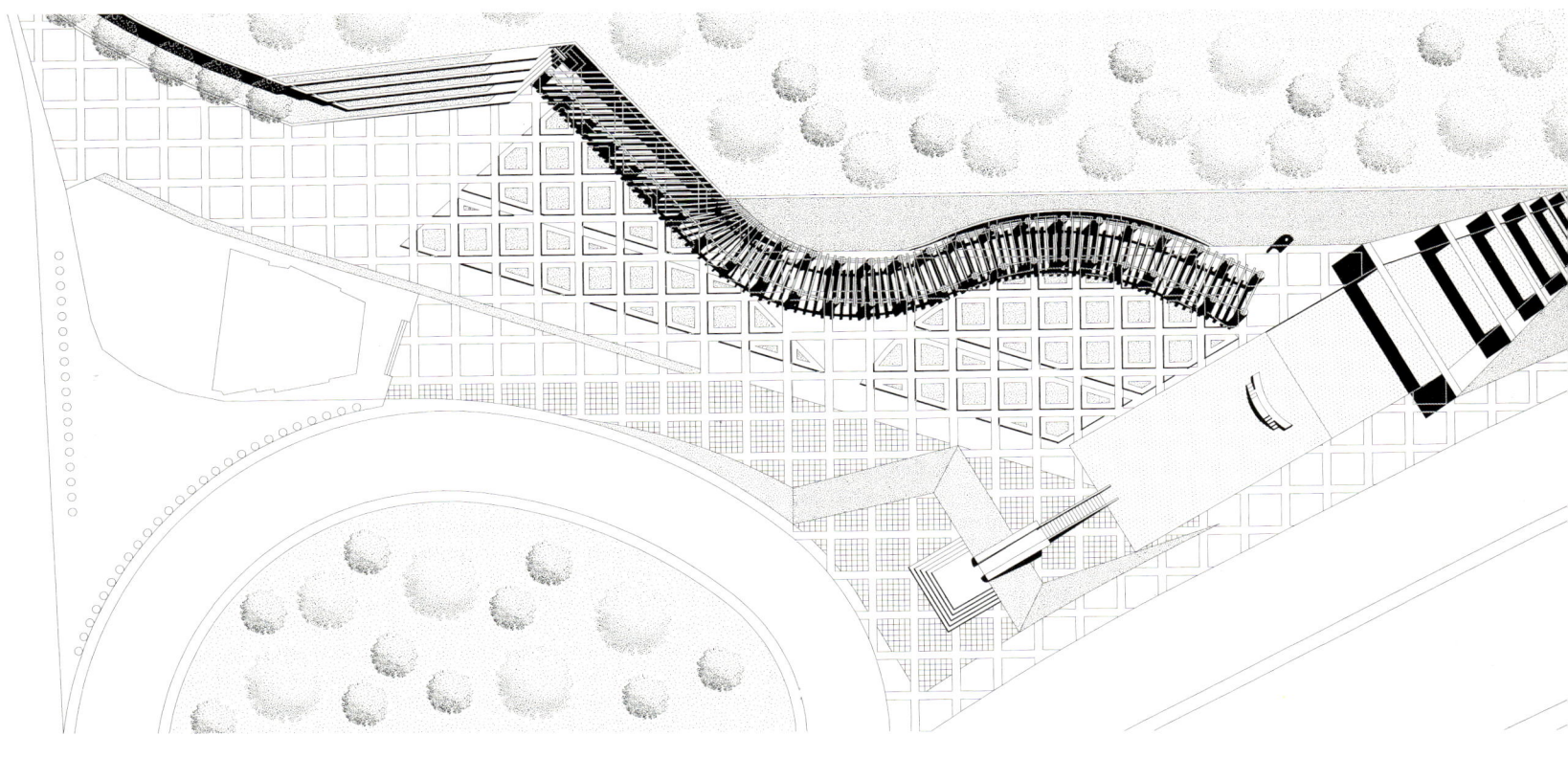
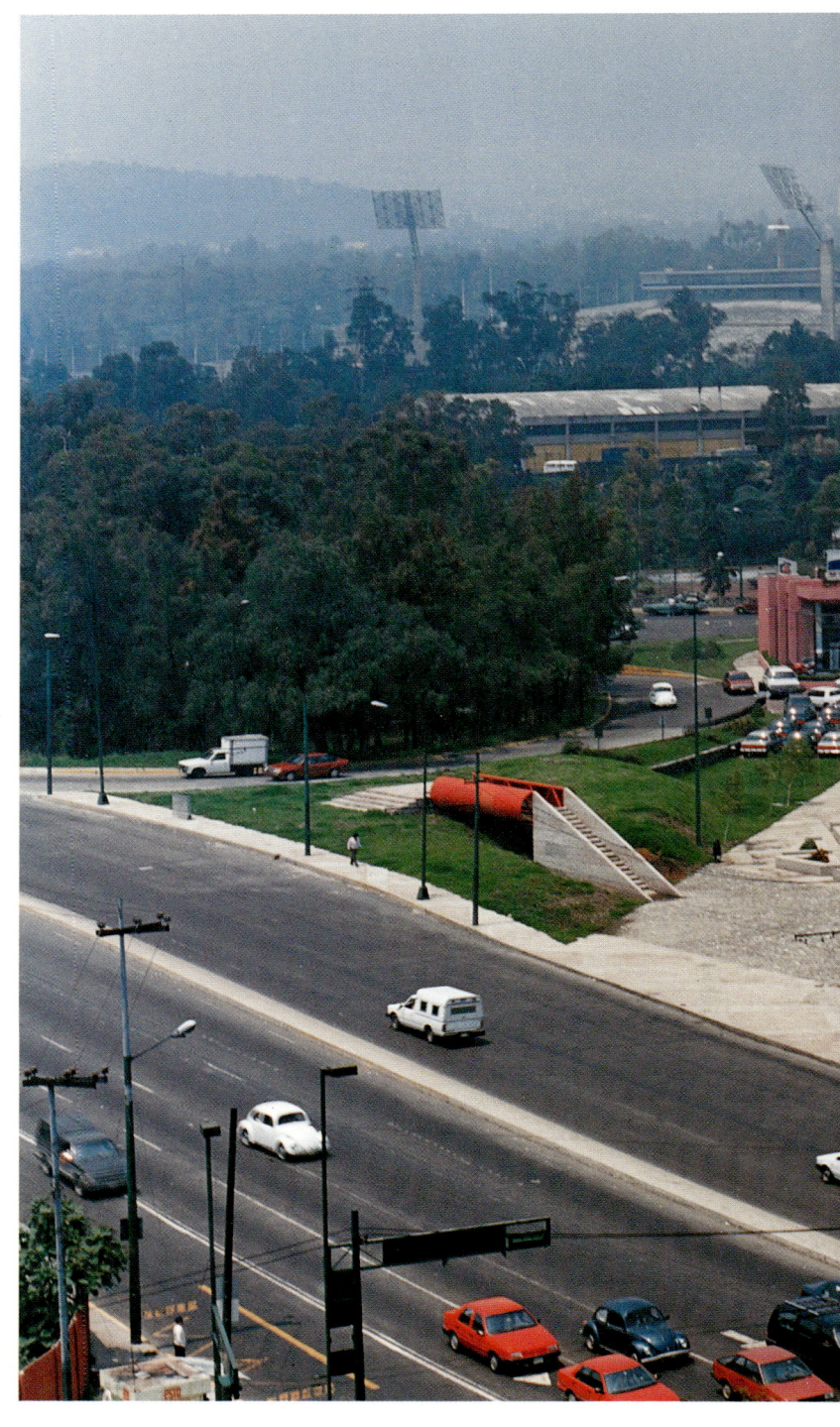

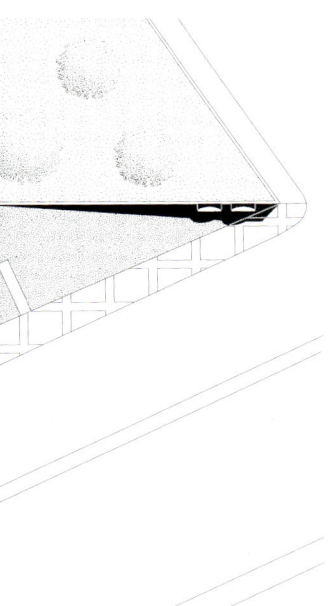

Site plan and, below, aerial view of Plaza Rufino Tamayo, located in a narrow urban space widened by the streamlined, scenographic perspectives created by González de León.

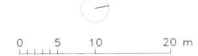

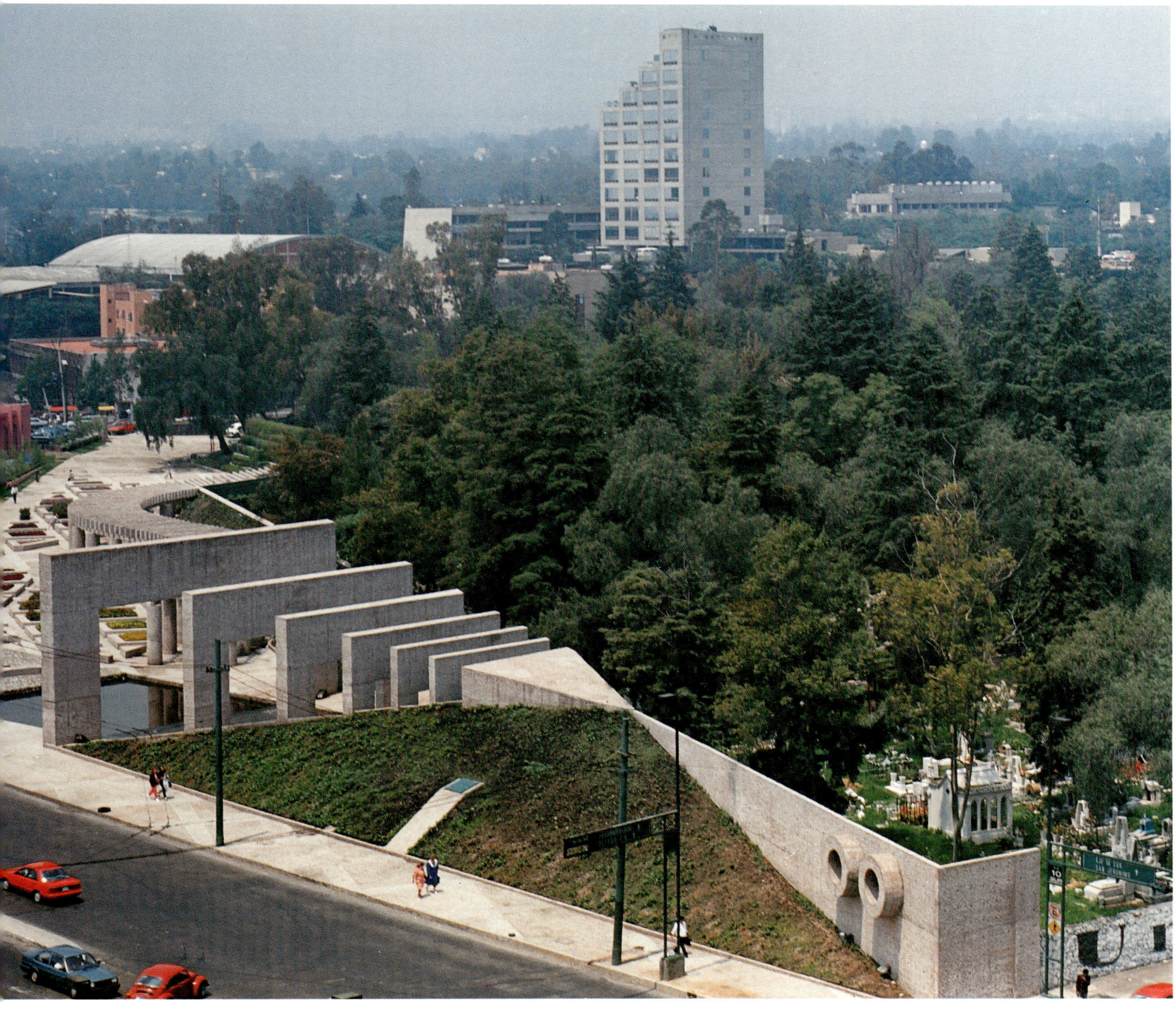

Perspective view of the plaza, bordered by a trellised path to the west and fountain to the north.

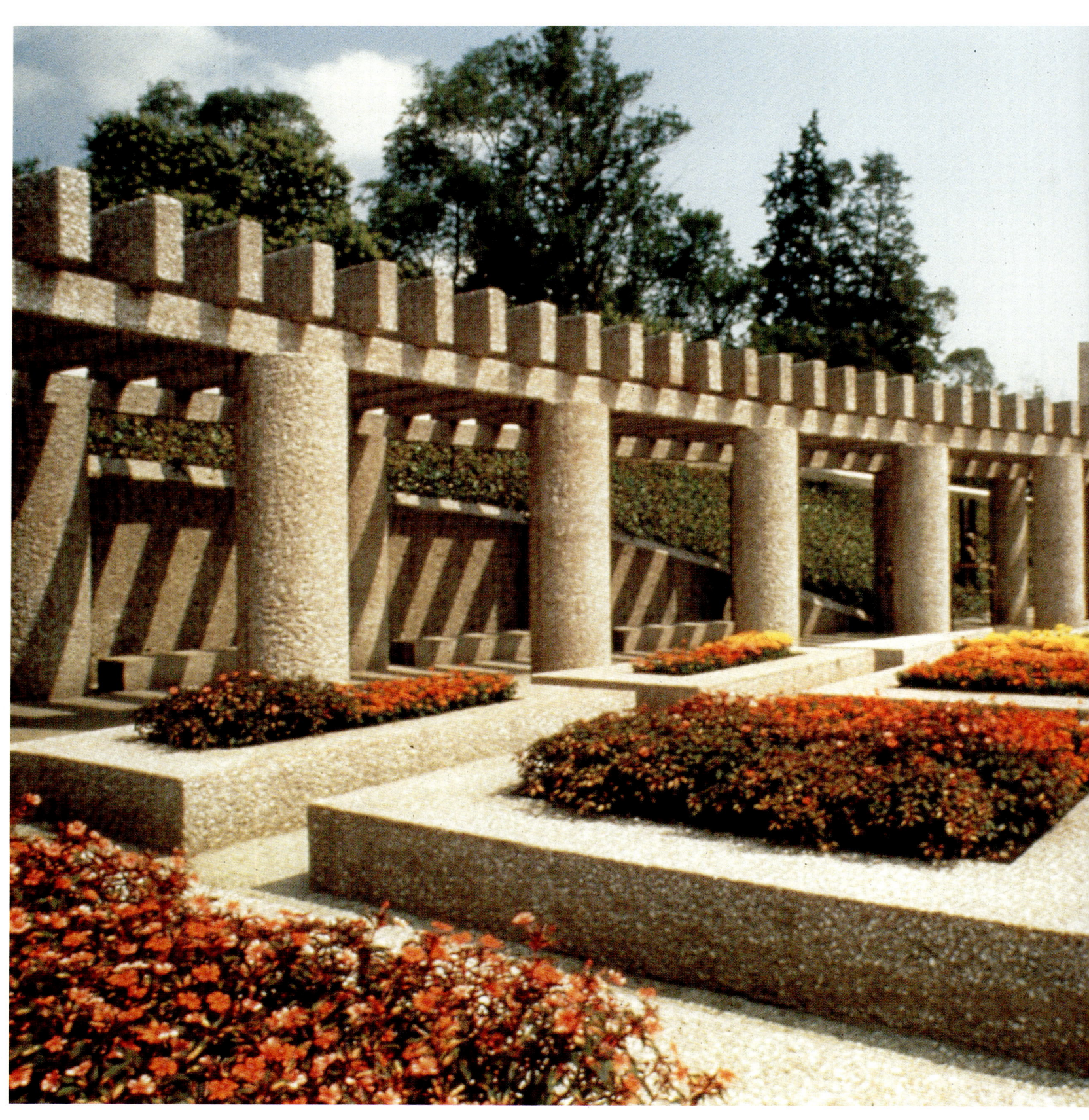

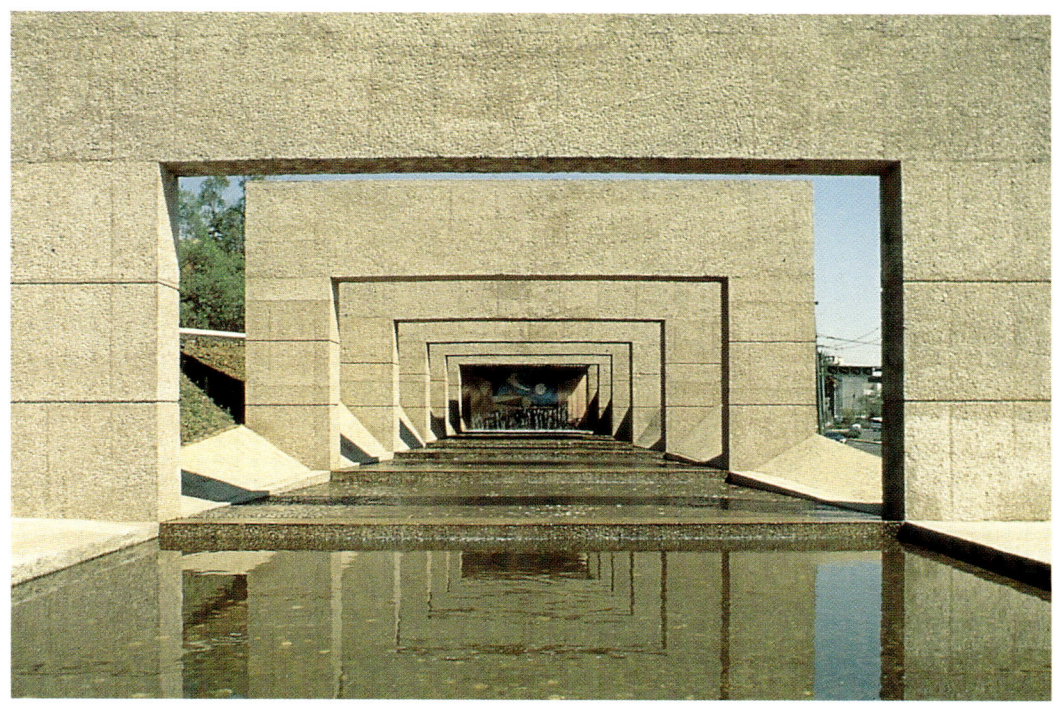
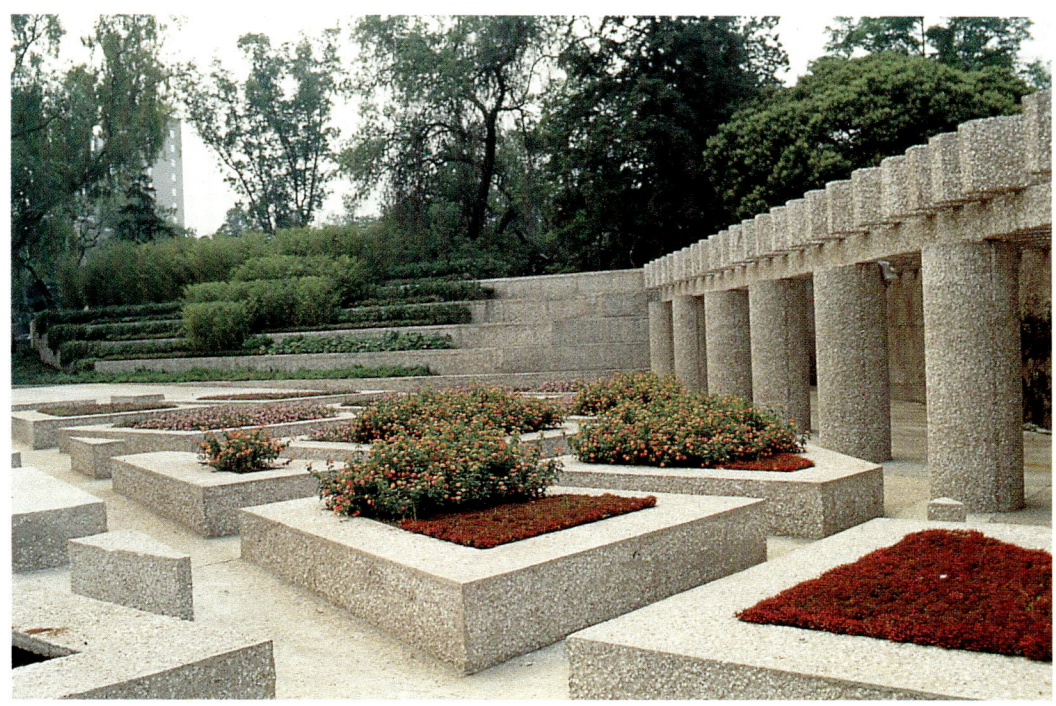
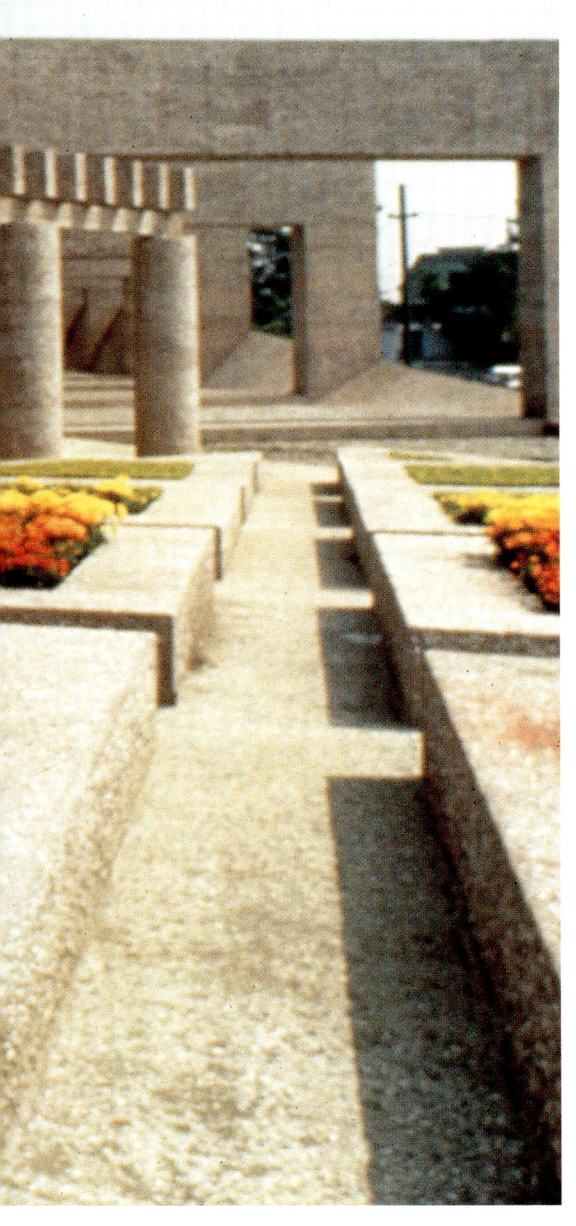

Details of the fountain and concrete fixtures holding the flowers.

Belmopan, 1992-1996

Mexican Embassy in Belize

Owner
Secretaria de Relaciones Exteriores

Architect
Teodoro González de León

Collaborator
Guillermo Díaz de Sandi

Interior design
Luis de Regil

Structural design
Héctor Margain

Electrical and air conditioning design
Ingenieria RIM, S.A.

Hydraulics and sanitary design
Ingenieria RIM, S.A.

Lighting
Gustavo Avilés

Construction area
1,320 sq.m.

The project for the Mexican Embassy in Belmopan, Belize, contains some important new design features. Teodoro González de León draws on elements from other projects to create a close correlation between material and design. A diagonal line, curve, and prominent structures, are cut through by light so that they stand out with great clarity: these are the elements of the design idiom González de León's draws on to create new spatial patterns. All this, which clearly evokes the old formalist approach to architecture, provides useful new indications for the future of architectural design, further underlining González de León plastic skills and stylistic expertise. This proves that it is only in small things and in the recurring features of experimentation that we can identify the formal layout of space.

These spaces, if they are carefully organised across their planes, as in the case of the Mexican Embassy in Belize, instantly embody the functional purposes of the basic architectural layout. We will never tire of pointing out González de León's skill at using the same forms and materials to create architecture capable of existing on its own and, at the same time, of embodying extraordinary design style.

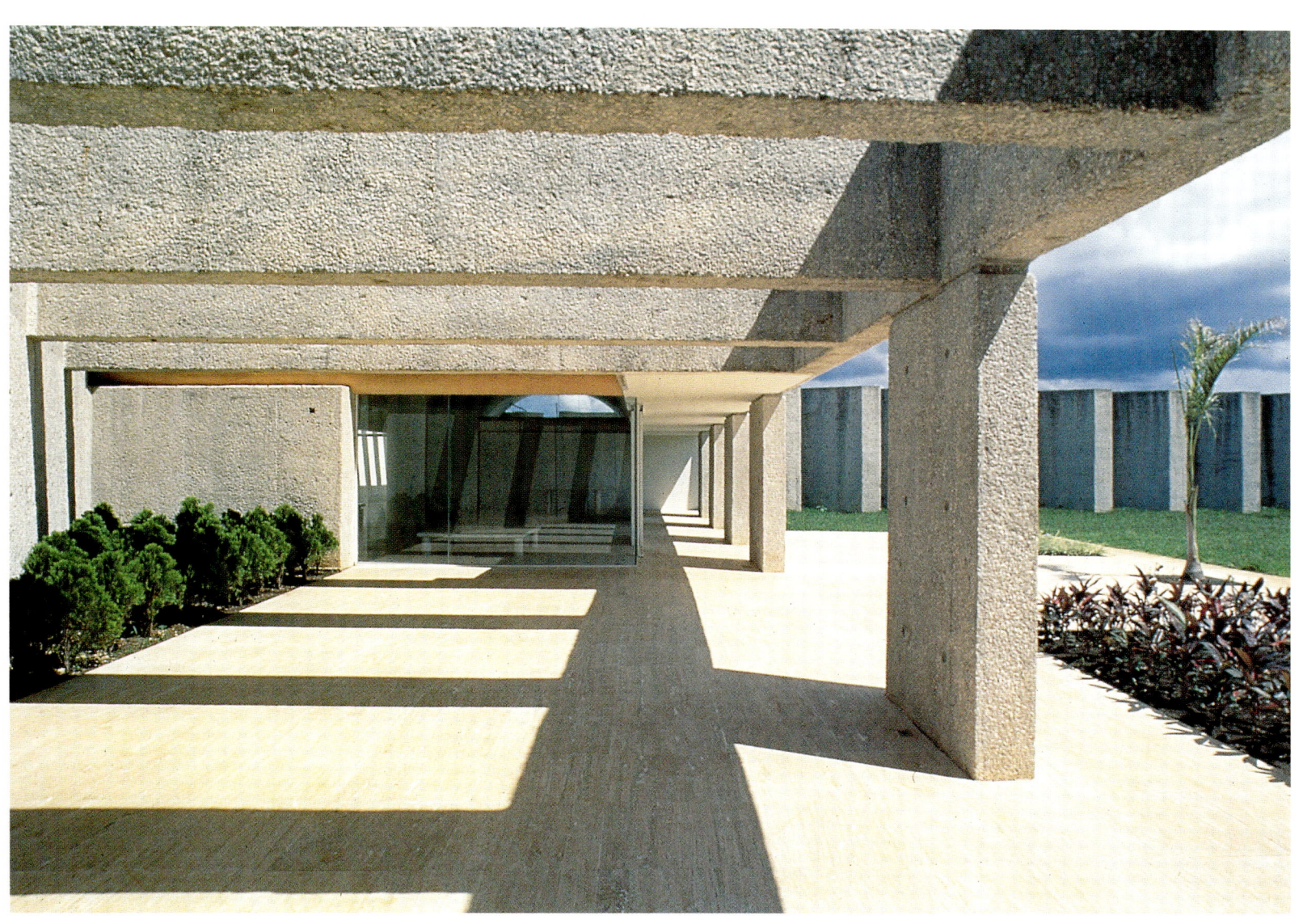

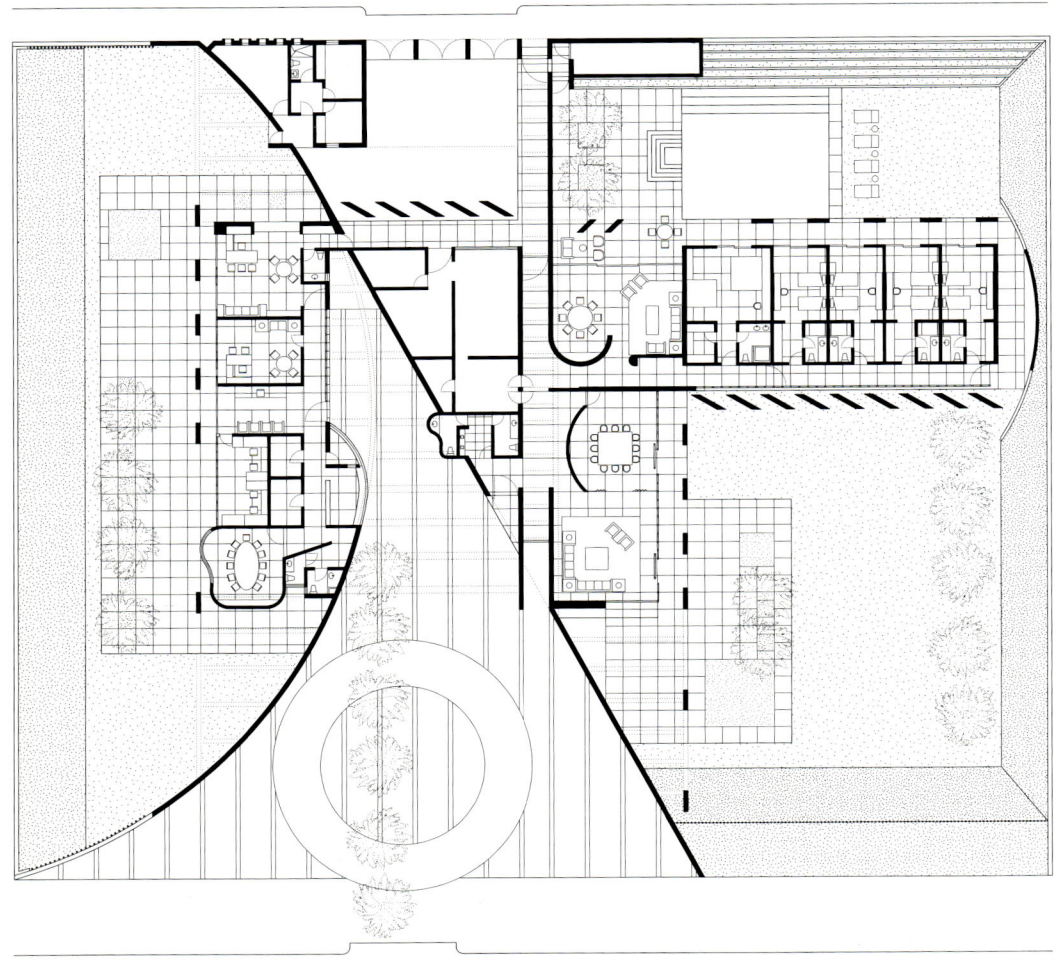

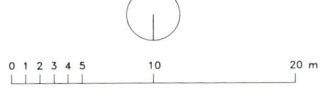

Ground floor plan. Right and opposite page, details of the plaza and entrance canopy to the Embassy.

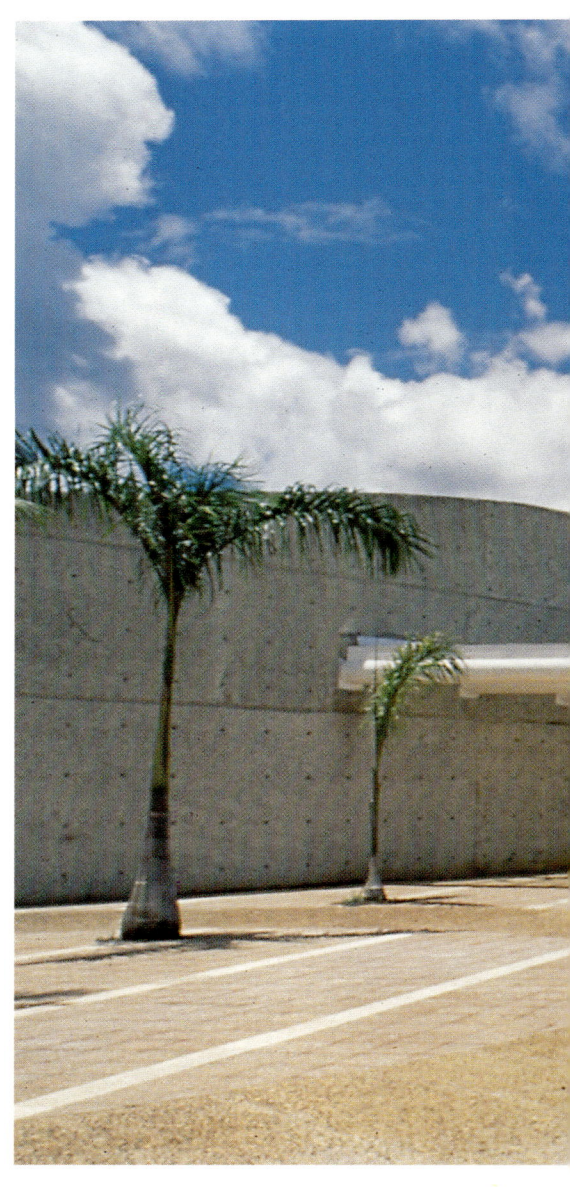

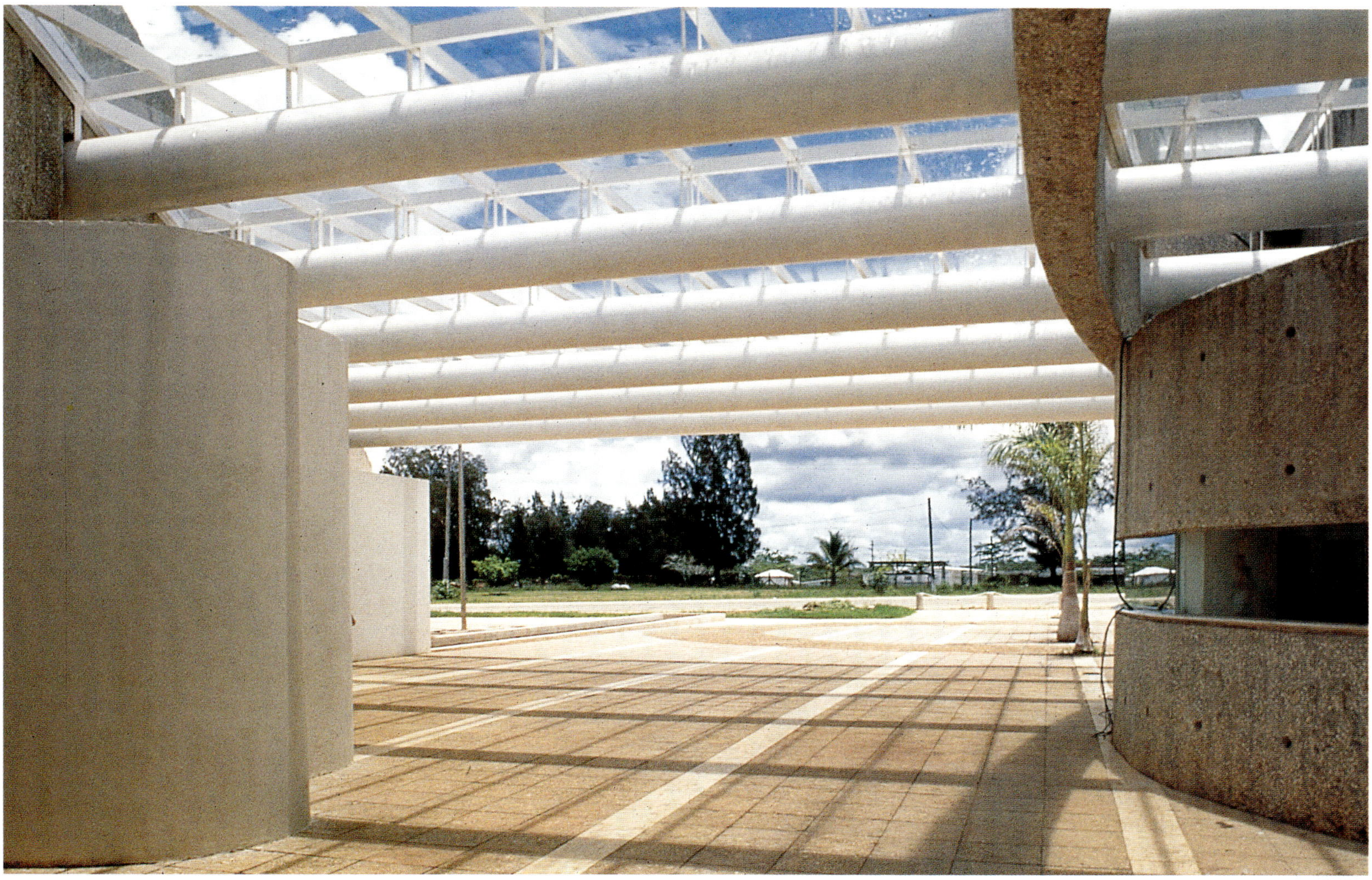

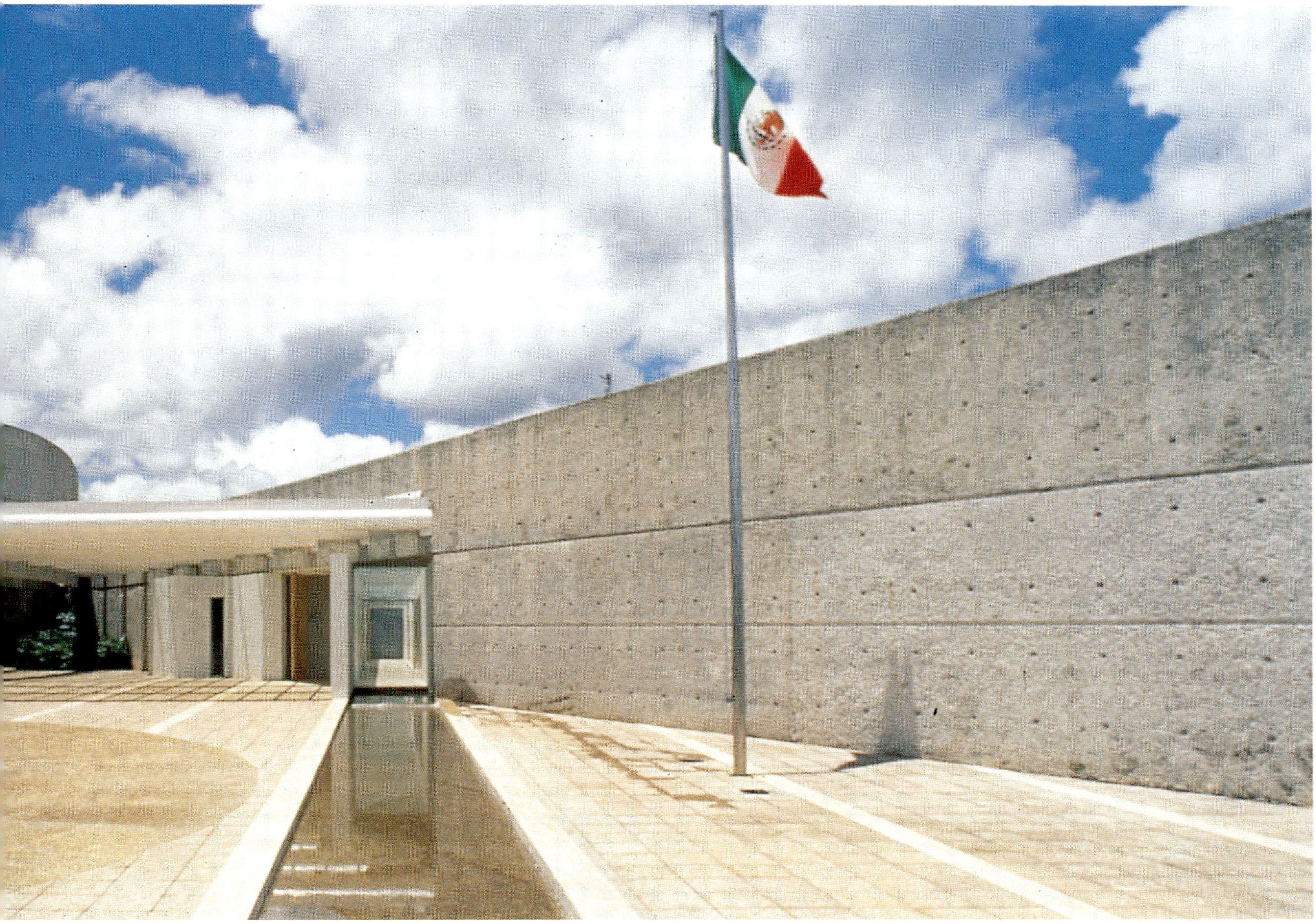

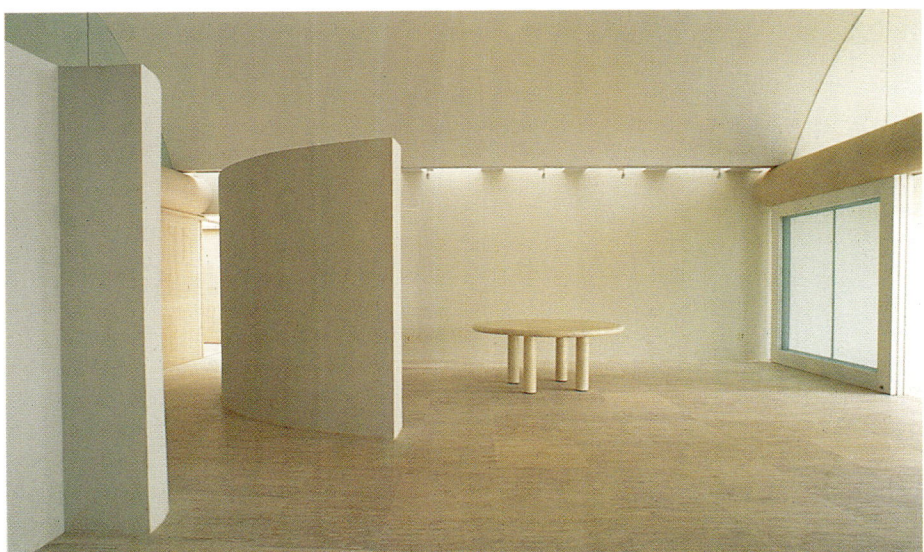

Left, one of the inside rooms. Below and opposite page, details of the outside trellised paths linking together the various building features.

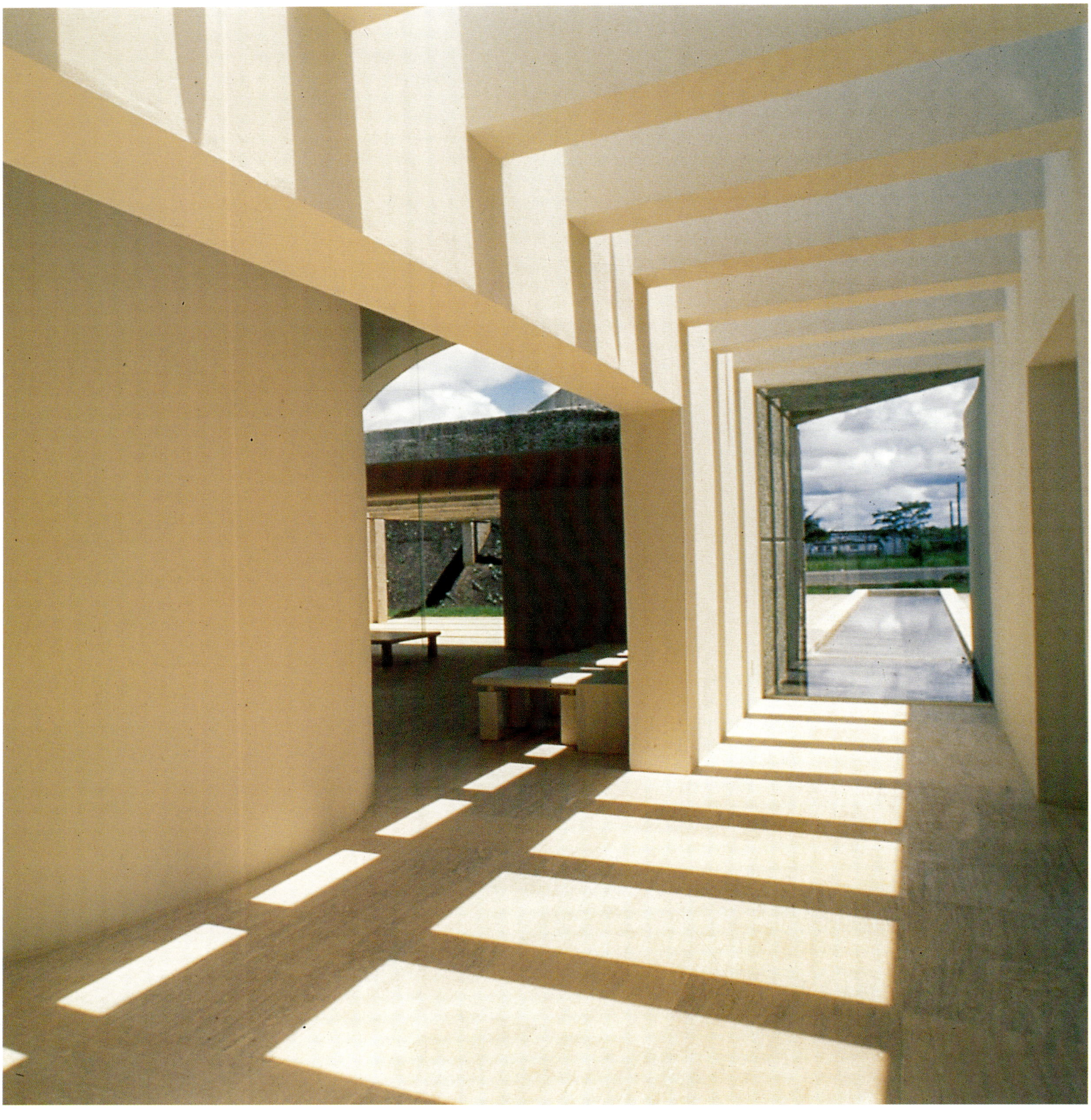

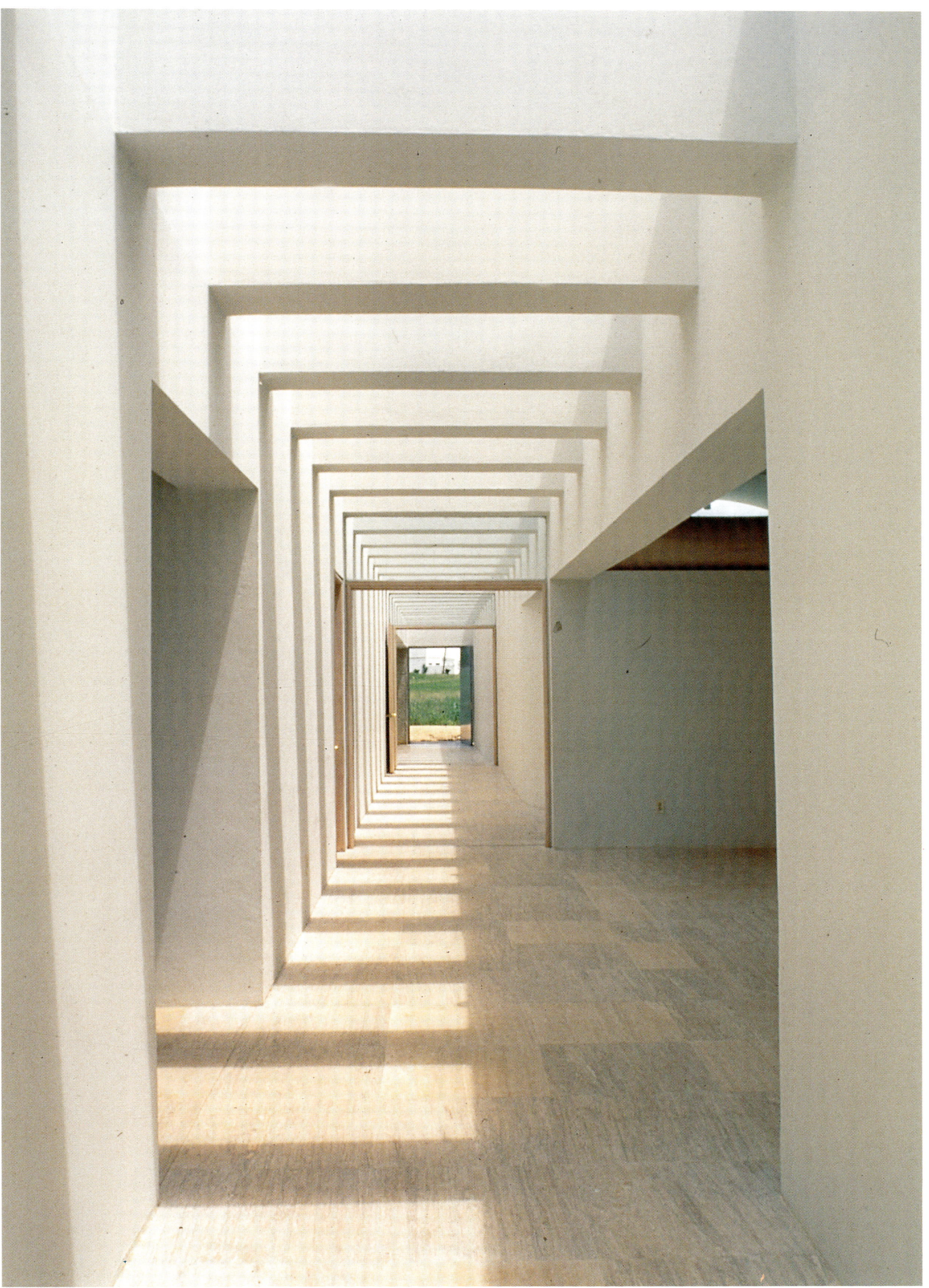

London, 1993-1994

The Mexican Gallery at the British Museum

Owner
Instituto Nacional de Antropologia e Historia

Architect
Teodoro González de León

Collaborator
Ernesto Betancourt

Designer
Miguel Cervantes

Structural engineer
F.J. Samuely and Partners

Services engineer
Hoare Lea and Partners

Lightning
Fisher Marantz
Rentro Stone Inc.

Project management
British Museum Architecture and Building Services
British Museum Design Office

Quantity surveyor
William C. Inman and Partners

Construction area
187 sq.m.

The room reserved for Mexican art inside the British Museum in London is designed to display pre-Columbian Aztec art from Mexico in all its splendour. The exhibition takes on a rather permanent nature inside the museum, which is why the project had to be commissioned to a real artist.

Here again González de León's architecture is characterised by features suitable for this kind of museum space.

The room is on the ground floor of the British Museum, right alongside the King's Library in a highly prestigious position.

González de León has, therefore, used his triangles, cylinders and cubes to crown ancient Mexican art in the most dignified manner possible.

The design really has succeeded in displaying these works of art in all their glory. The geometric force of the structural volumes combined with the transparent, light-weight, glass showcases holding the old jewels provide the Museum's Mexican room with its own unitary image.
Teodoro González de León's design for this museum room is shot through with the force of South-American art by creating a perfect balance between design and the basic project theme. Light and darkness, vehicles of truth and legend, are the most eye-catching aspects of the overall design.

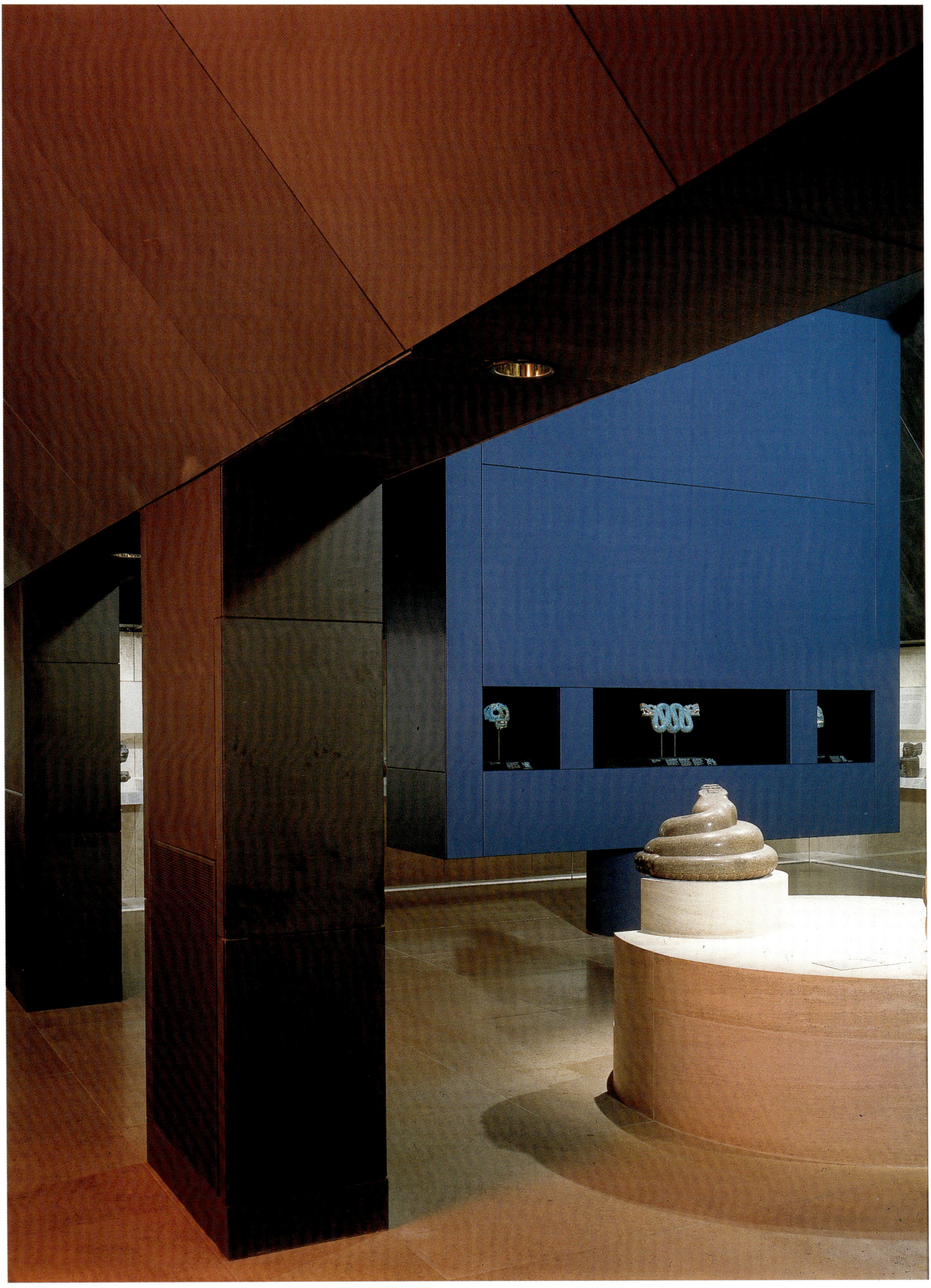

Plan of the room and, below, the triangular display platform for the pre-Columbian art relics. Following spreads, sections and details of the room showing the interior entrance portico.

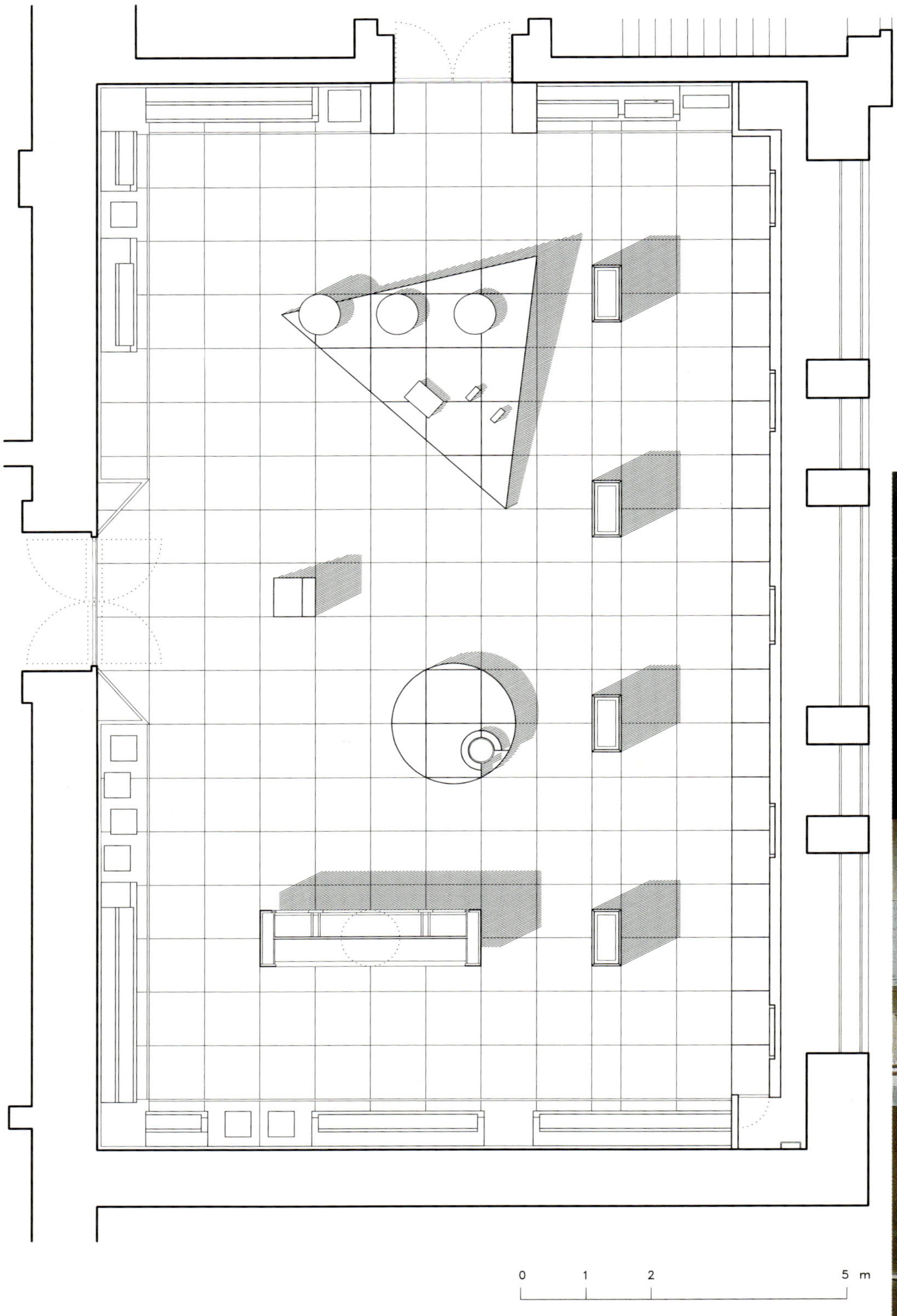

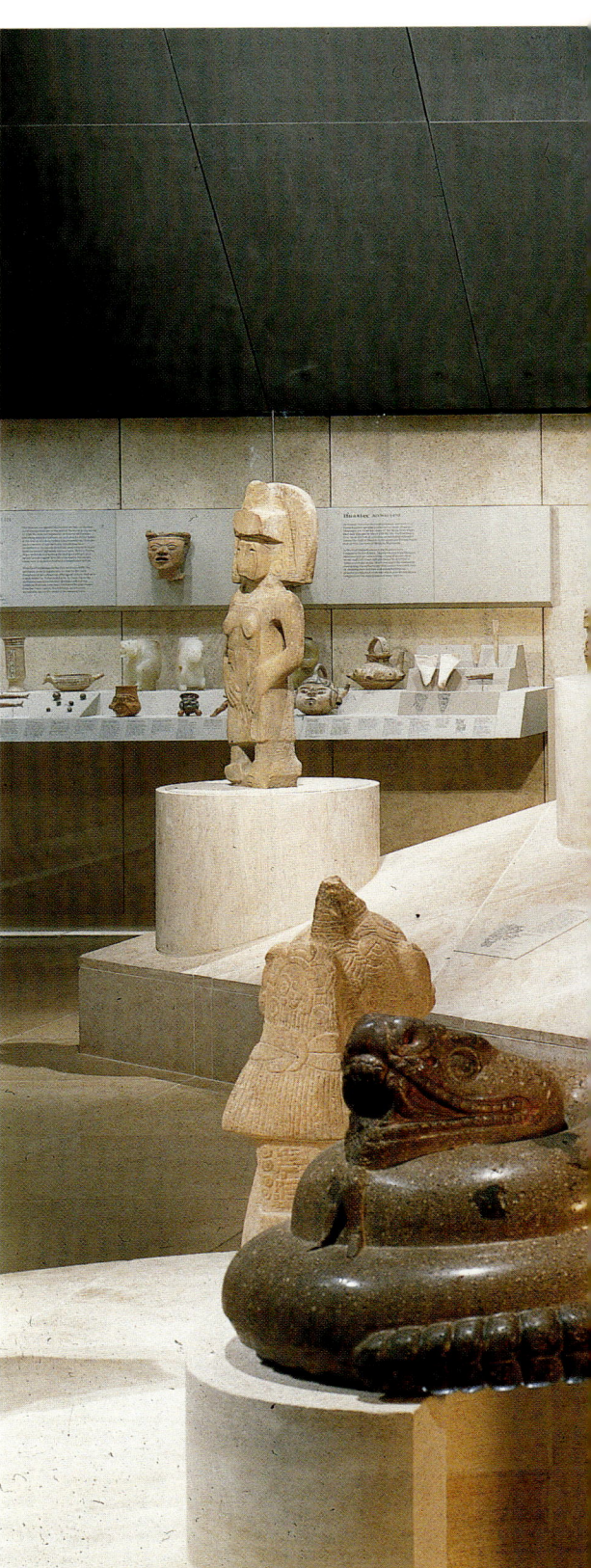

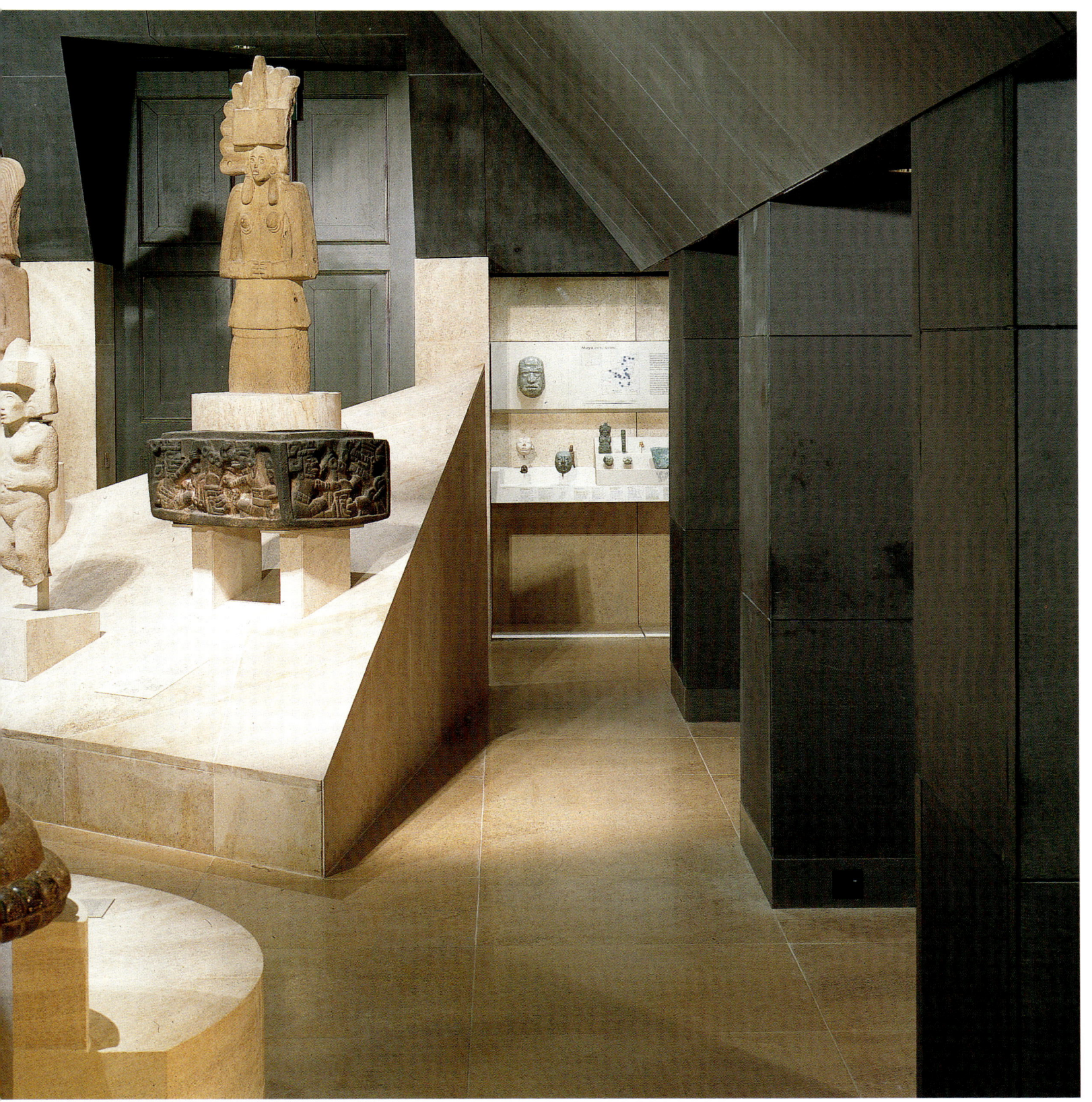

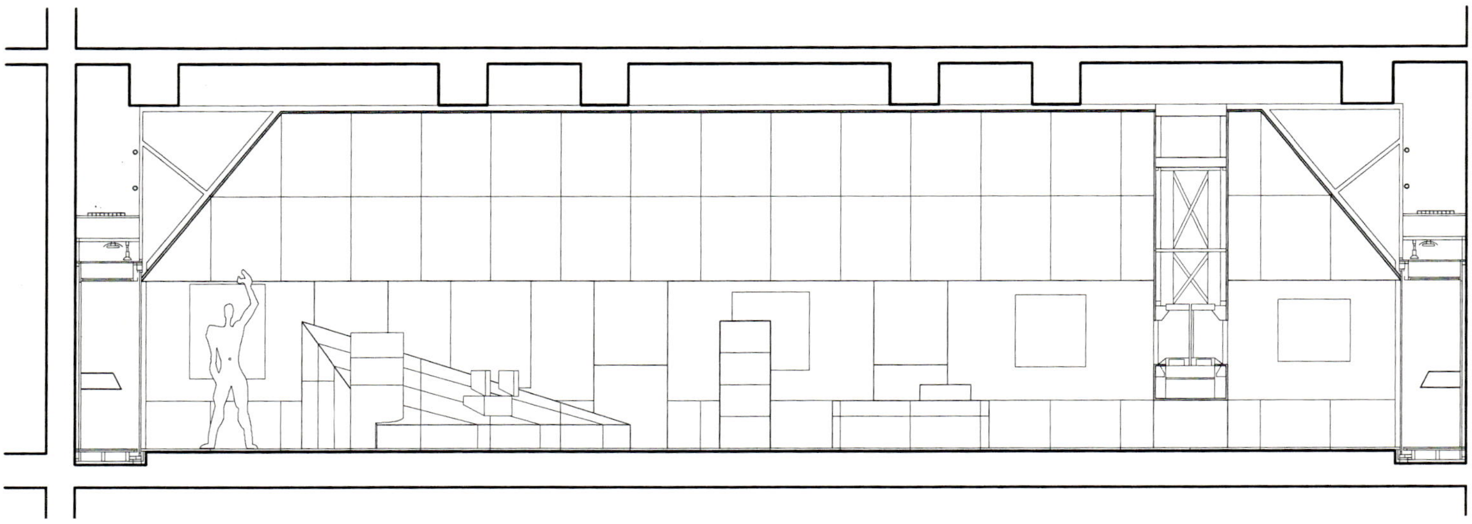

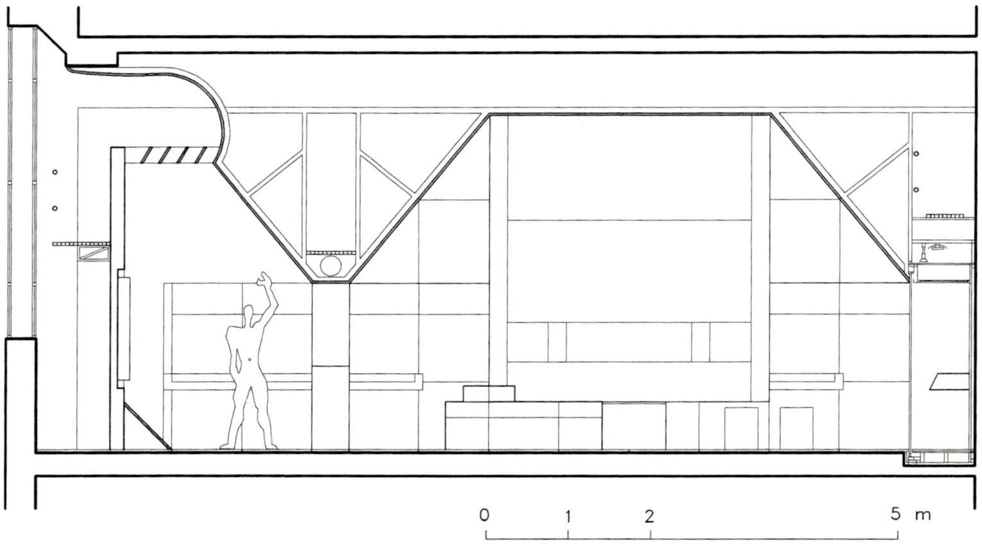

0 1 2 5 m

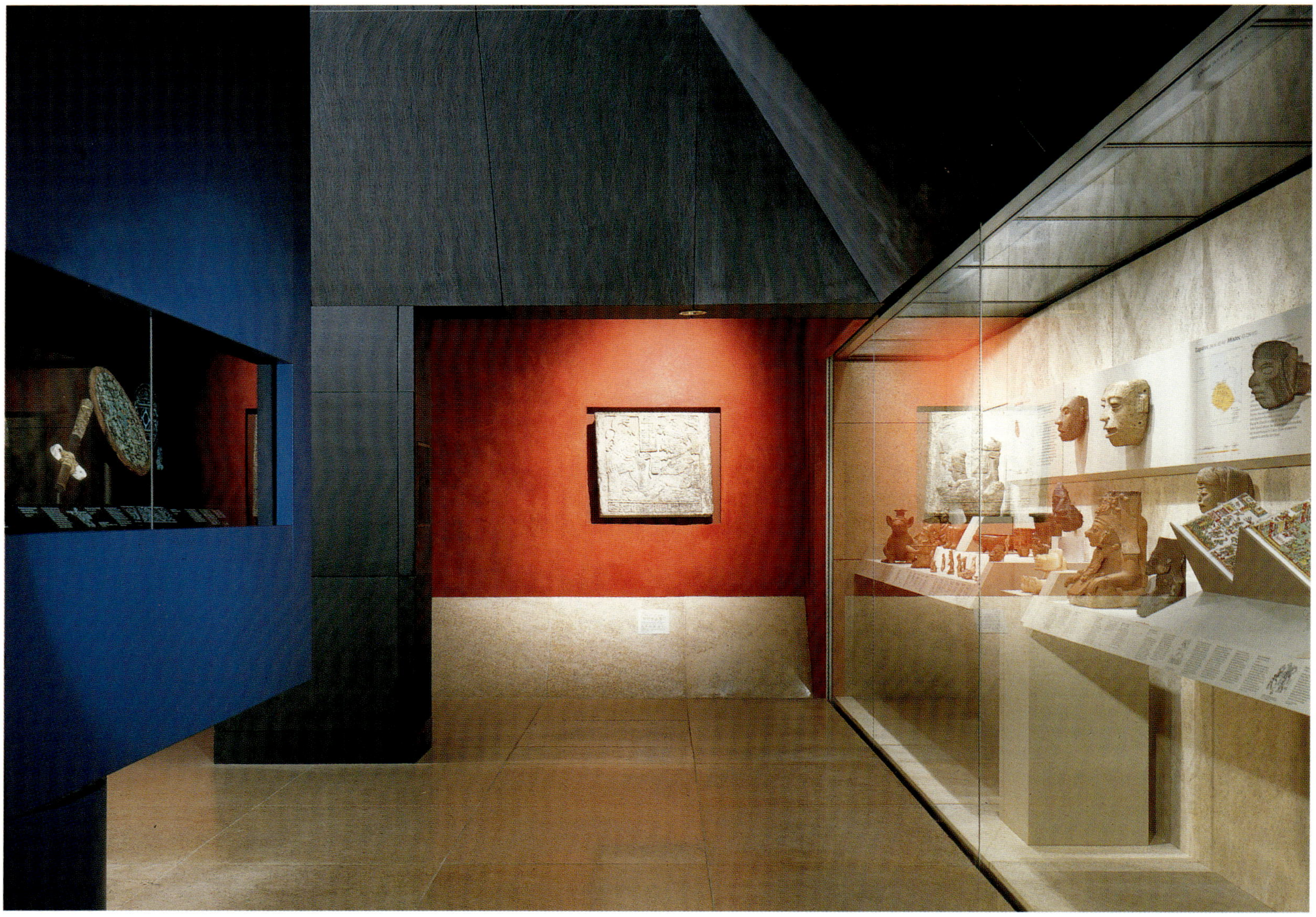

88

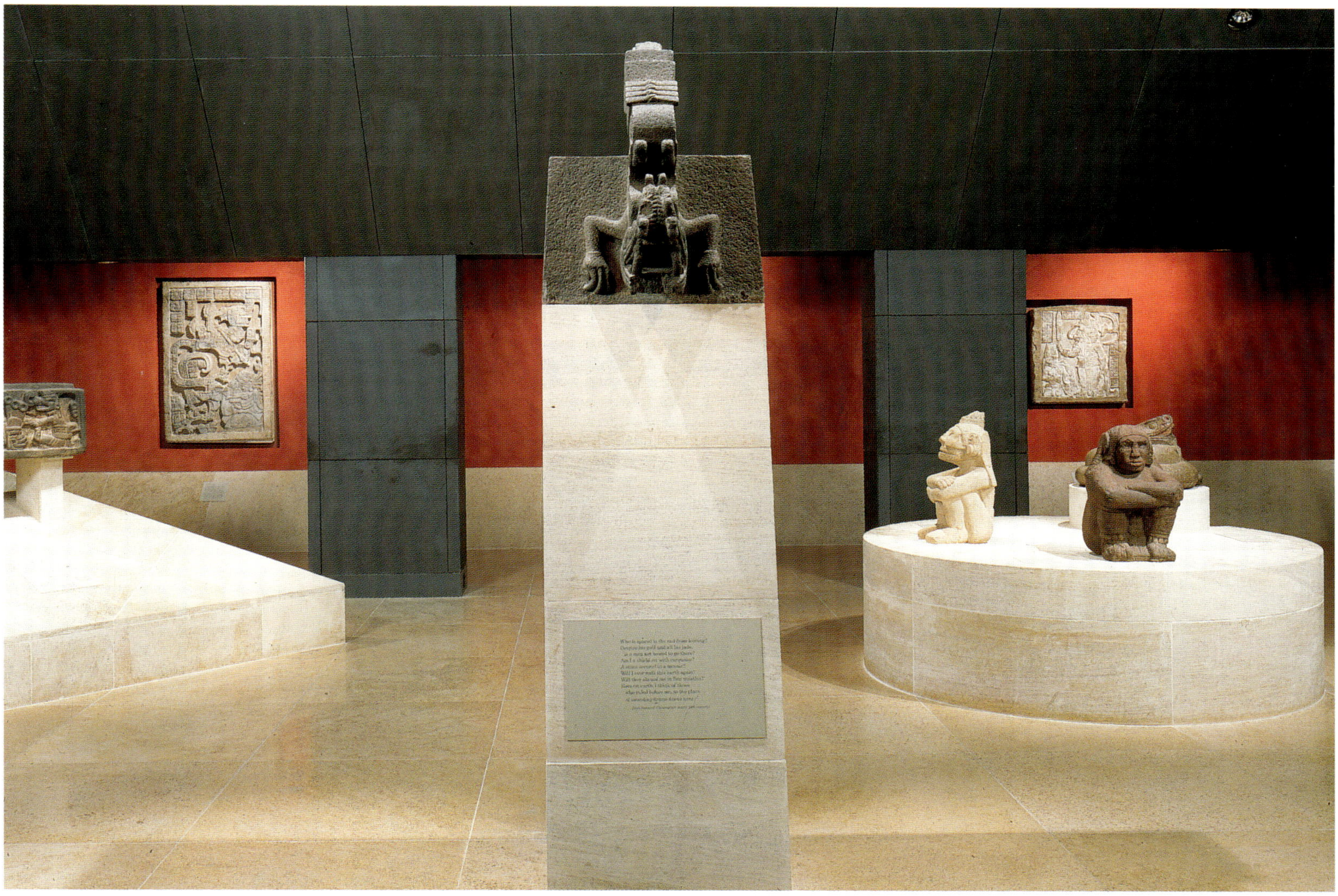

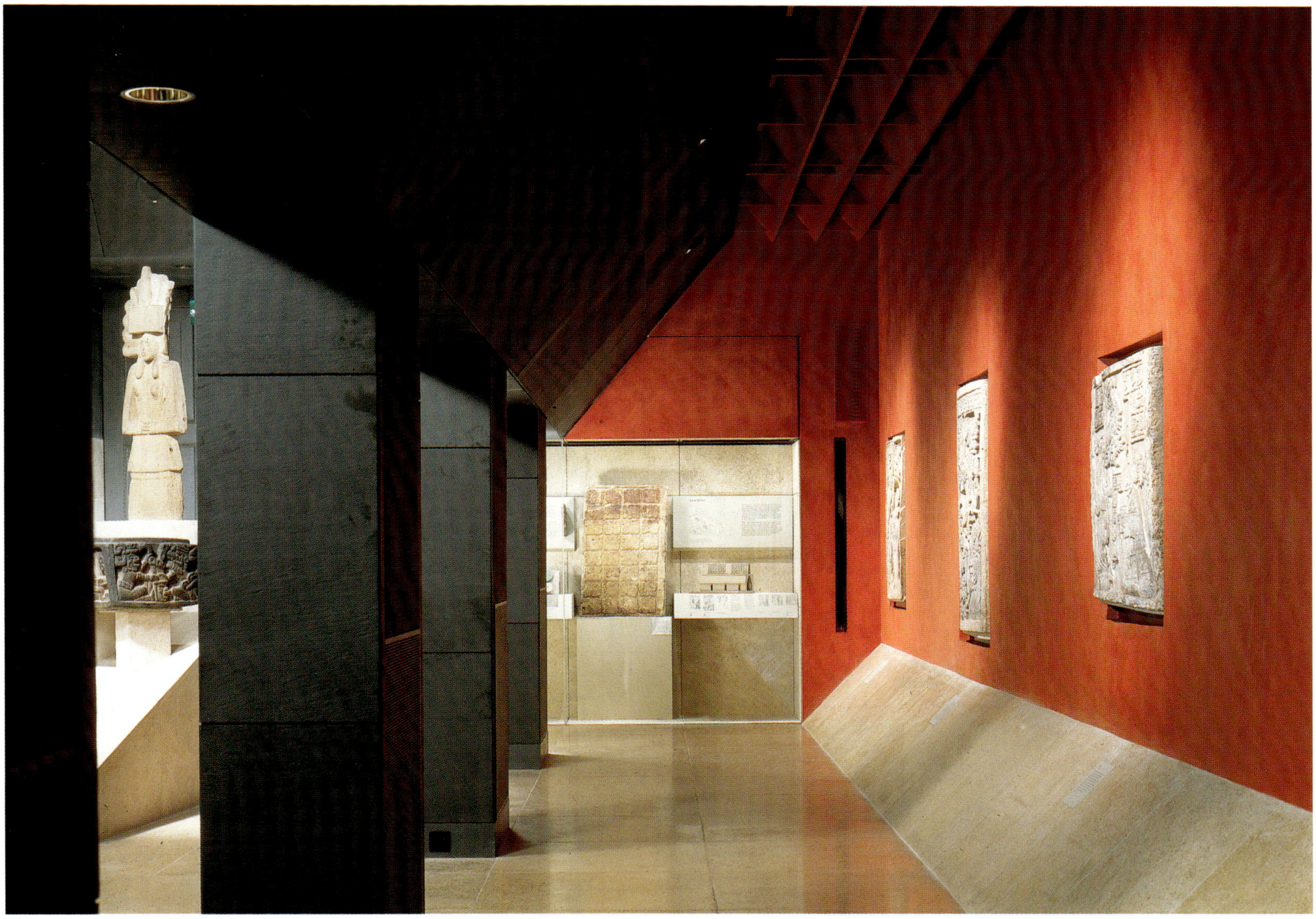

89

The geometric forms of the support structures and the lightness of the glass showcases emphasise the importance of the art works on display in the room.

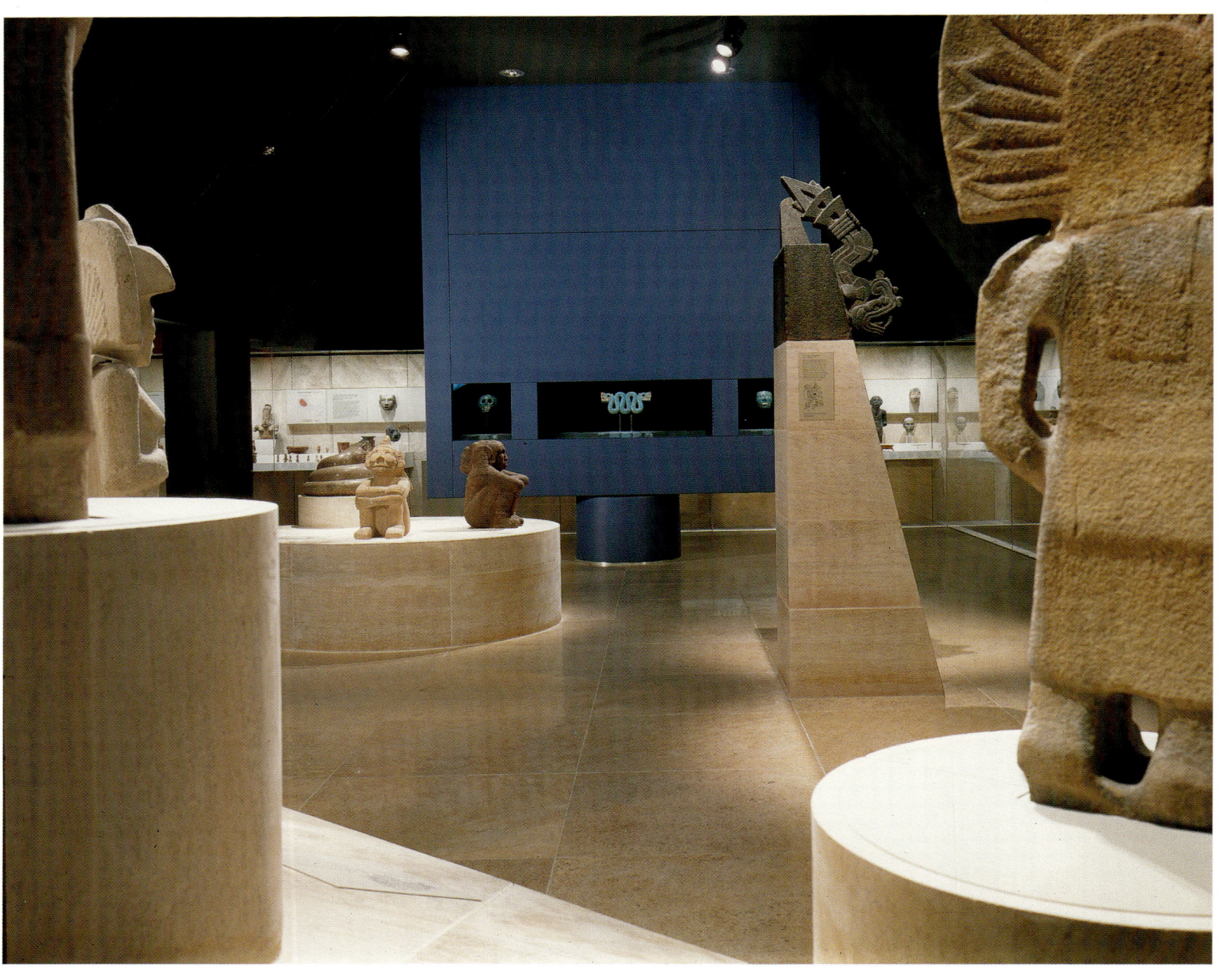

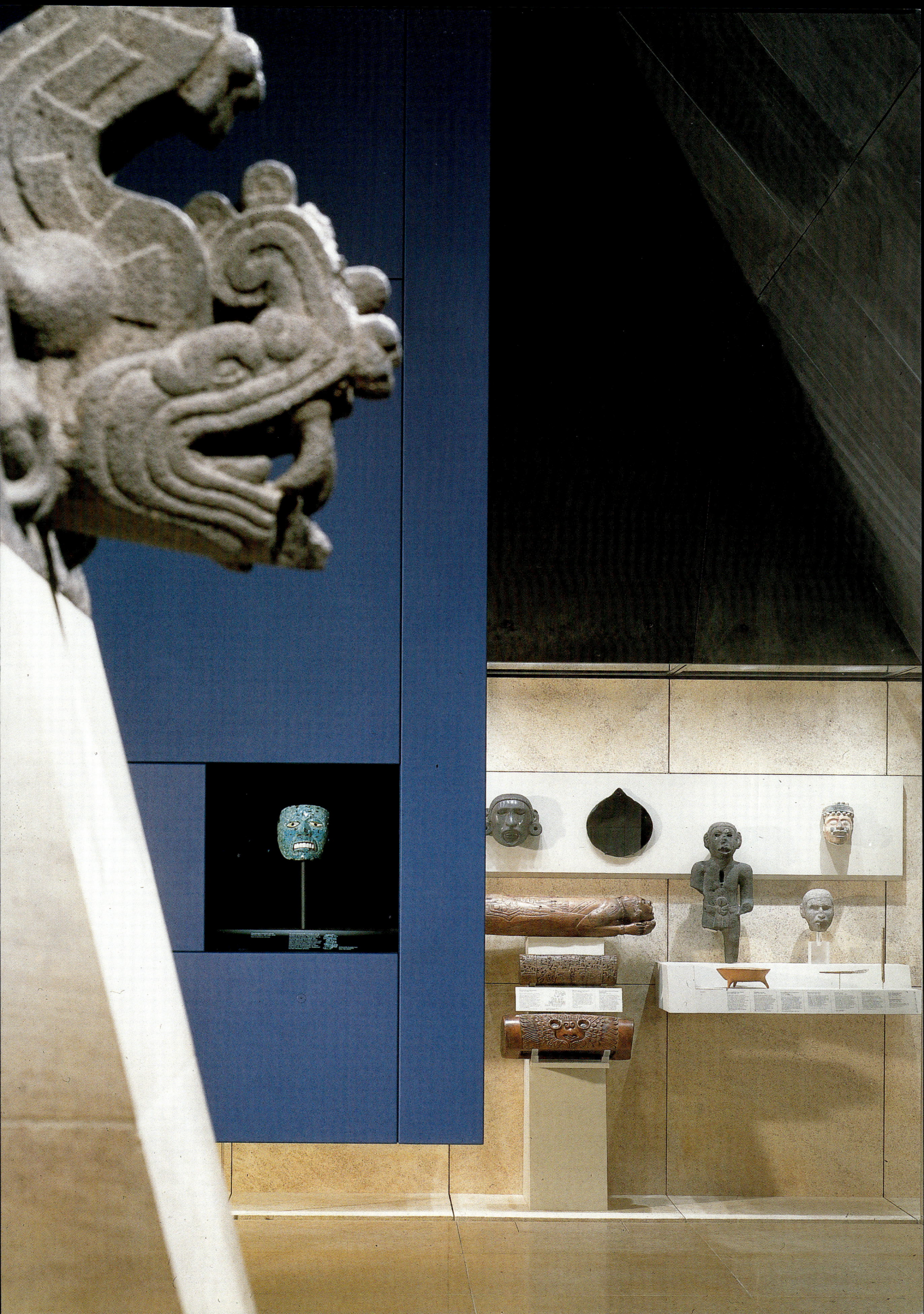

Mexico City, 1990-1996

Arcos Bosques Corporativo

Owner
Desc, S.A. de C.V.

Architects
Teodoro González de León
J Francisco Serrano
Carlos Tejeda

Collaborators
Antonio Rodríguez
José Arce Gargollo
José Ma. Larios
Juan Espinoza
Carlos Gutiérrez Juarez

Mural painting design
Teodoro González de León

Collaborator for mural paintings
Miguel Barbachano Ponce

Structural design
Diseño y Supervisión, "DYS", S. C.

Hydraulics and sanitary design:
Garza Maldonado y Asociados, S.C.

Air-conditioning design
Calefacción y Ventilación, S.A. de C.V.
Industrias Garvel, S.A. de C.V.

Electrical design
Instalaciones y Mantenimiento
Ing Ignacio González Castillo
Tecnoproyectos

Special Installations
LOGEN

Construction area
234,880 sq.m. offices
19,120 sq.m. shopping area
367,560 sq.m parkings
621,560 sq.m. Total

The Arcos Bosques Corporativo designed by Teodoro González de León in Mexico City is certainly one of his most tricky projects.

The sheer size of the building makes it a sort of small city.

The Arcos Bosques Corporativo design epitomises his great expressive force. More than ever before, he has shown his faith in the evolutionary progress of architectural form. There can be no doubt that this contemporary master has the ability to draw on technically correct rationalism to move beyond the bounds of cold numerical precision. This imposing architectural image epitomises the real force of South-American tradition that he himself has helped to forge. Drawing on a carefully constructed framework, he depicts nature as the real inspiration behind human creativity, carefully scrutinising cause and form, he produces synthesises what are really genuine organisms. The trick lies in the way he uses the numerical logic of architectural patterns to forge new spatial arrhythmias. The design themes underlying this project are also key factors in instilling the work with stylistic force. The offices, flats and sports facility make this a truly community project, in which González de León strives to represent his country's most deeply rooted architectural traditions. Its roots are deeply entrenched in the ground forming the service areas, warehouses and car parks, while the service facilities are situated above grade level. Together they can be interpreted as a sort of Le Corbusier-type dream of the vertical stratification of the urban environment. Its functions are designed to incorporate both public and private services, rather than just a carefully devised functional programme.

This fragment of vertical city has its own self-contained structure capable of meeting all the qualitative-quantitative demands emerging from its urban surroundings.

It is hardly surprising that González de León has once again incorporated a diagonal feature in this new project, almost as if he wanted to thrust the design into a different three-dimensional dynamic relation to its surroundings, within what is still a symmetrically precise and highly rational composition. Often, as in this case, it is the material used in the construction of a building that epitomises the design philosophy and stylistic diversity of a new project sewn into the surrounding urban fabric. It is no coincidence that a light-weight, transparent material like glass has been chosen here to allow light to shine through in its own peculiar way, creating a powerful architectural landmark narrated in a distinctly desecrating form.

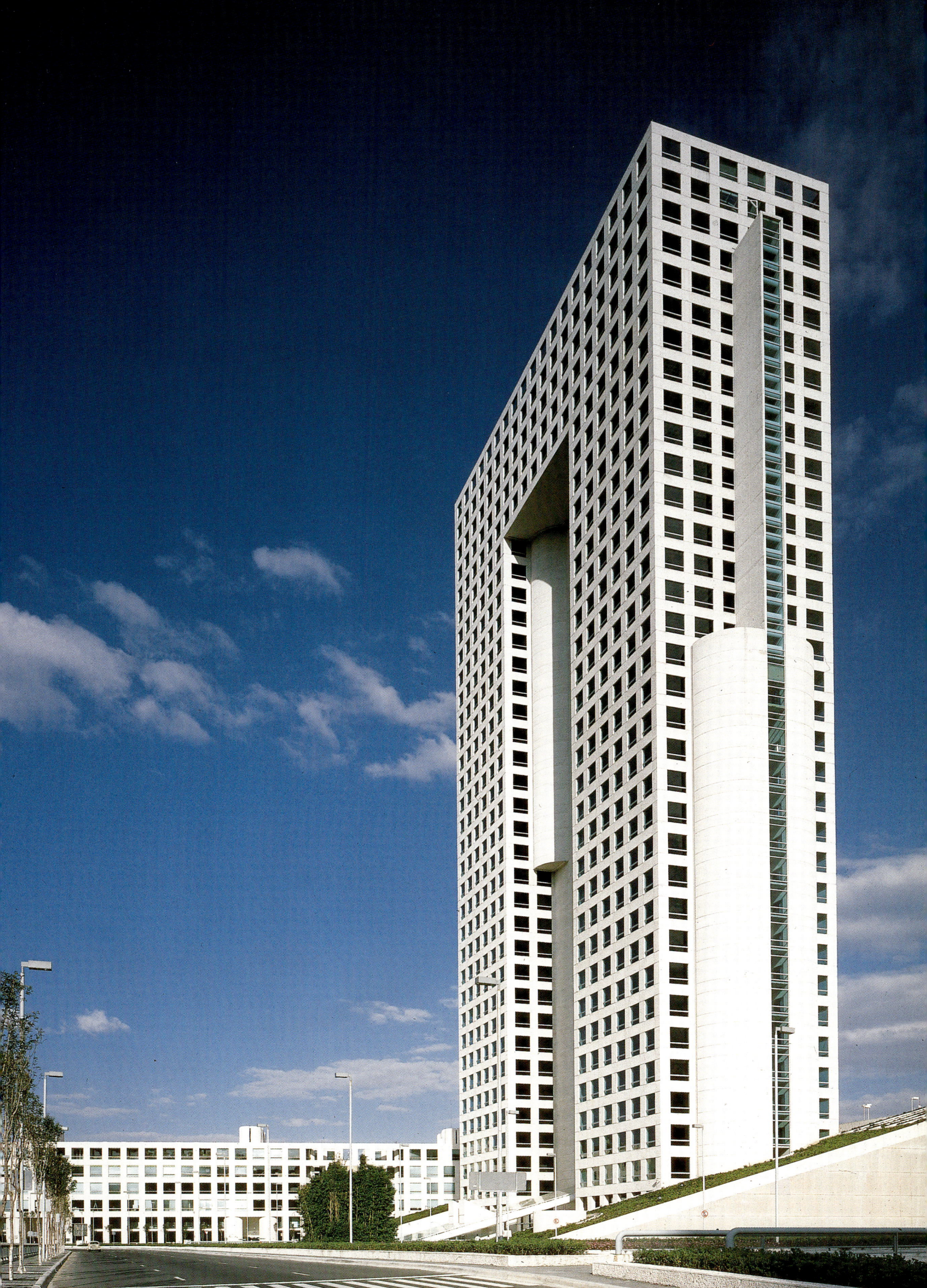

Typical plans of floors from level 3 to 14. Opposite page, typical plans of floors from level 18 to 28. Below, detail of the sloping-based building.

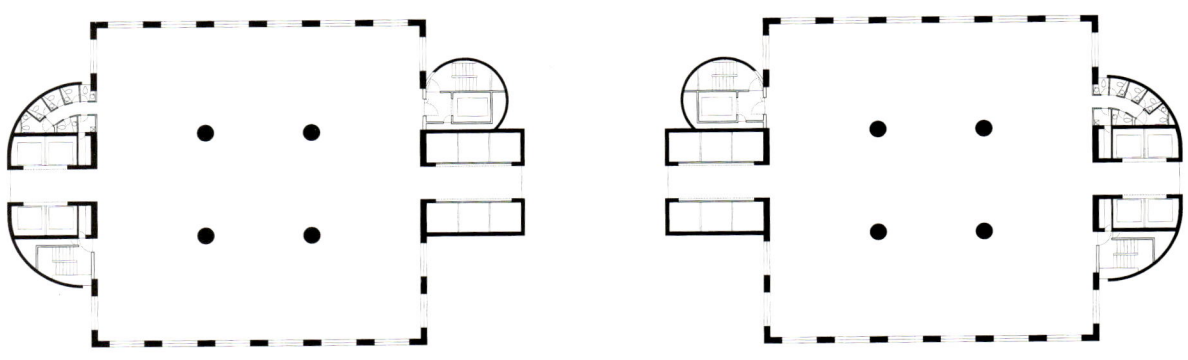

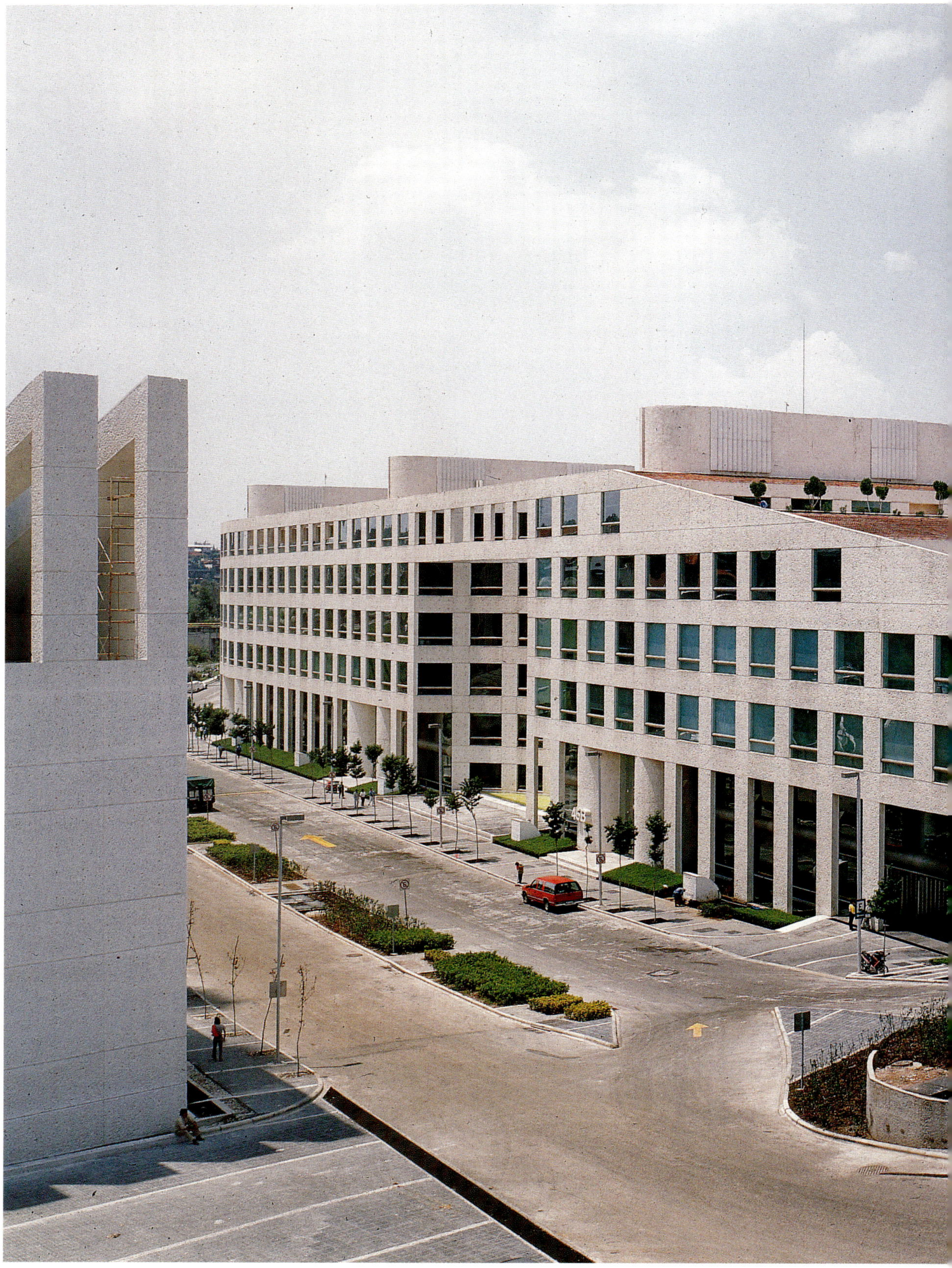

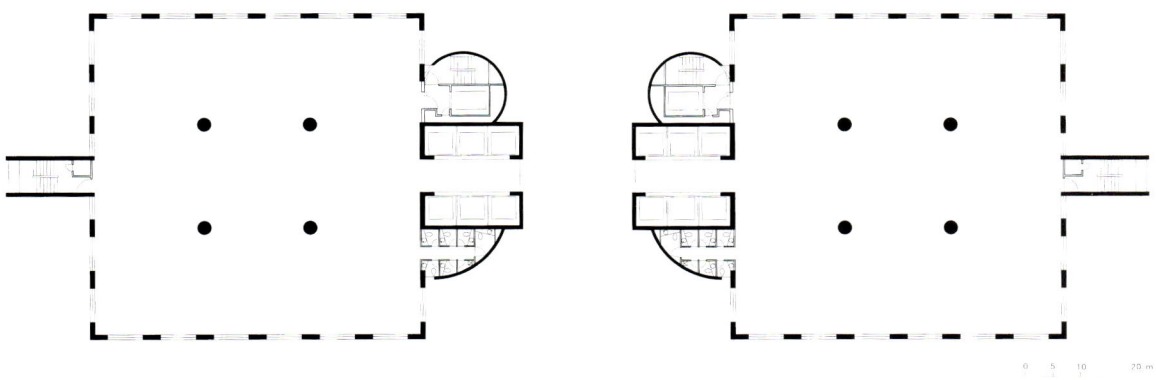

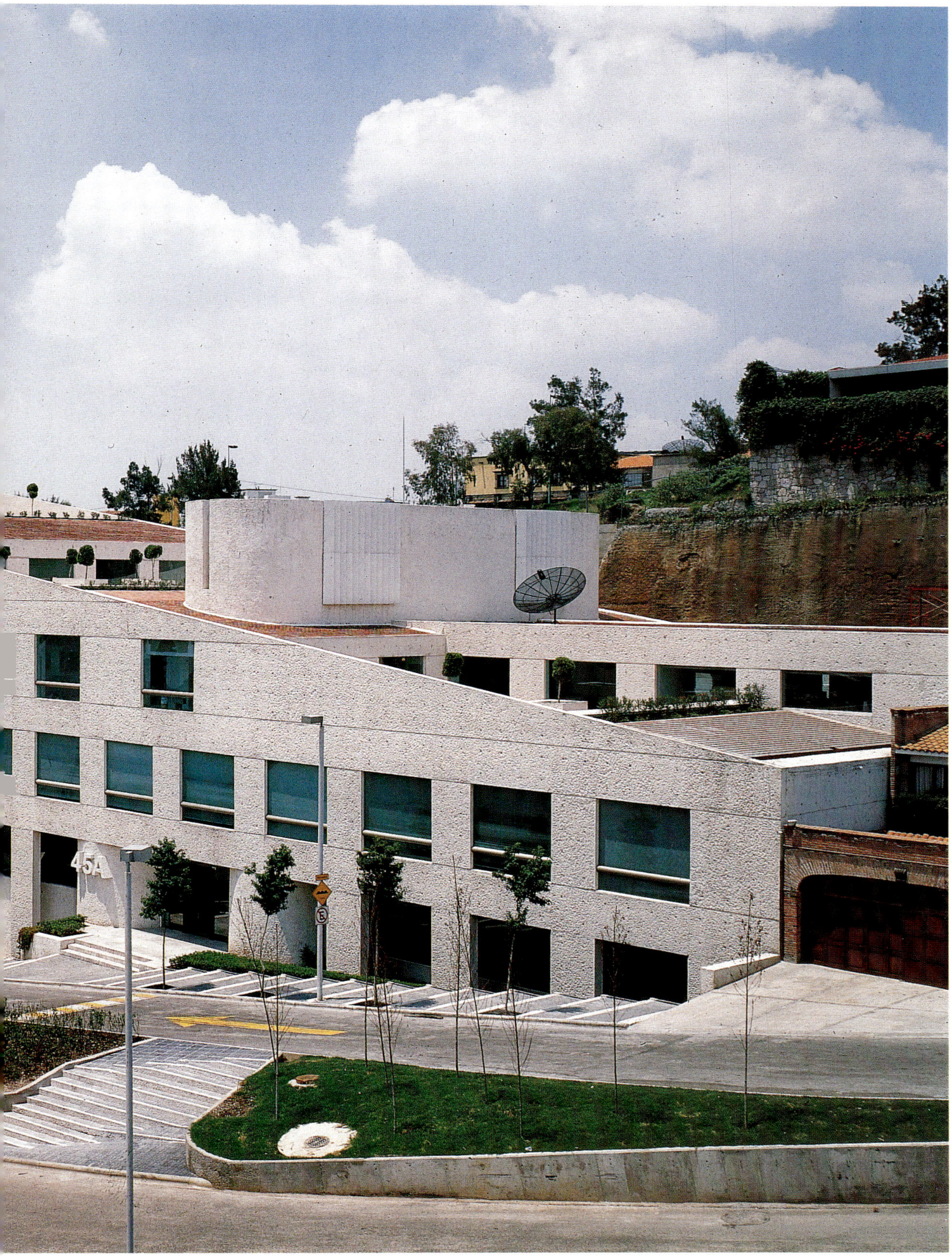

Site plan and section of the Arcos Bosque Corporativo high-rise building in Mexico City.

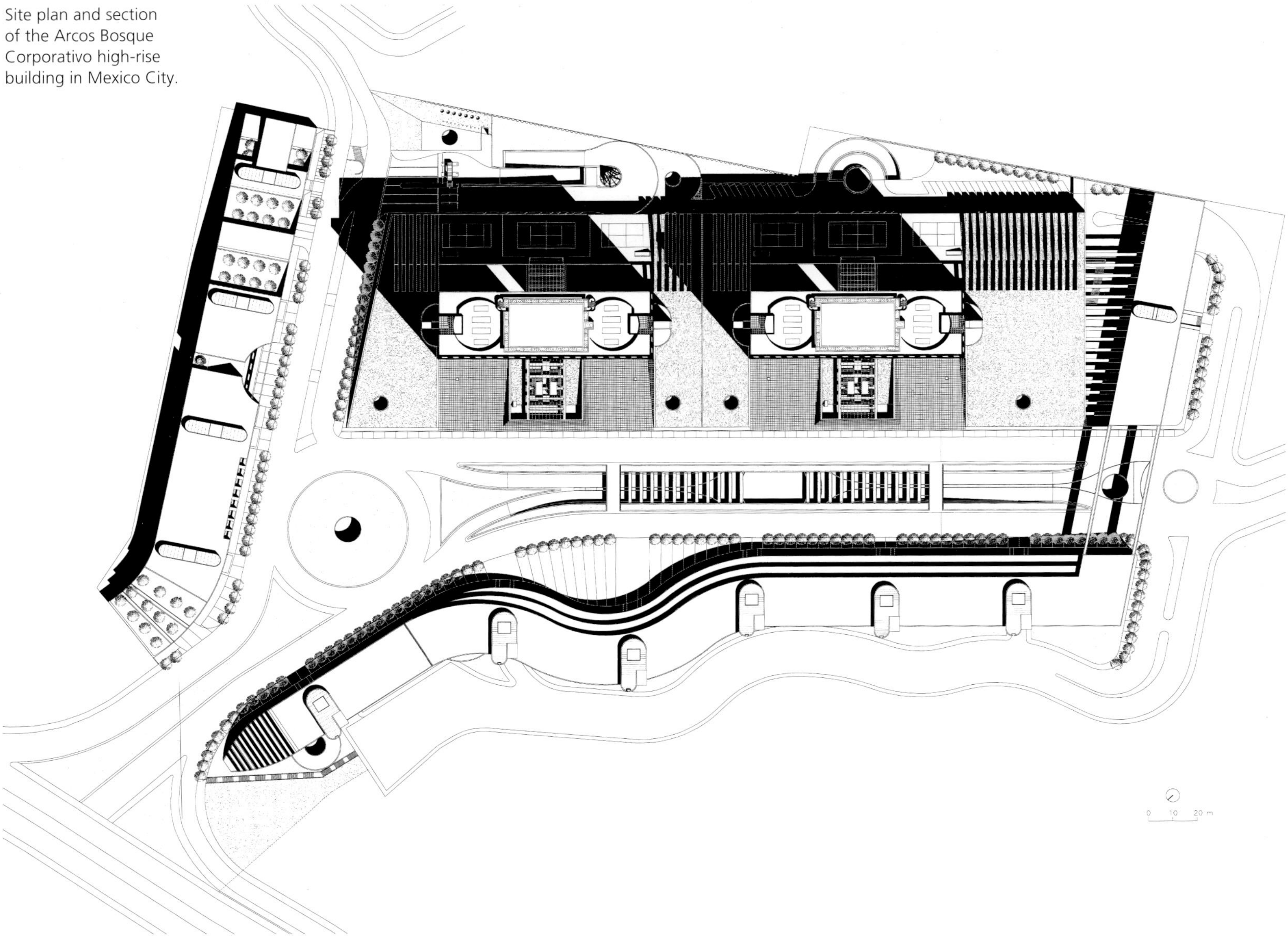

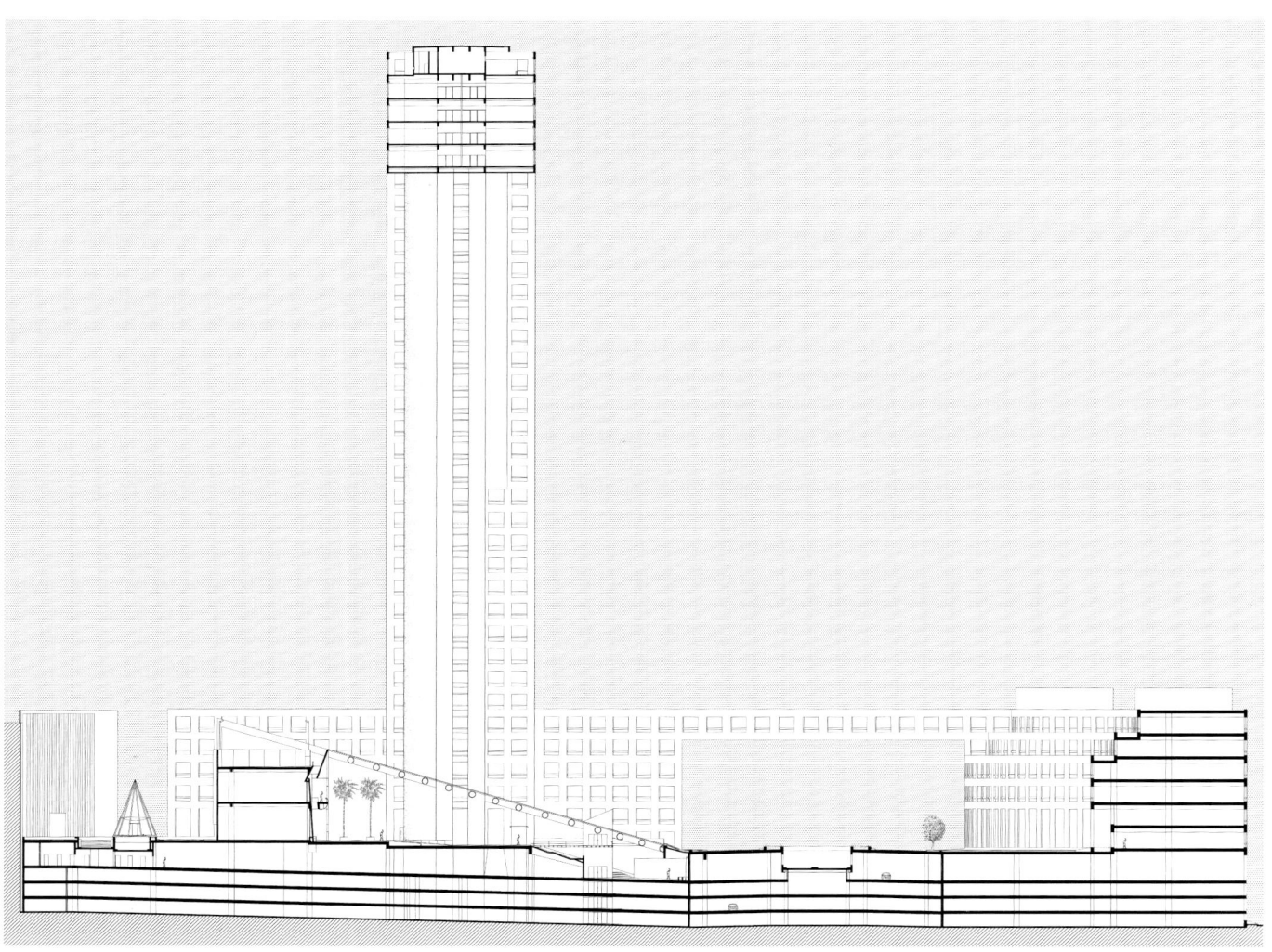

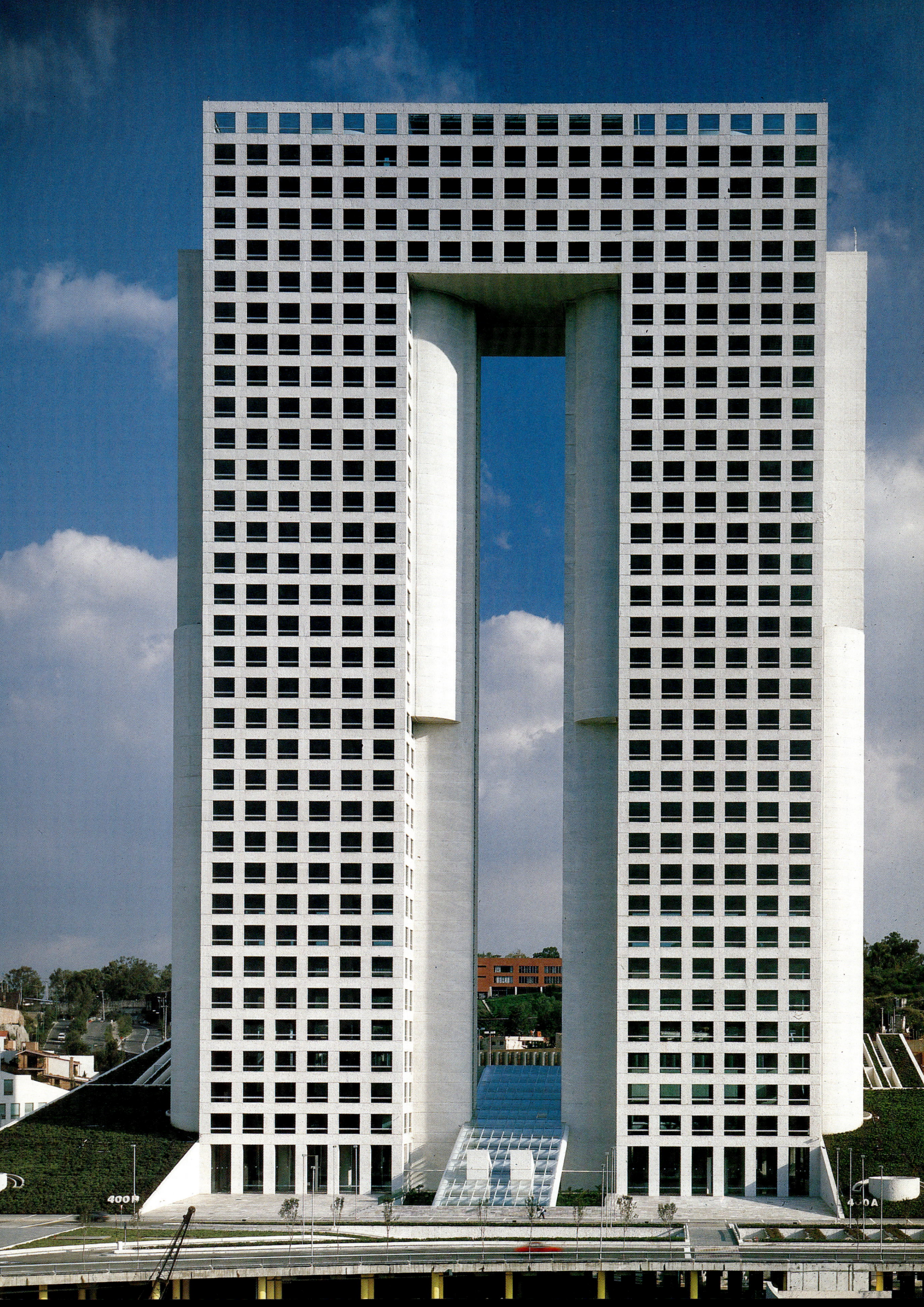

Detail of the facade
of the base building.

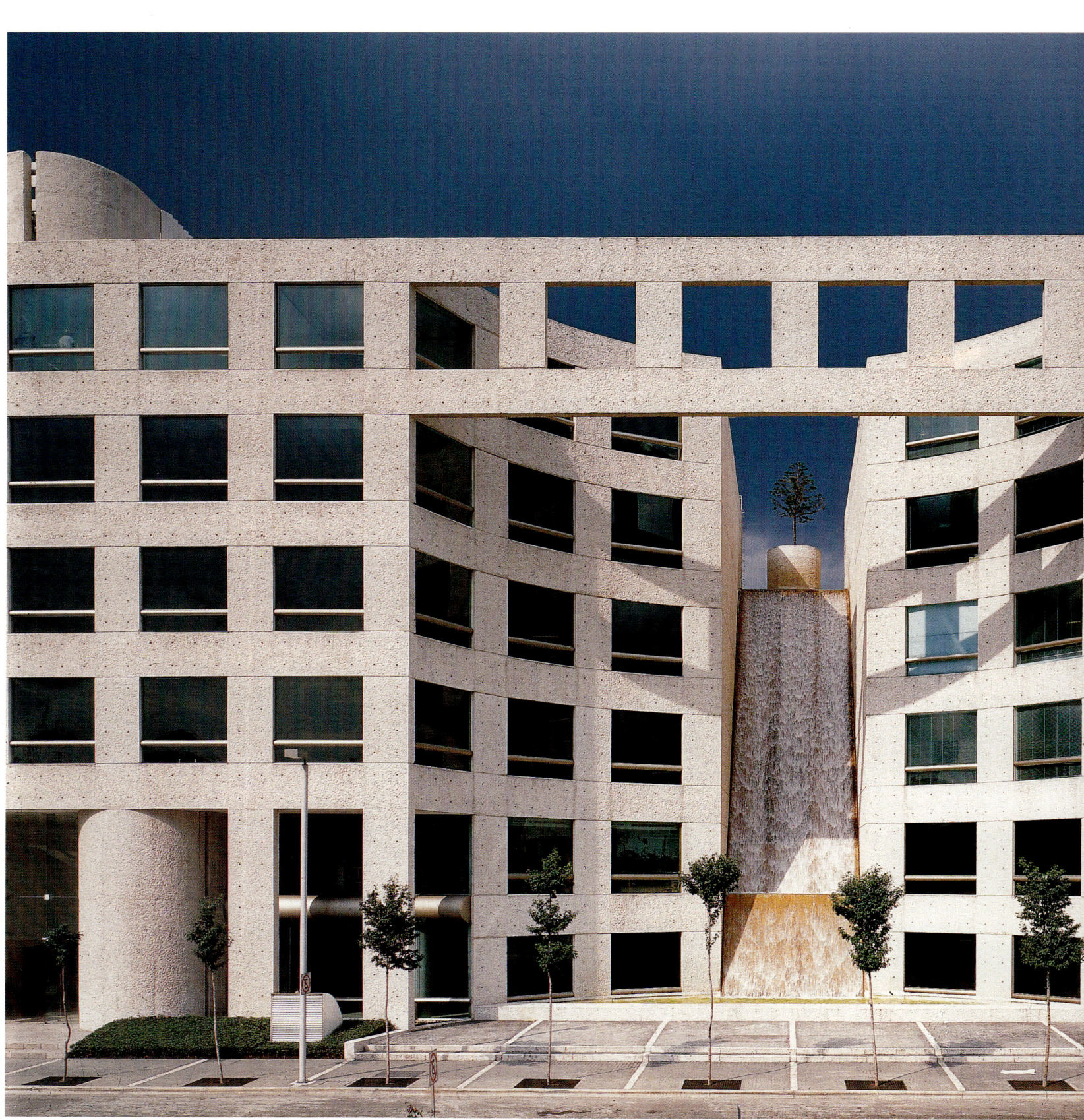

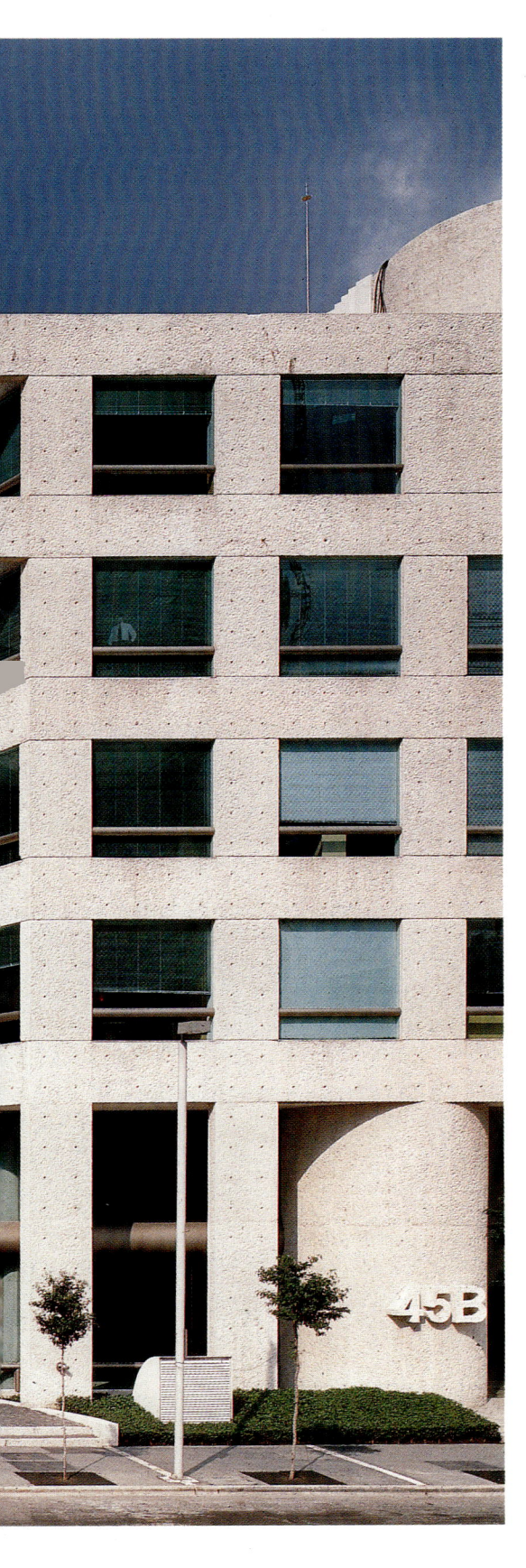

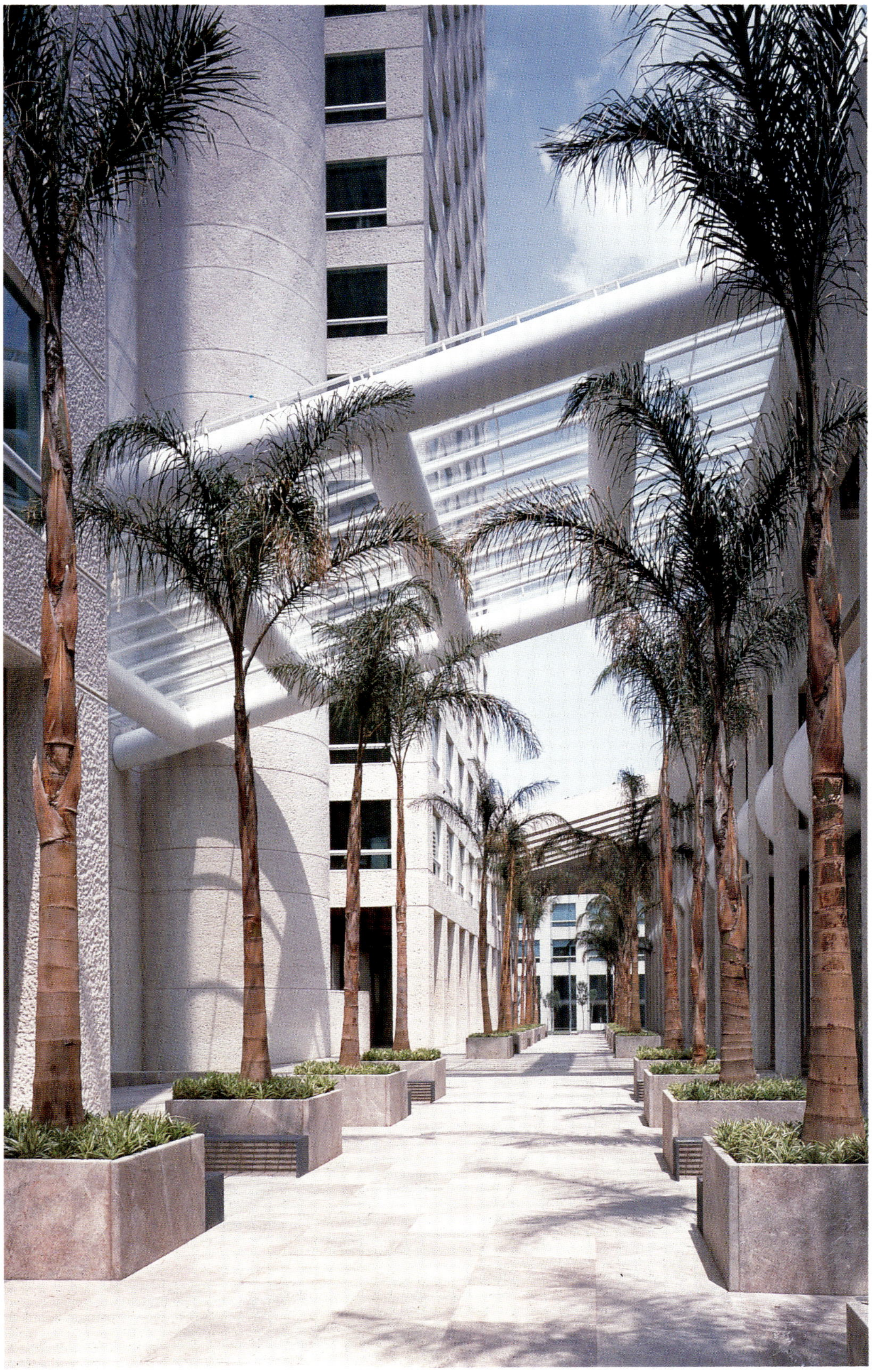

Detail of the internal "road" covered by a sloping glass and steel roof, under which the shopping arcade is also located.

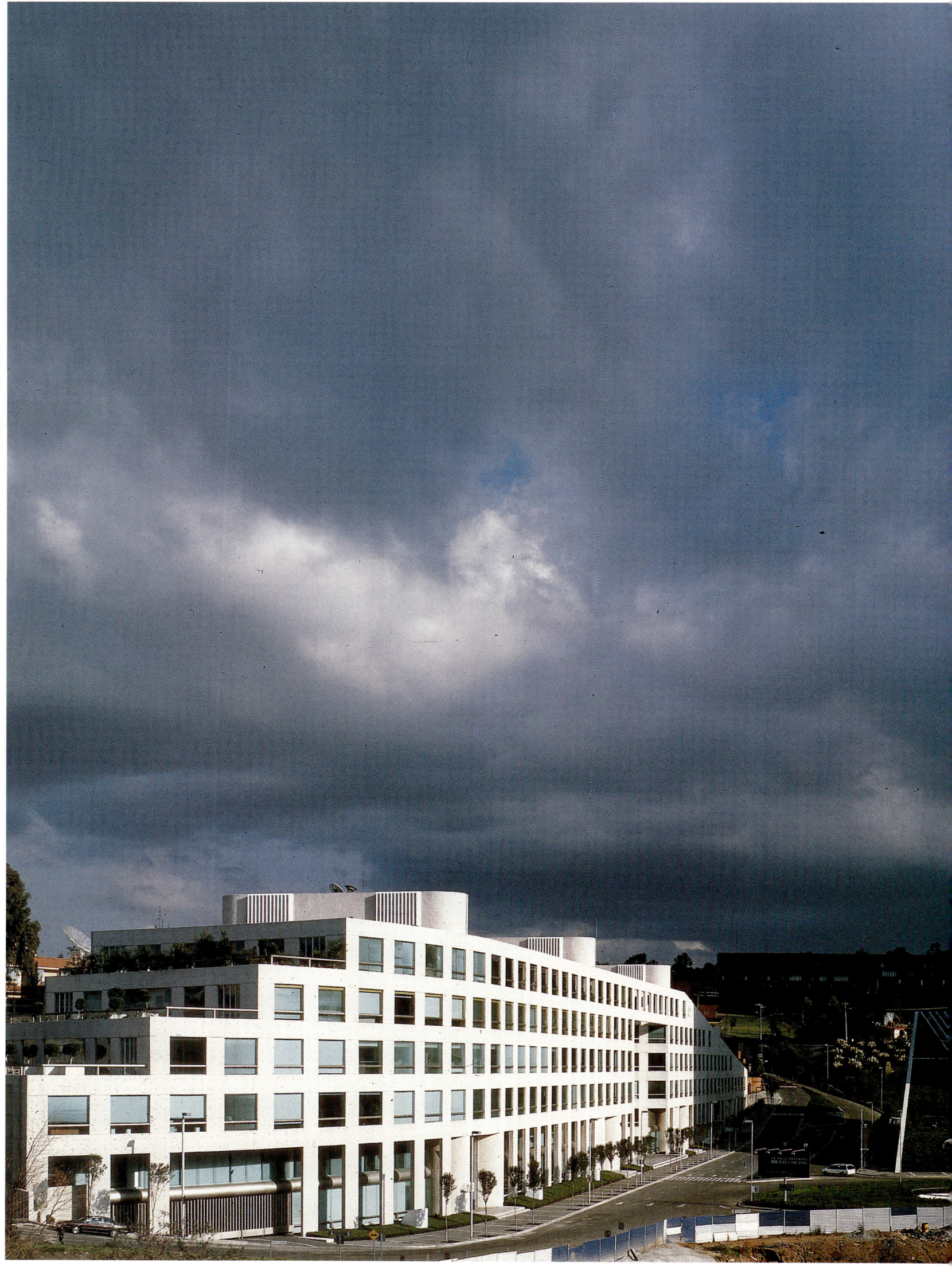

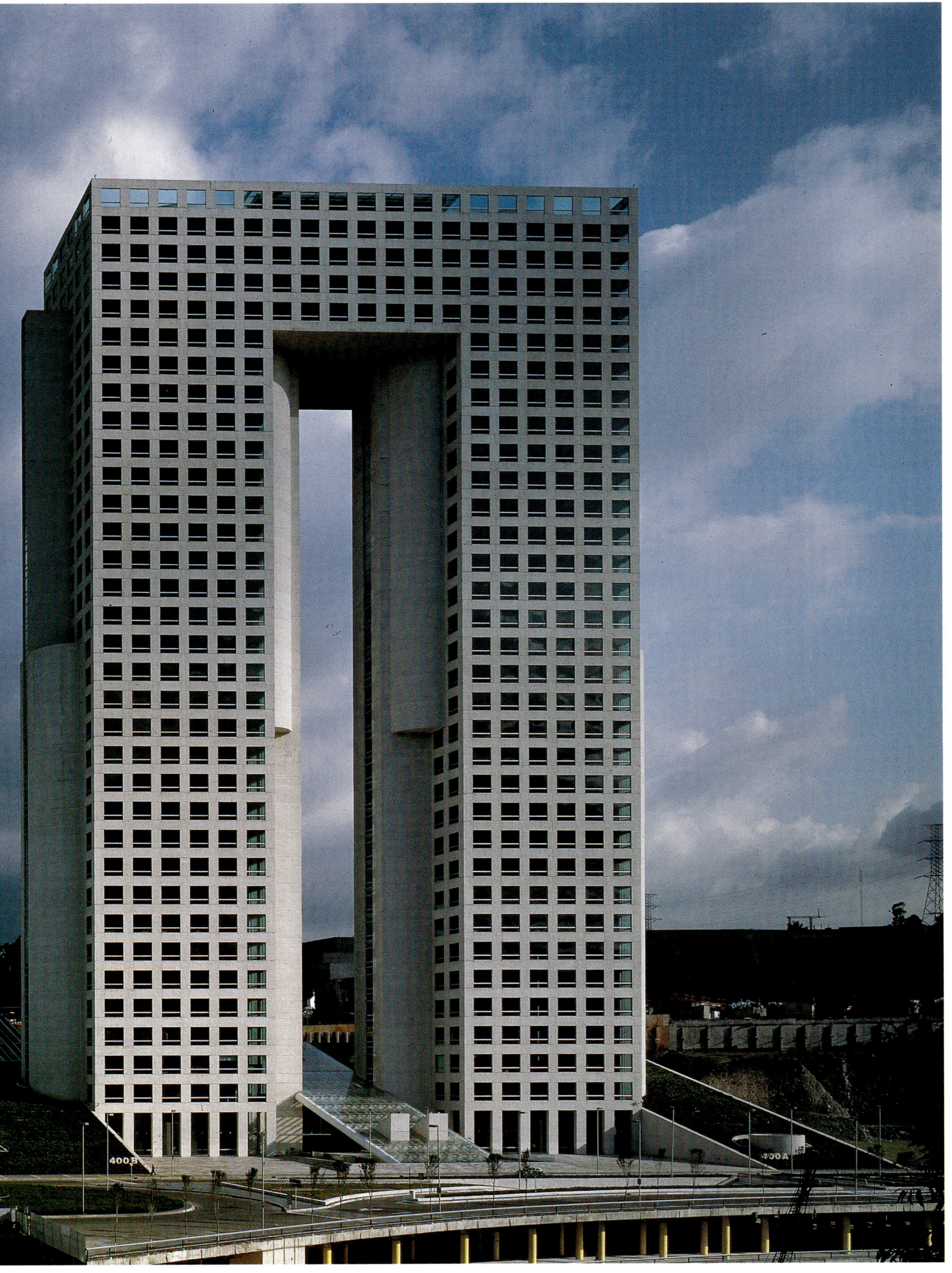

Mexico City, 1993-1994

National Music Conservatory

Owner
Consejo Nacional para la Cultura y las Artes

Architect
Teodoro González de León

Collaborator
Ernesto Betancourt

Acoustics
Jaffe Holden Scarbrough Acoustics Inc.

Structural design
Diseño y Supervisión "DYS", S.C.

Air-conditioning, electric and hydraulics and sanitary design
Tecnoproyectos, S.C.

Construction area
7,800 sq.m.

This project, one of the most important of all Teodoro González de León's designs, features two main architectural constructions: the common rooms and a library. The National Music Conservatory's architectural layout is designed to create a fluid sense of functionality through the arched structure of the main rooms and library. This has produced a simple yet intricate architectural design projecting its own peculiar image. As with all buildings of this kind, acoustics played a vital part in the basic design. González de León has handled these problems with great manual precision and dexterity, successfully counteracting the difficulties associated with acoustic resonance: the soundproof concrete panels and, above all, the use of wood for the floors in the all various rooms offered an ideal solution to sound distortions. The main auditorium hall, an interesting but highly unusual structural design for González de León featuring a cube rotated through 45 degrees, is buried below ground level to allow the public seating facilities to be placed along its diagonal axis.

This is a powerful sign of a new approach to design. Although some of González de León's other projects were devised to counteract the basic staticness of his architecture, here he has made a much braver and more determined attempt to forcibly adapt form to function.

The result is again worthy of attention and highlights his continuing experimentation into architectural design.

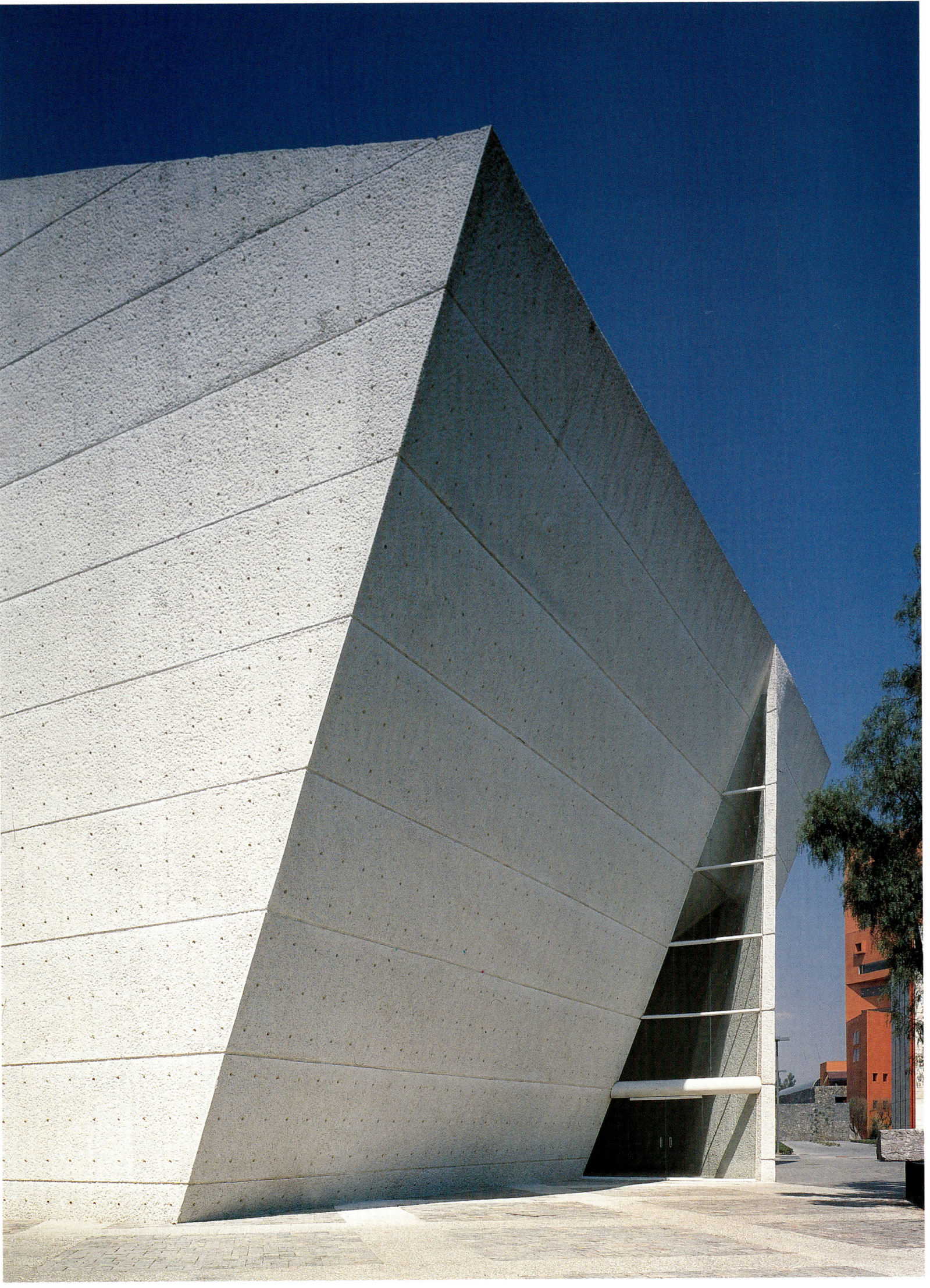

Site plan and, right, the end section of the arch-shaped volume to the east holding the rooms.

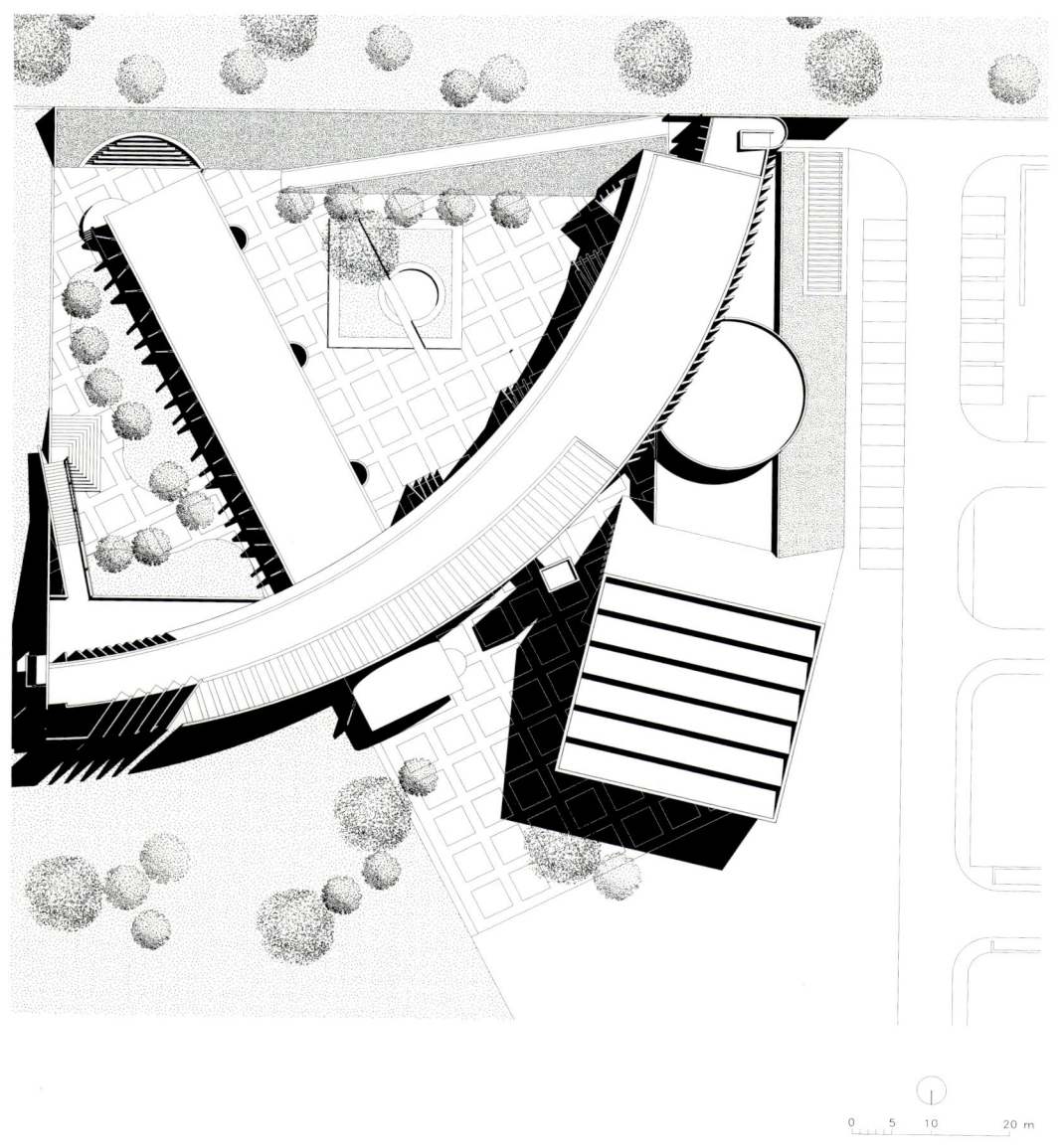
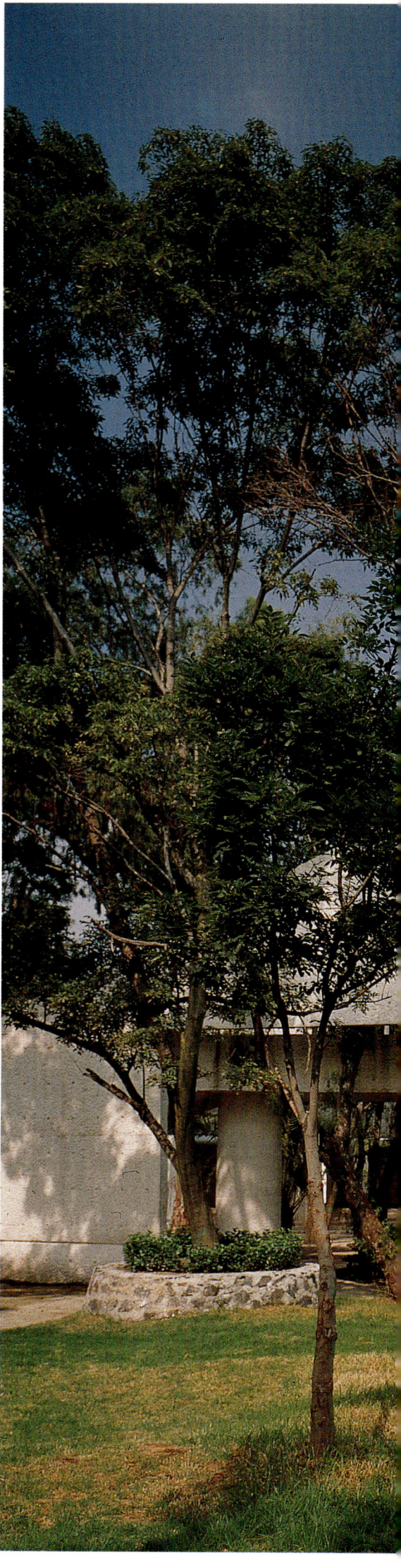

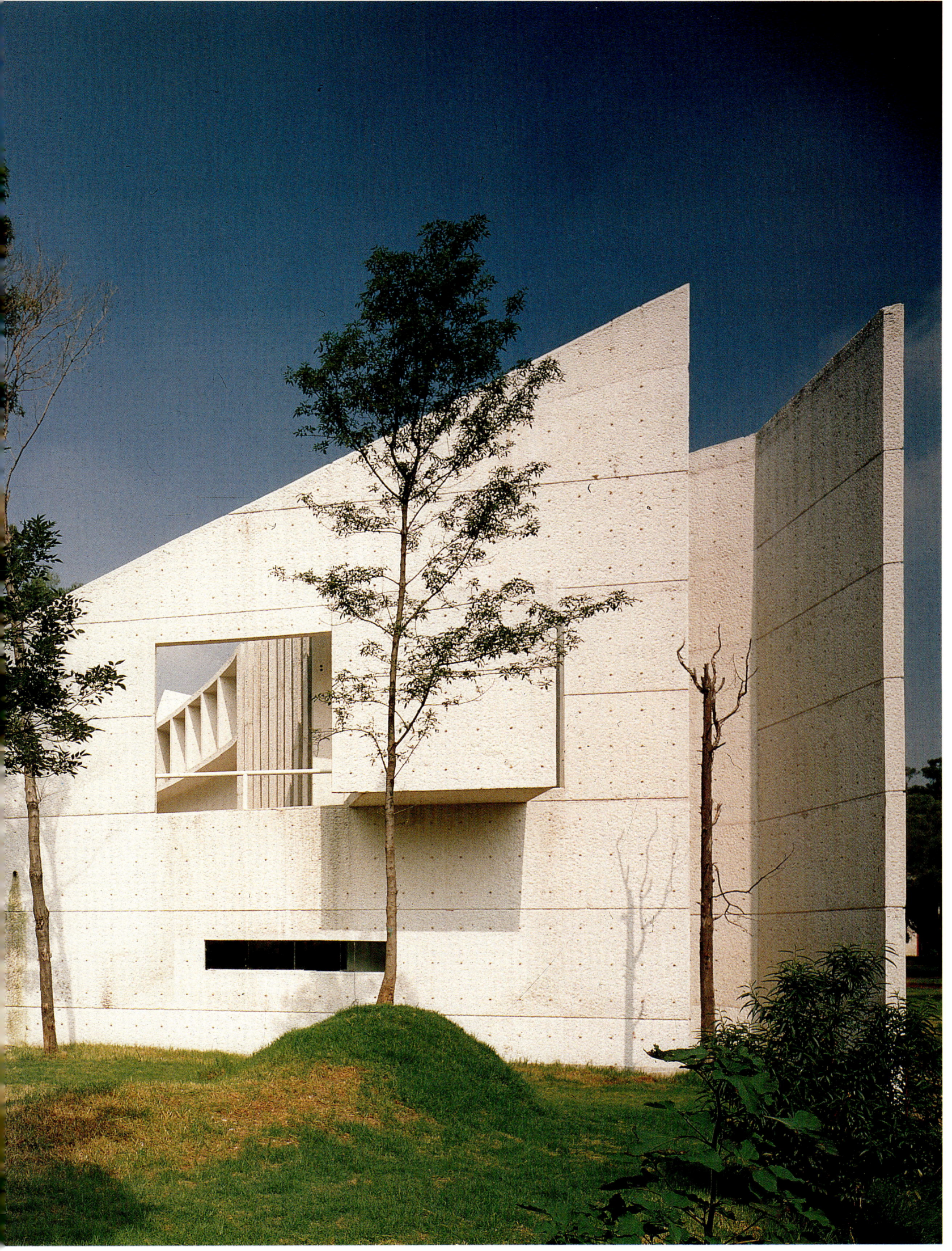

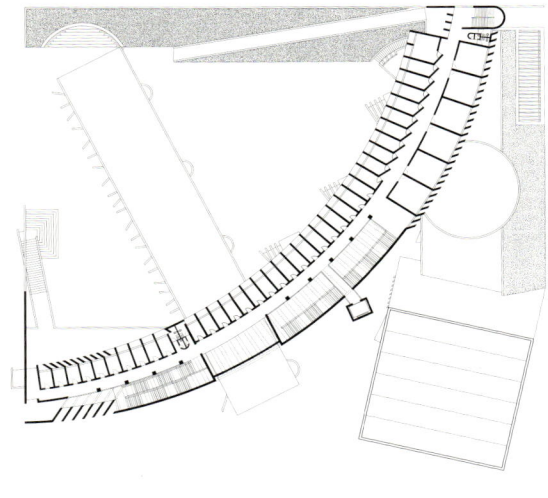
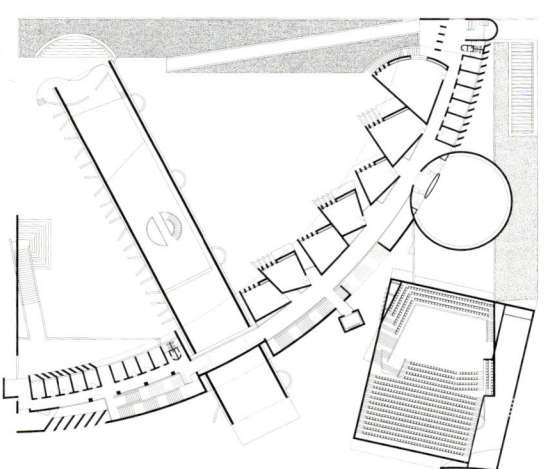
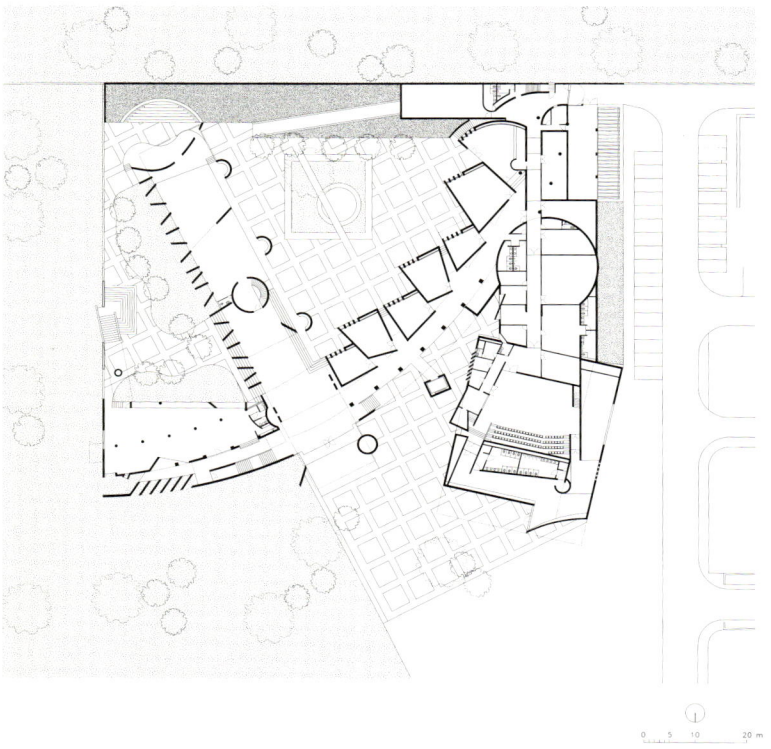

From bottom of page up, plans of the ground floor, first floor, and second floor. Below, the archway marking the entrance to the complex.

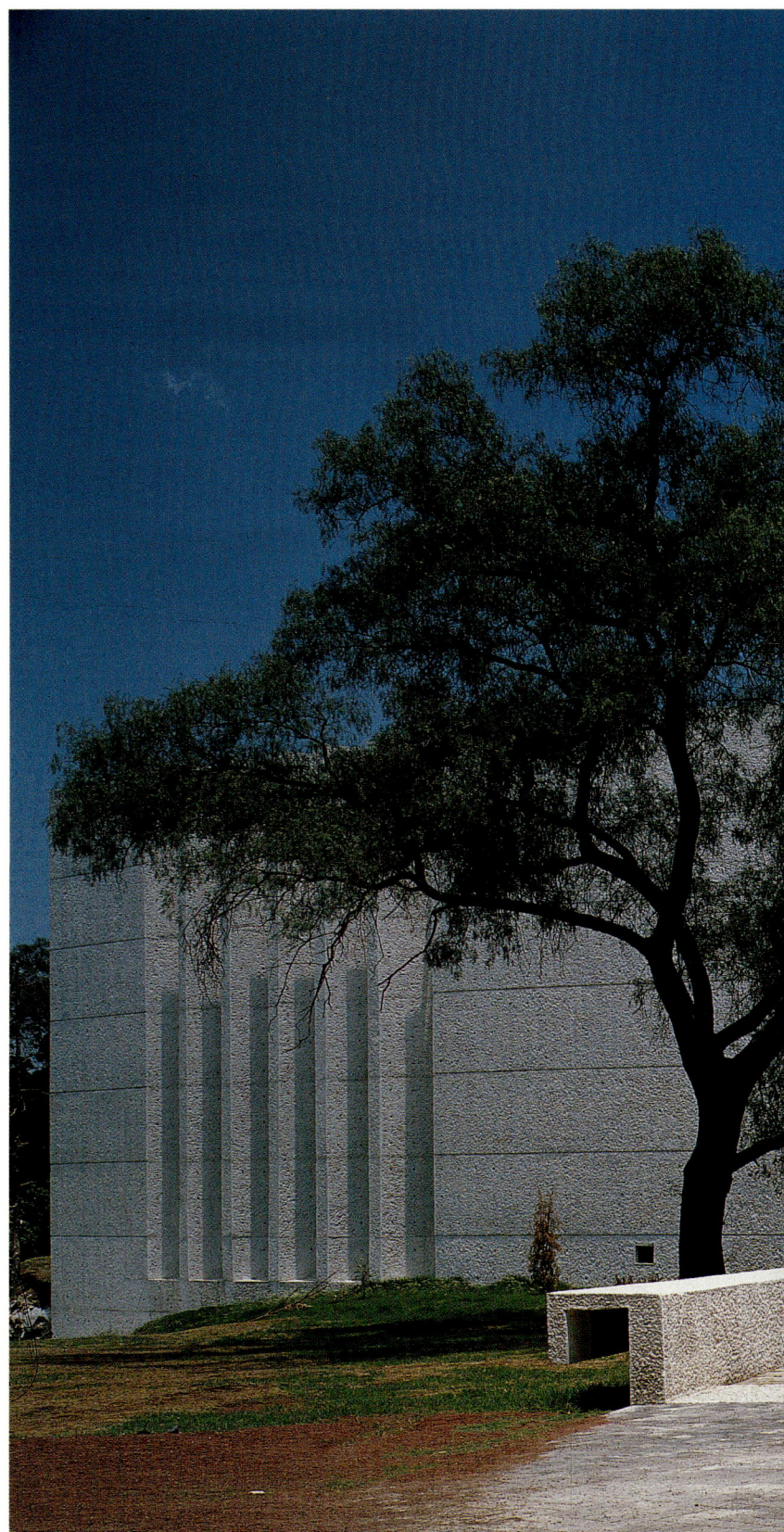

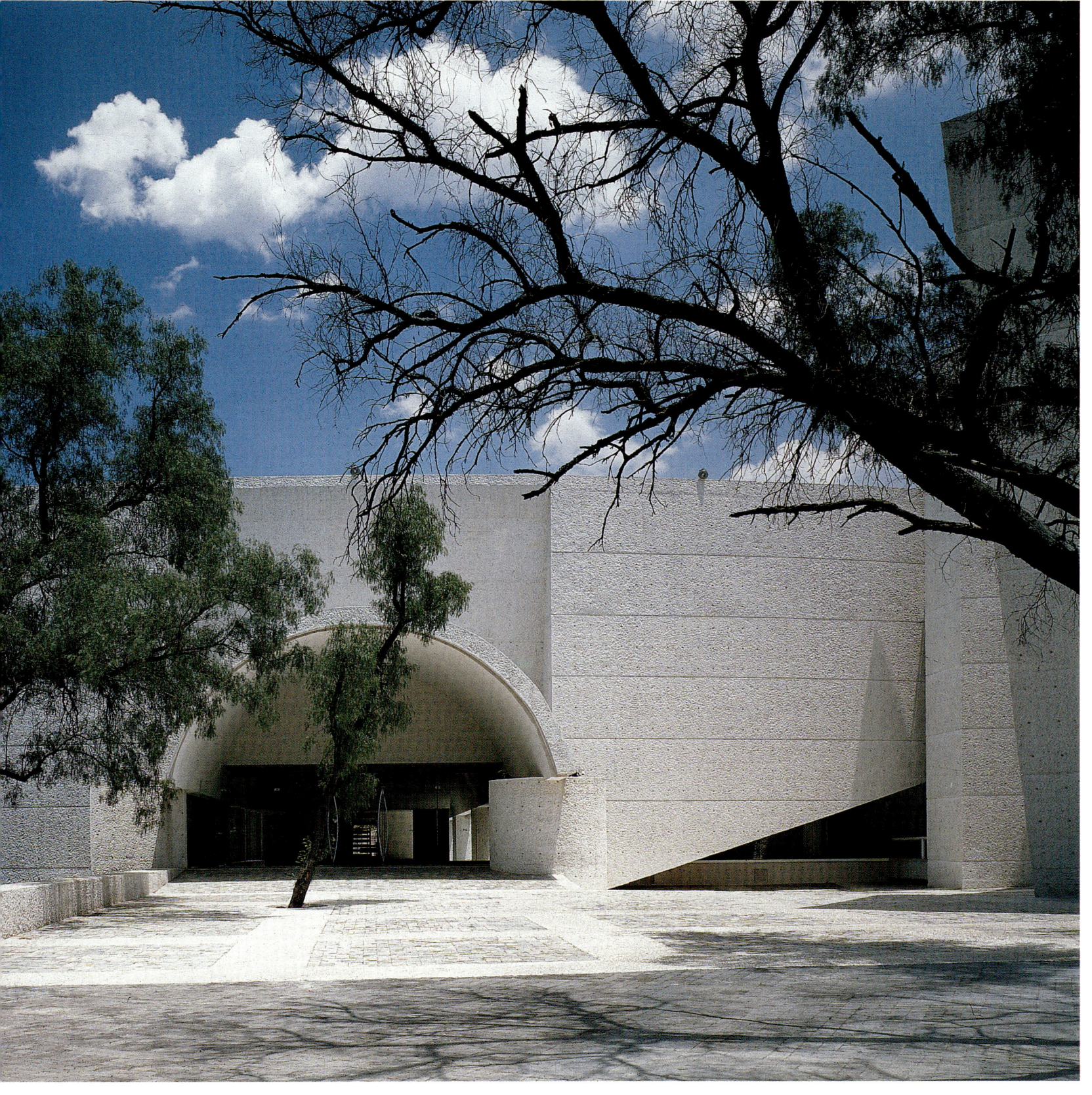

Detail of the entrance plaza.
Cross and longitudinal sections, section of the rooms, and section of concert hall.

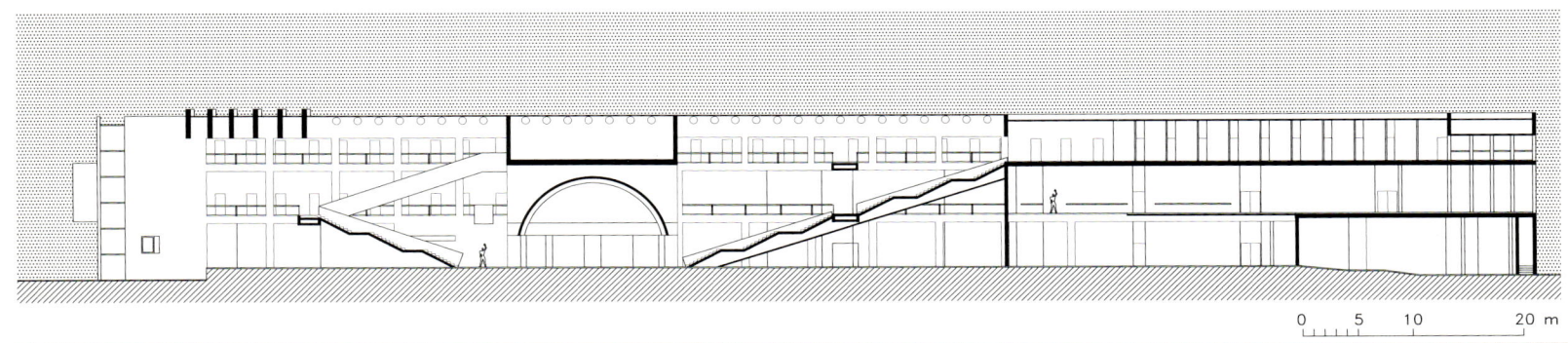

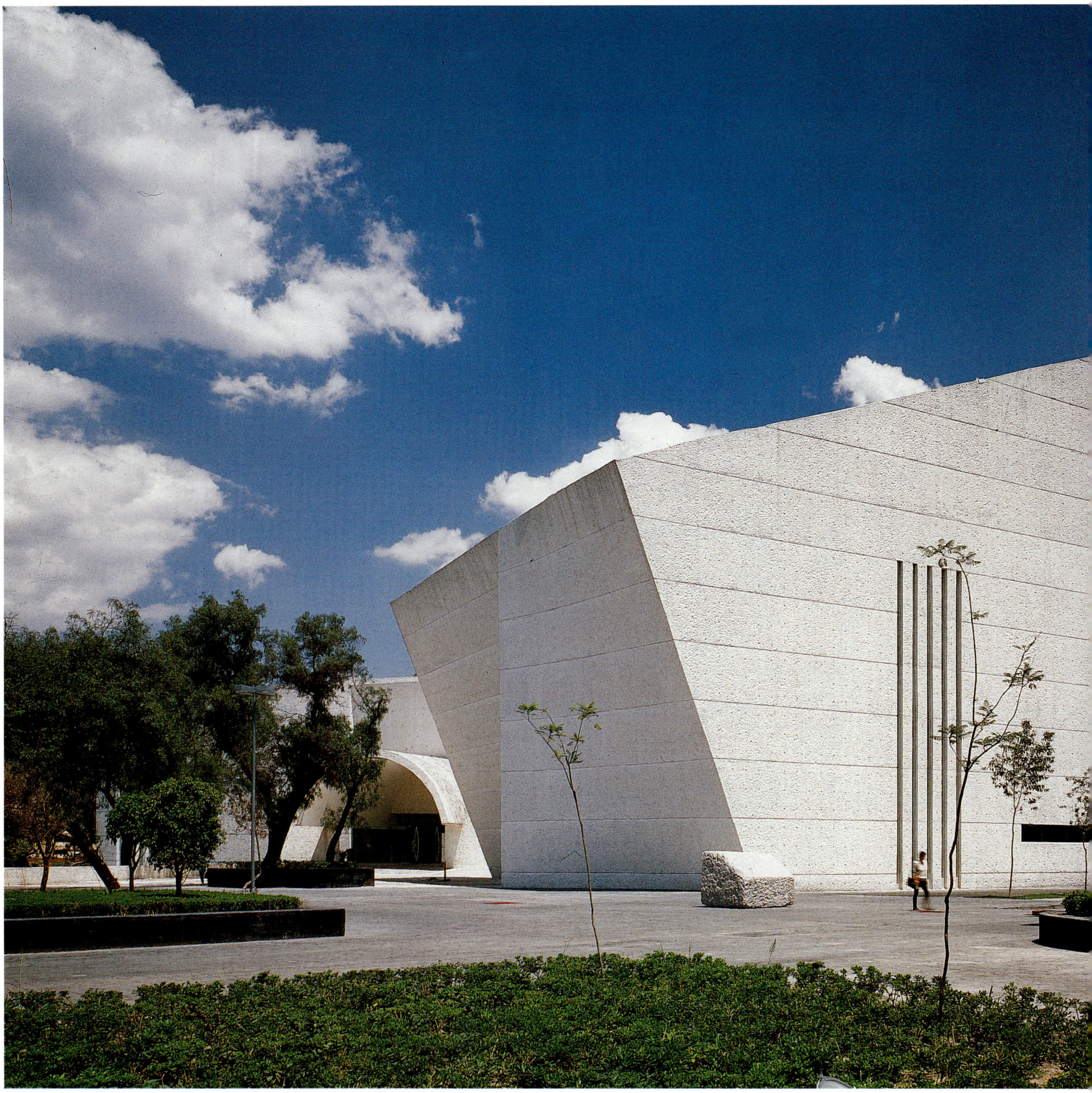

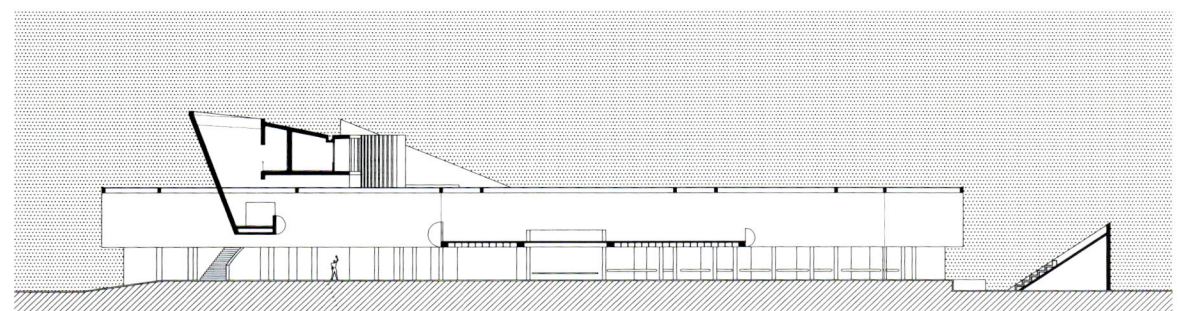
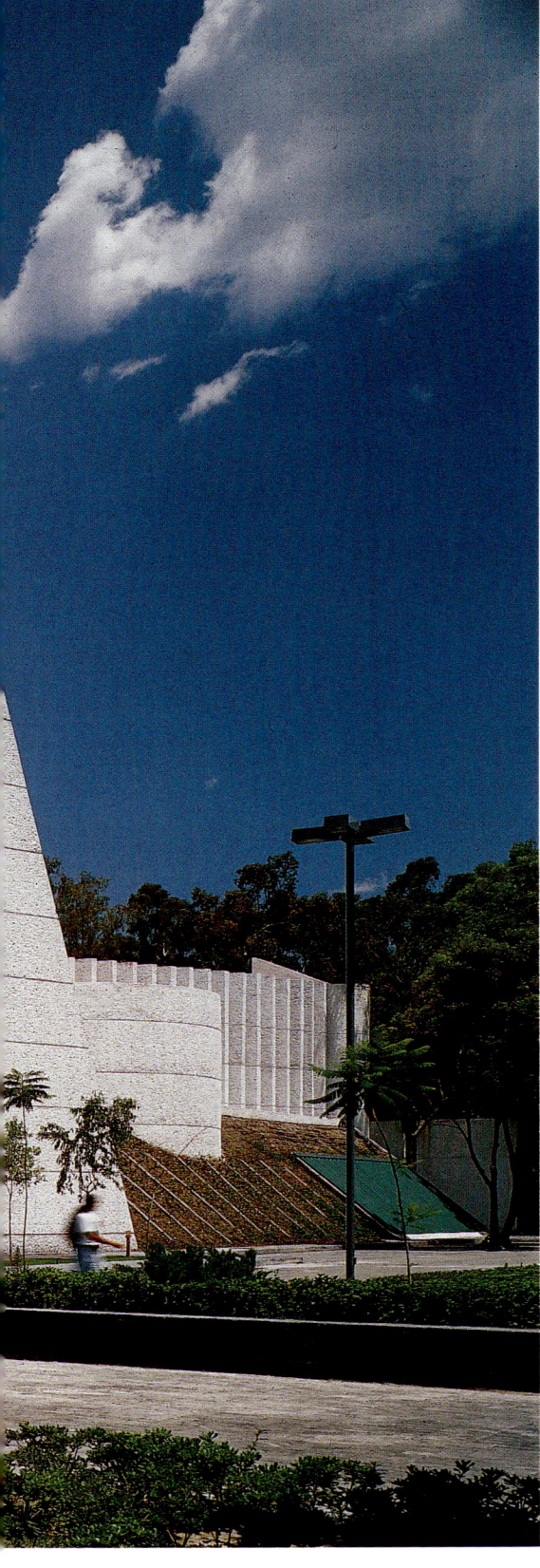
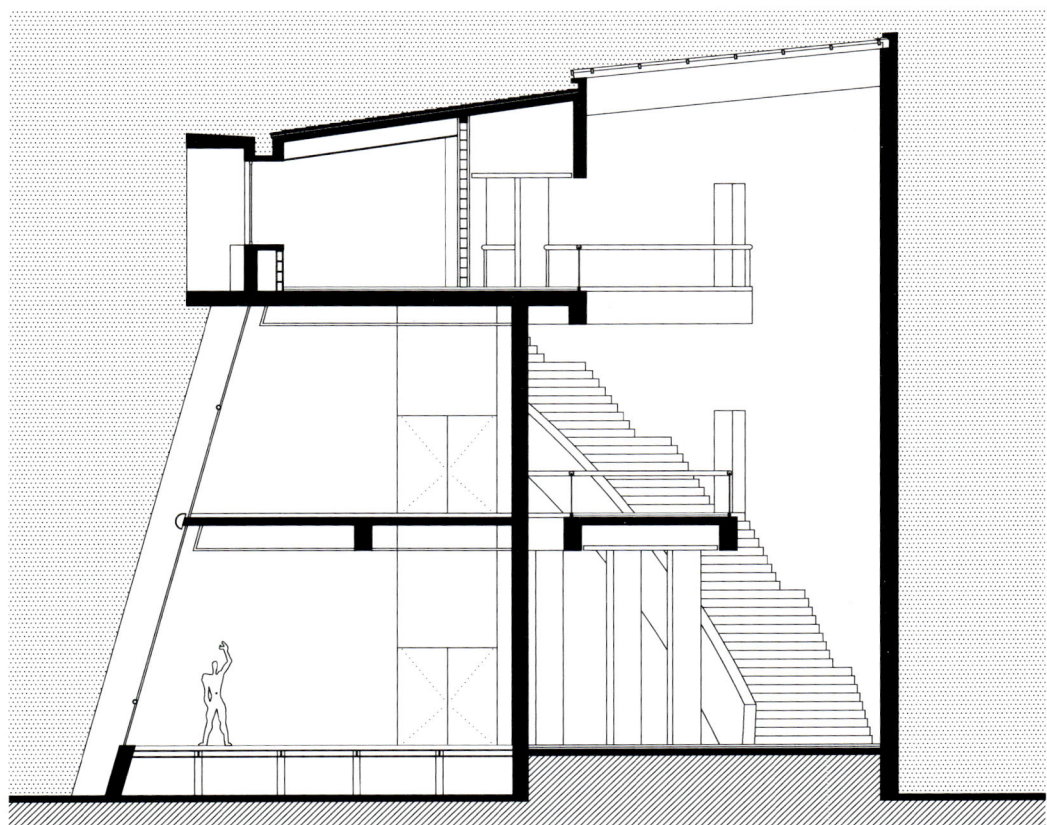
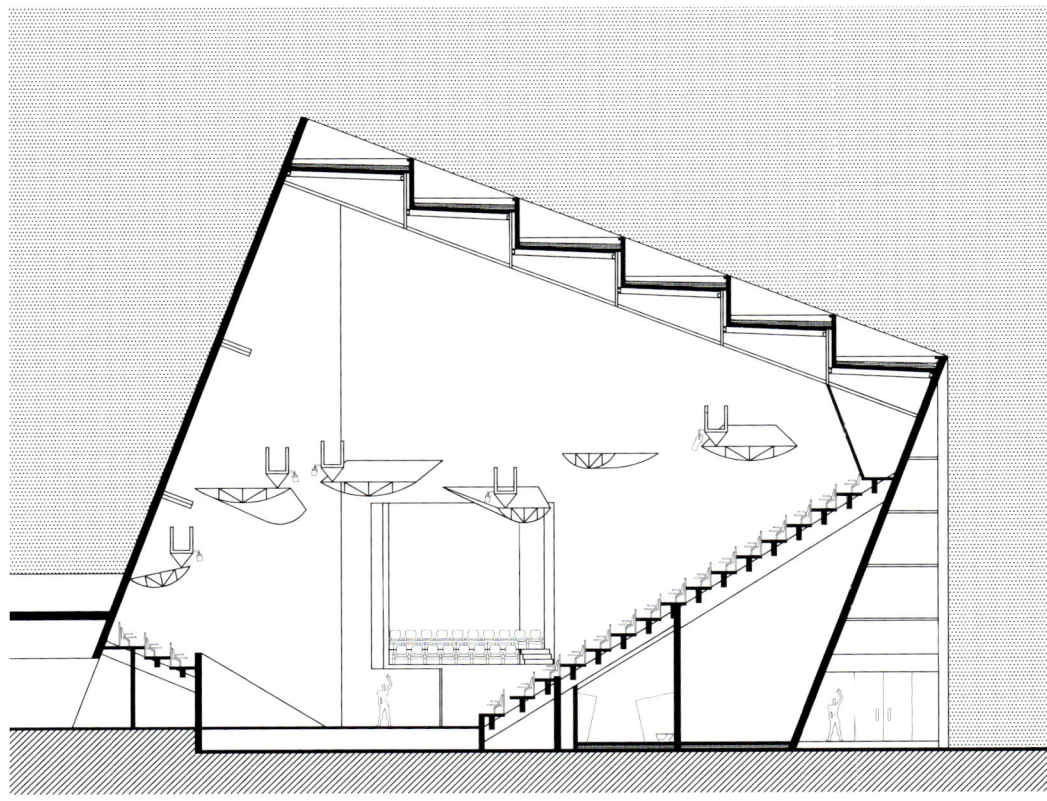

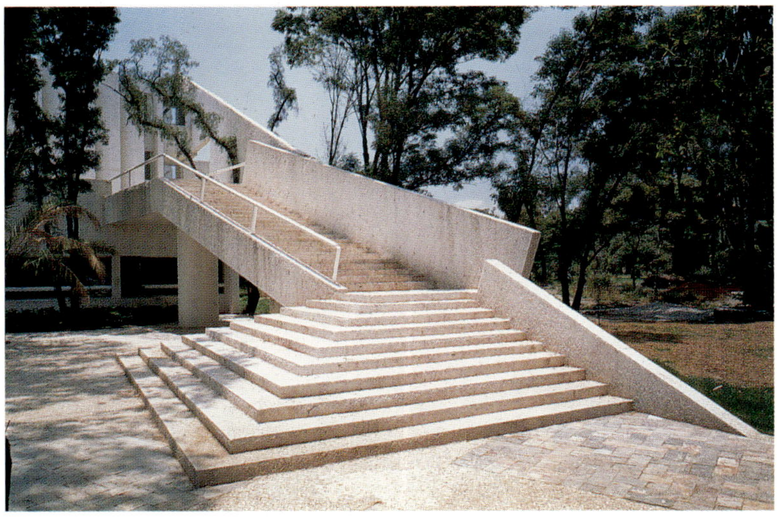

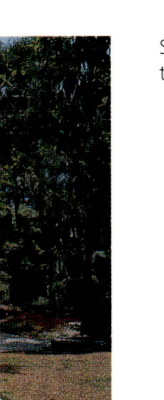

Stairway connecting
the patio to the first floor.

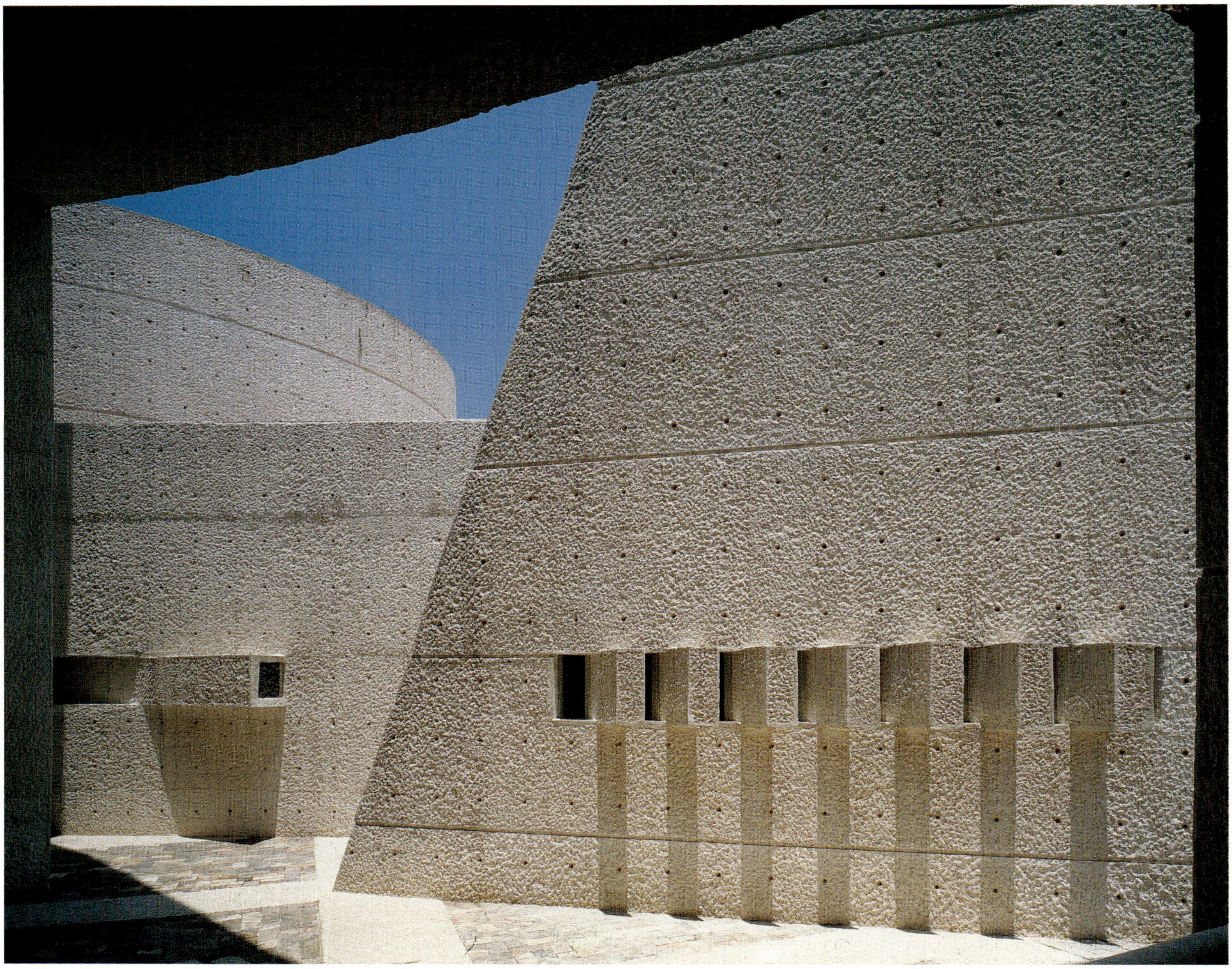

Details of the outside
curtain walls made
of soundproof concrete
panels to solve acoustic
resonance problems.

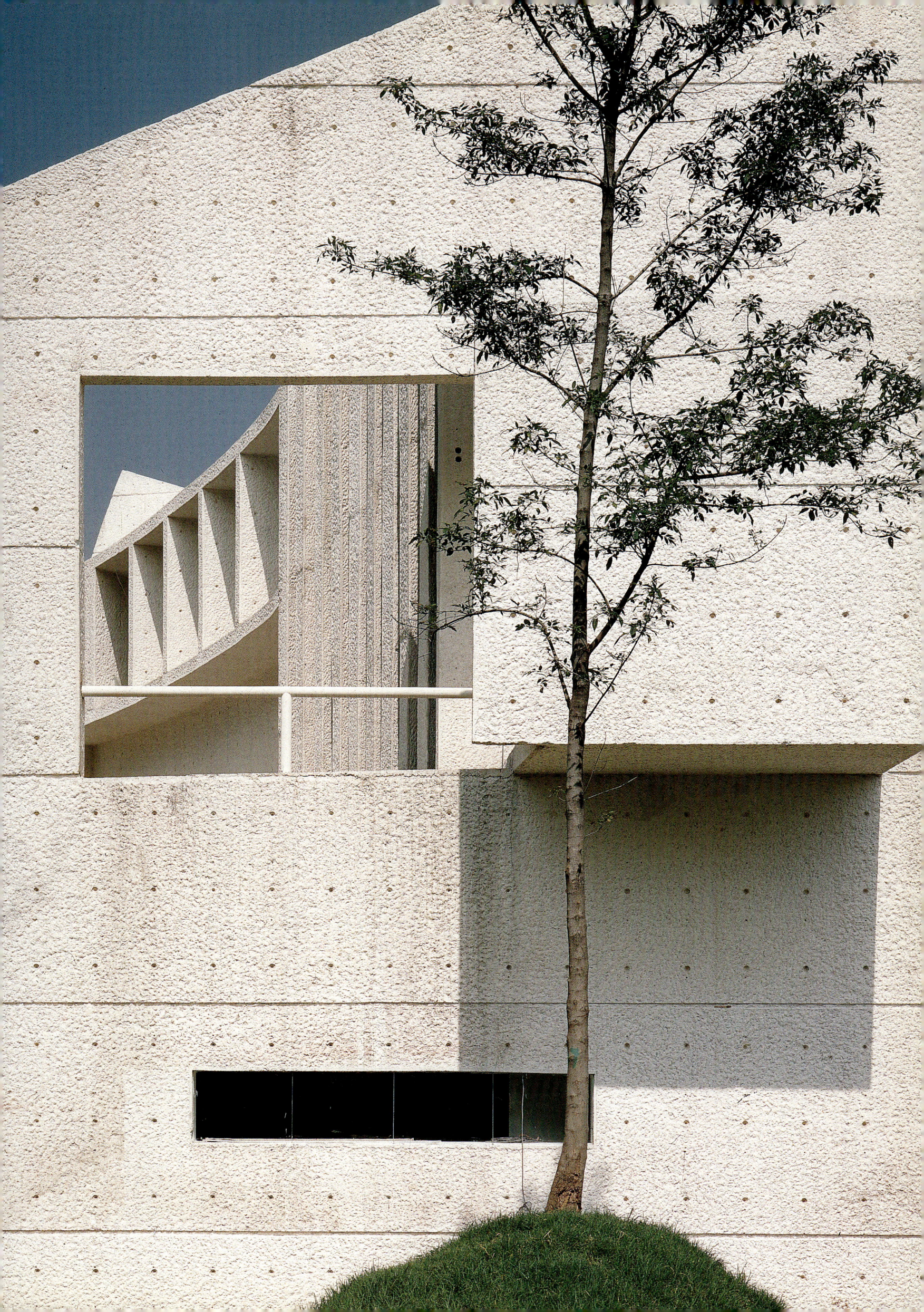

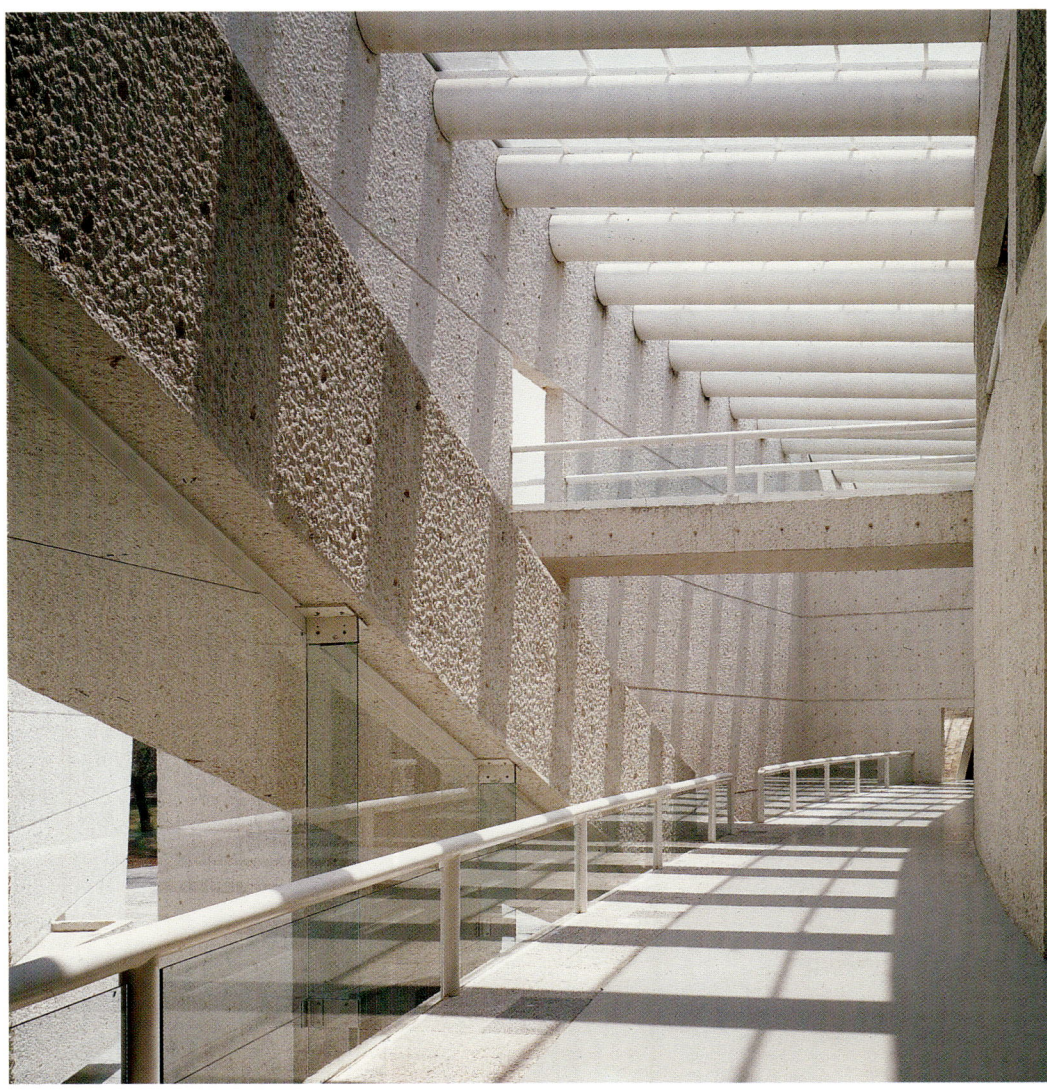

Details of the pathways weaving in and out to smoothly interconnect the various parts of the complex.

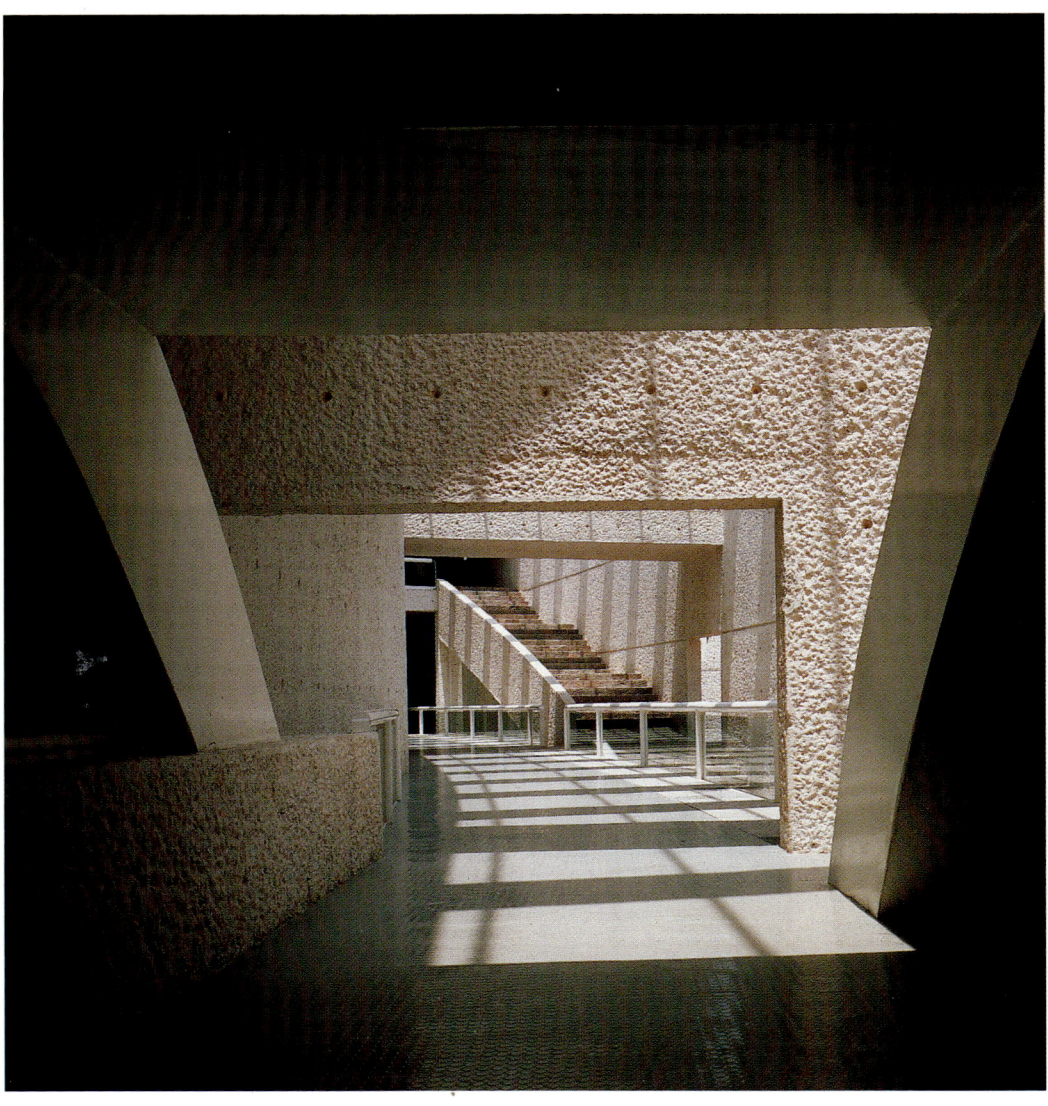

112

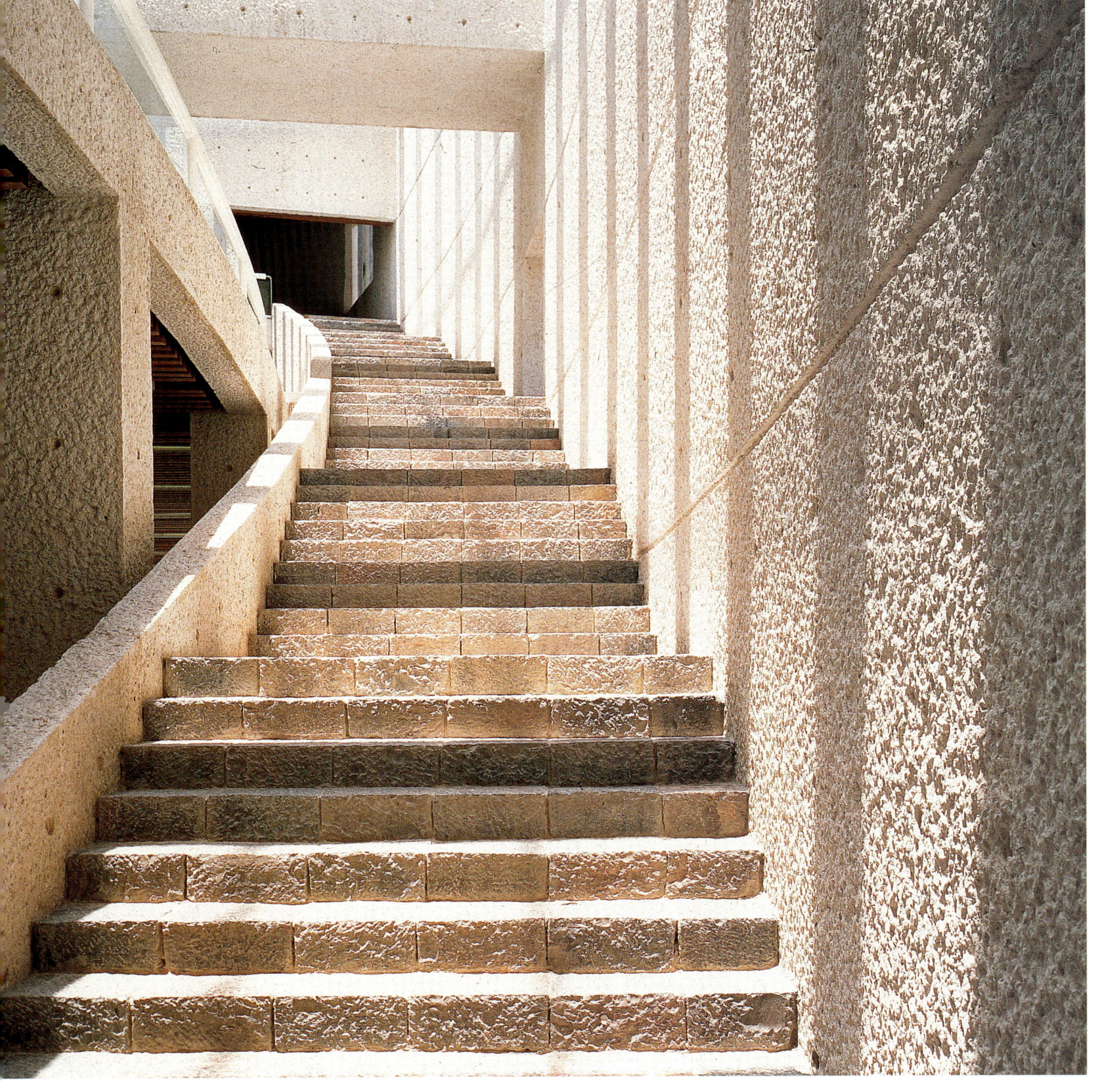

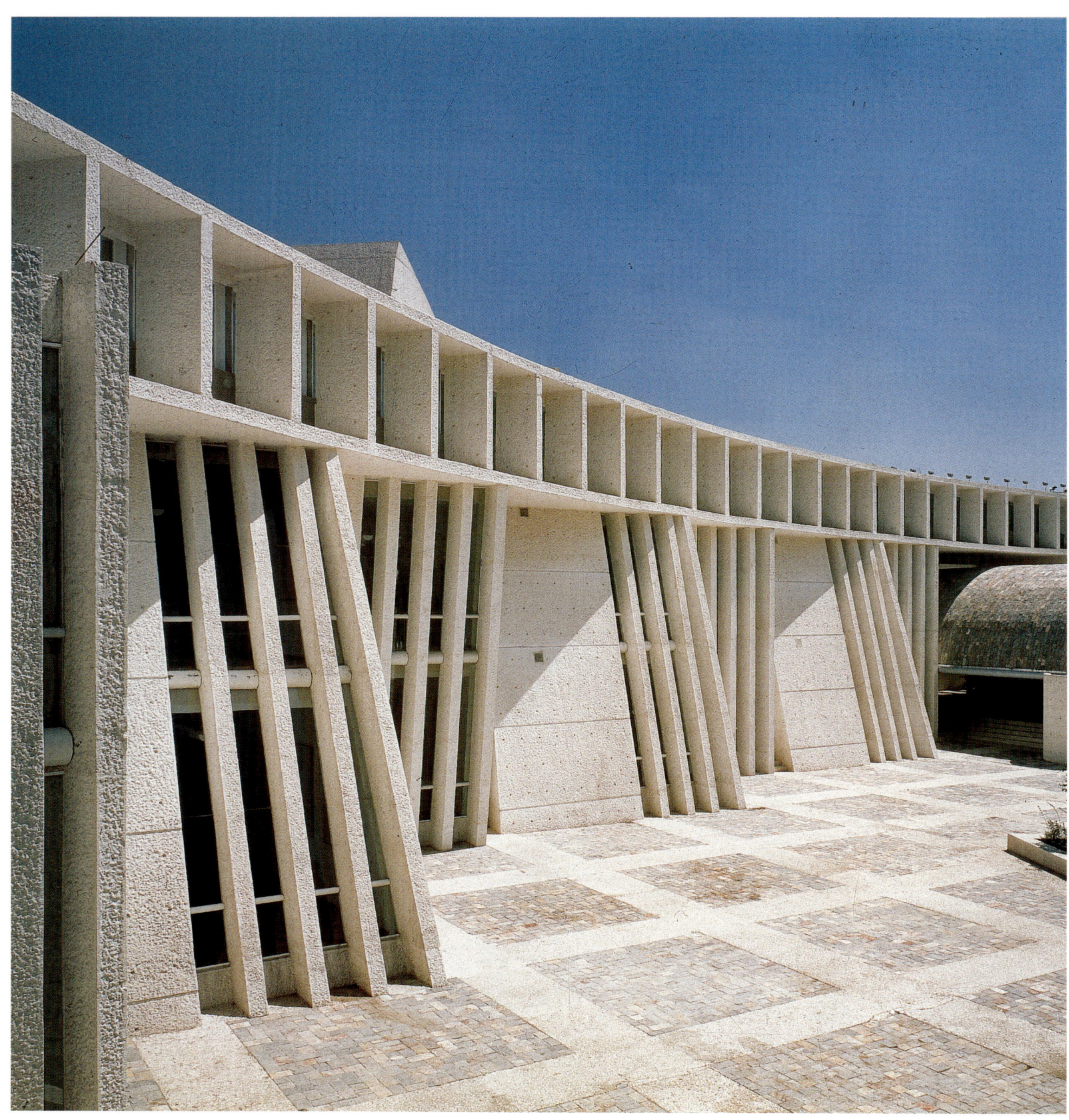

The internal courtyard cut through by the semi-cylindrical structure housing the library. Opposite page, detail of the outside of the cube-shaped concert hall inclined to allow the seating facilities to be inserted diagonally between the roof and floor.

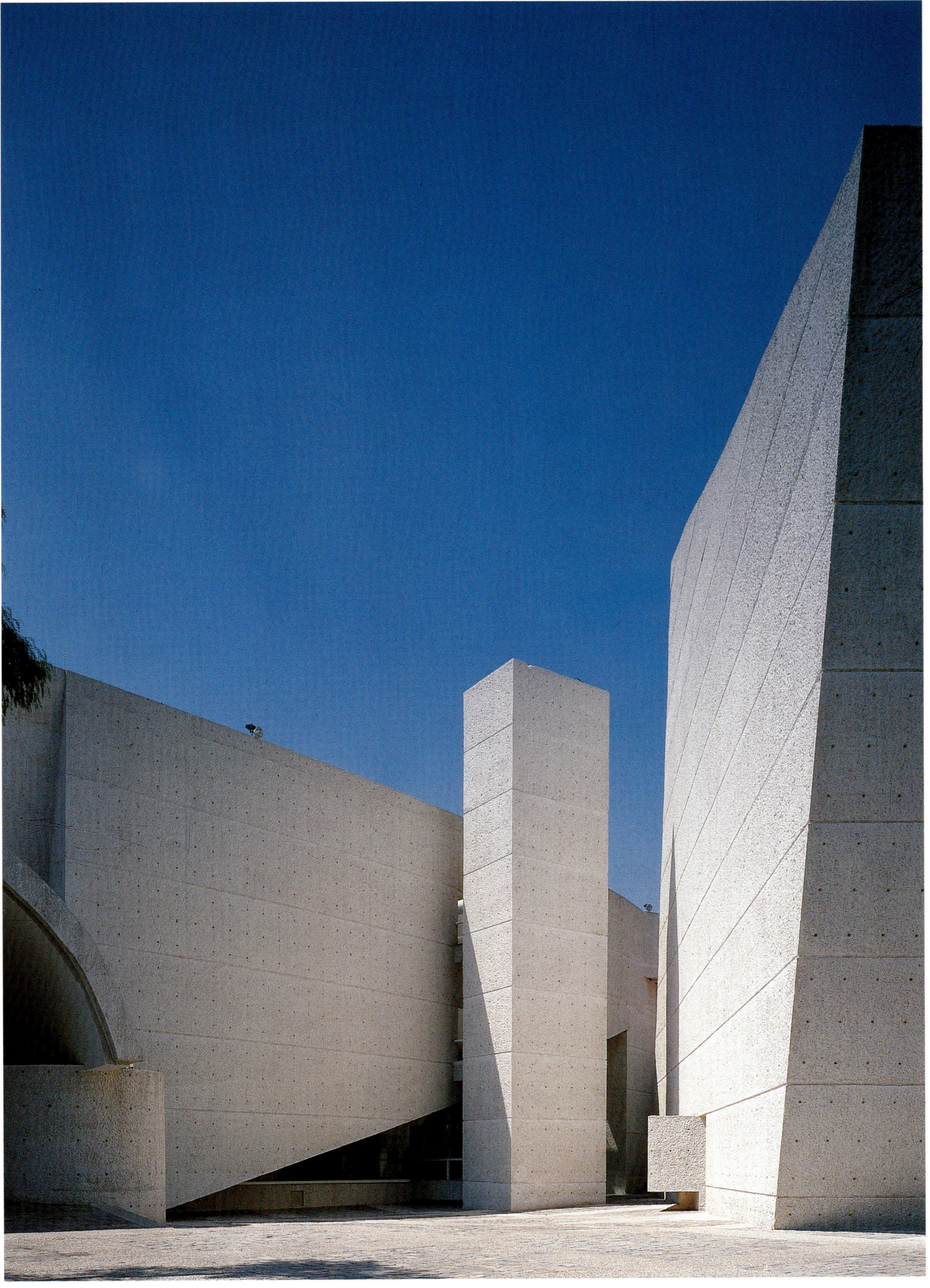

Mexico City, 1995

Senate Building

Architects
Teodoro González de León
J. Francisco Serrano

Collaborator
José Arce Gargollo

Project area
39,340 sq.m.

This project was designed to stitch up a hole in the urban fabric and, most importantly, to salvage a plot of land that had fallen into a terrible state of disrepair over the last sixty years. Four buildings have actually collapsed on this site creating an urban void full of ruins. The idea was to create a "tough" hinge across the city capable of giving the immediate surroundings their own powerful landmark. The building faces onto a Baroque church on the edge of Central Alameda Park that stretches out in front of the plot of land chosen for the new Senate Building. The project is also carefully geared to the heights of the surrounding buildings, which González de León has used to gauge his own structural design.

This creates a strong sense of interaction with the local urban fabric, sewing the project into the surrounding cityscape. The Senate Building is the same height as the Fine Arts Building designed by Adamo Boari that backs onto the lot itself. It is also the same height as Correo Central, also designed by Boari, over on the other corner.

The architecture is intricately designed to spread powerfully across the city, creating a series of well defined and elegantly defined perspectives.

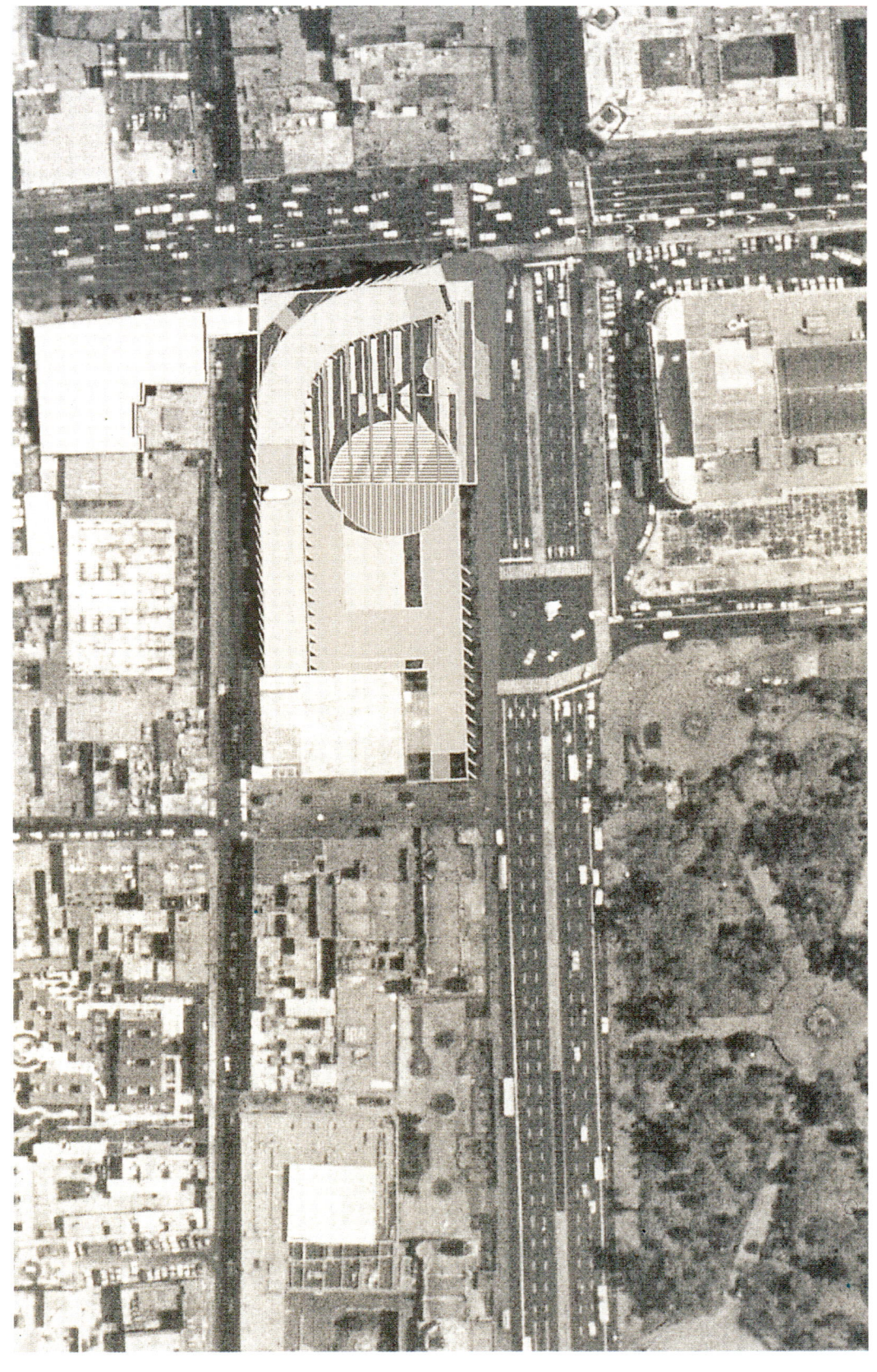

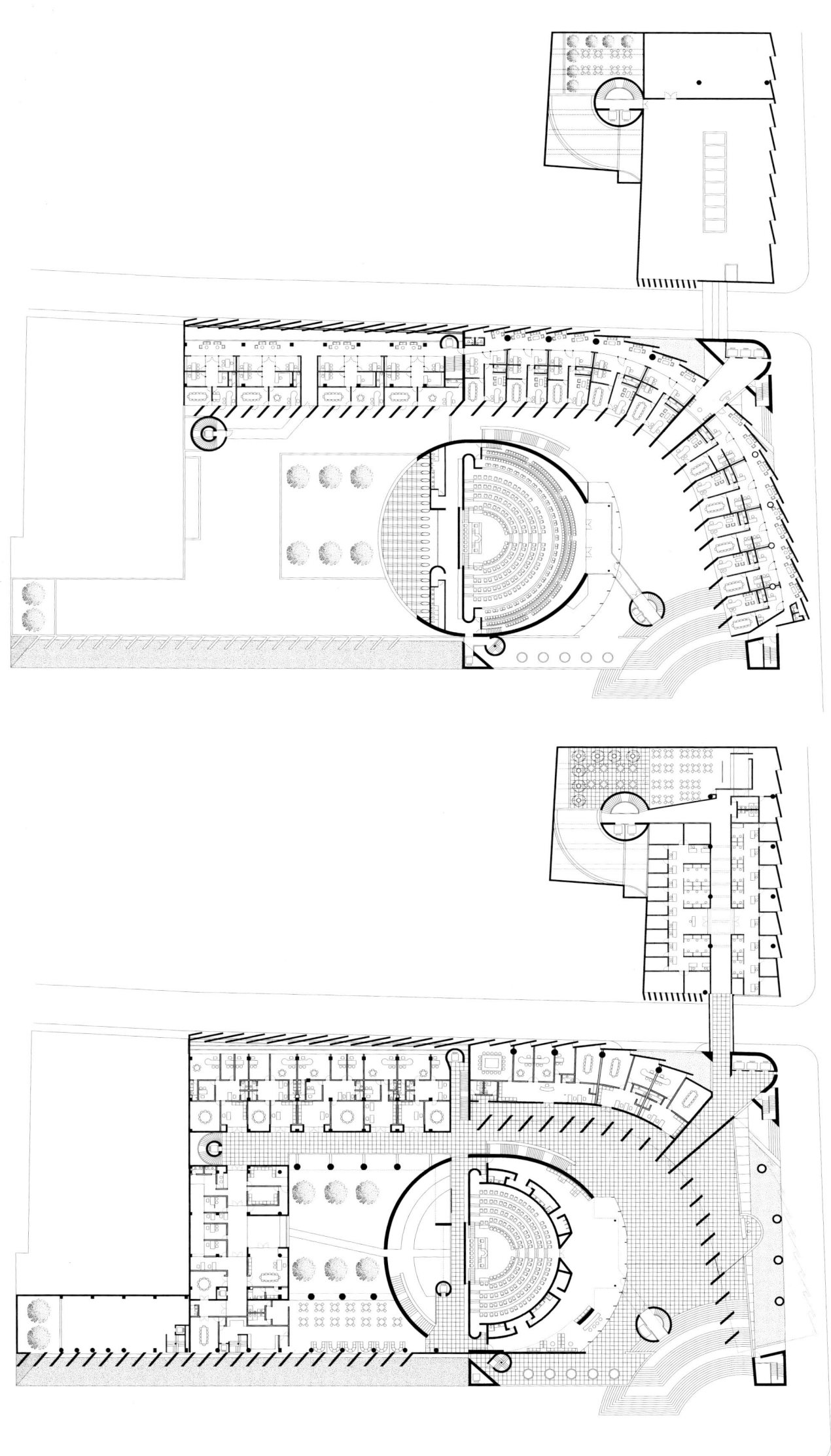

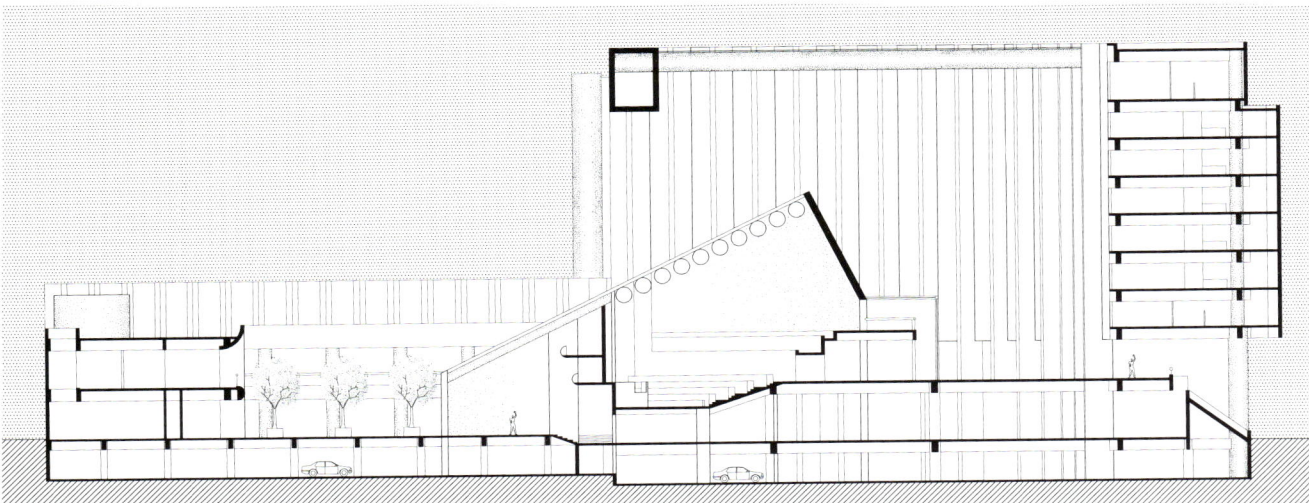

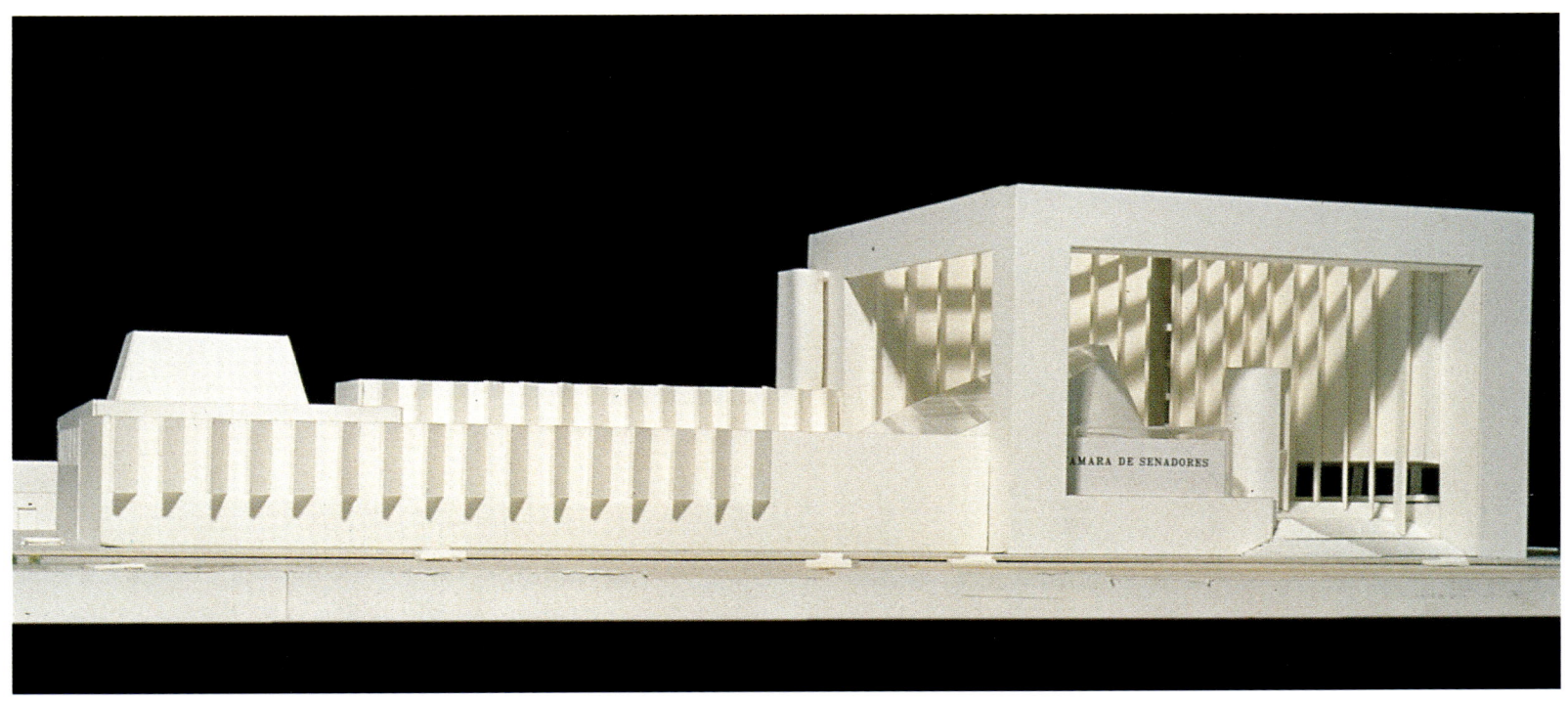

Opposite page, bottom, ground floor plan, below, first floor plan. Top of page, section and, below, model of the building designed to hold the House of Senate of the Mexican Republic

119

Perspective view of the building designed to provide this area alongside the Alameda Central and a Baroque church with its own new landmark.

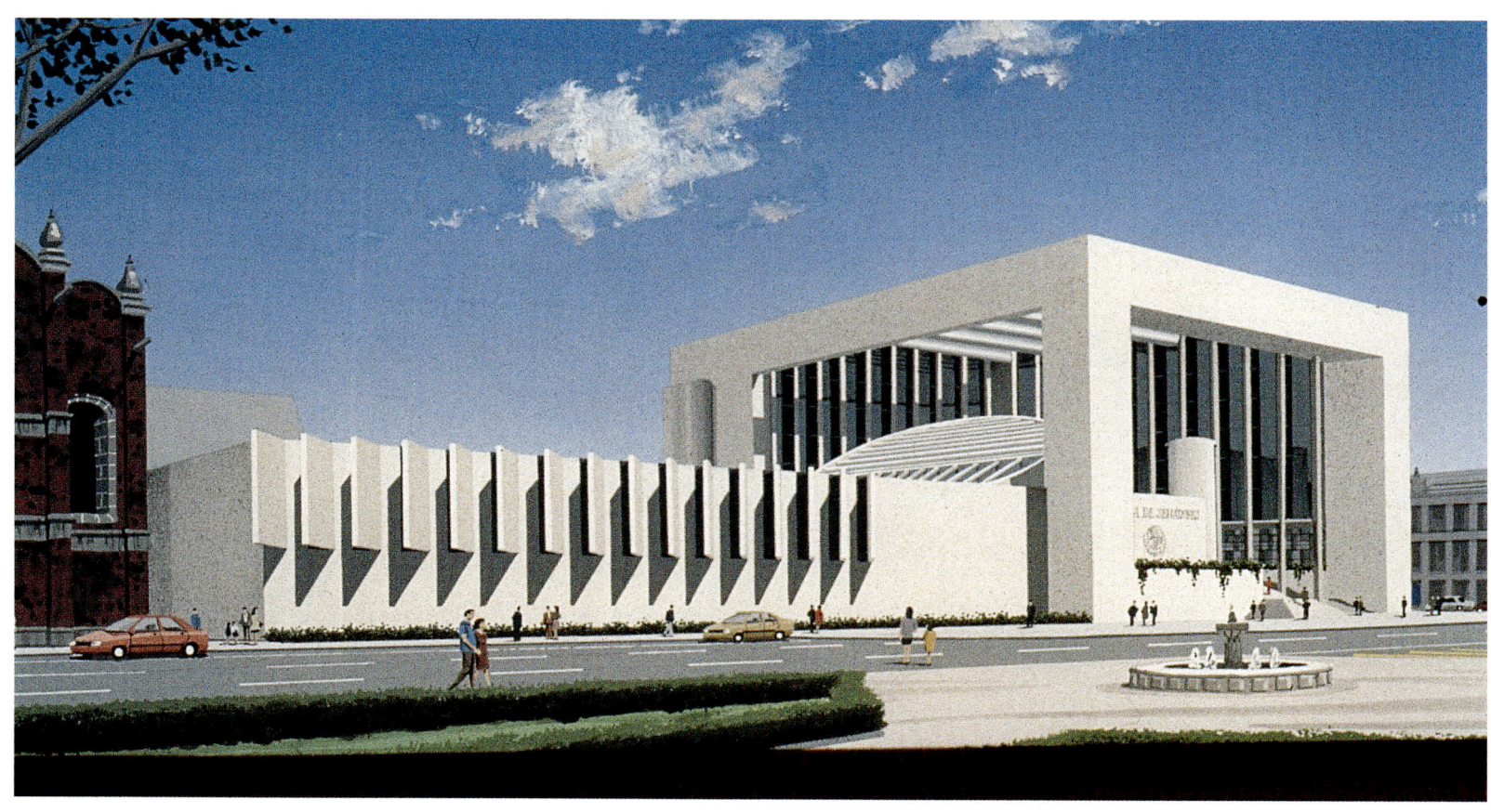

The building's imposing structure provides this urban area with its own modern landmark, without interfering with the surrounding buildings.

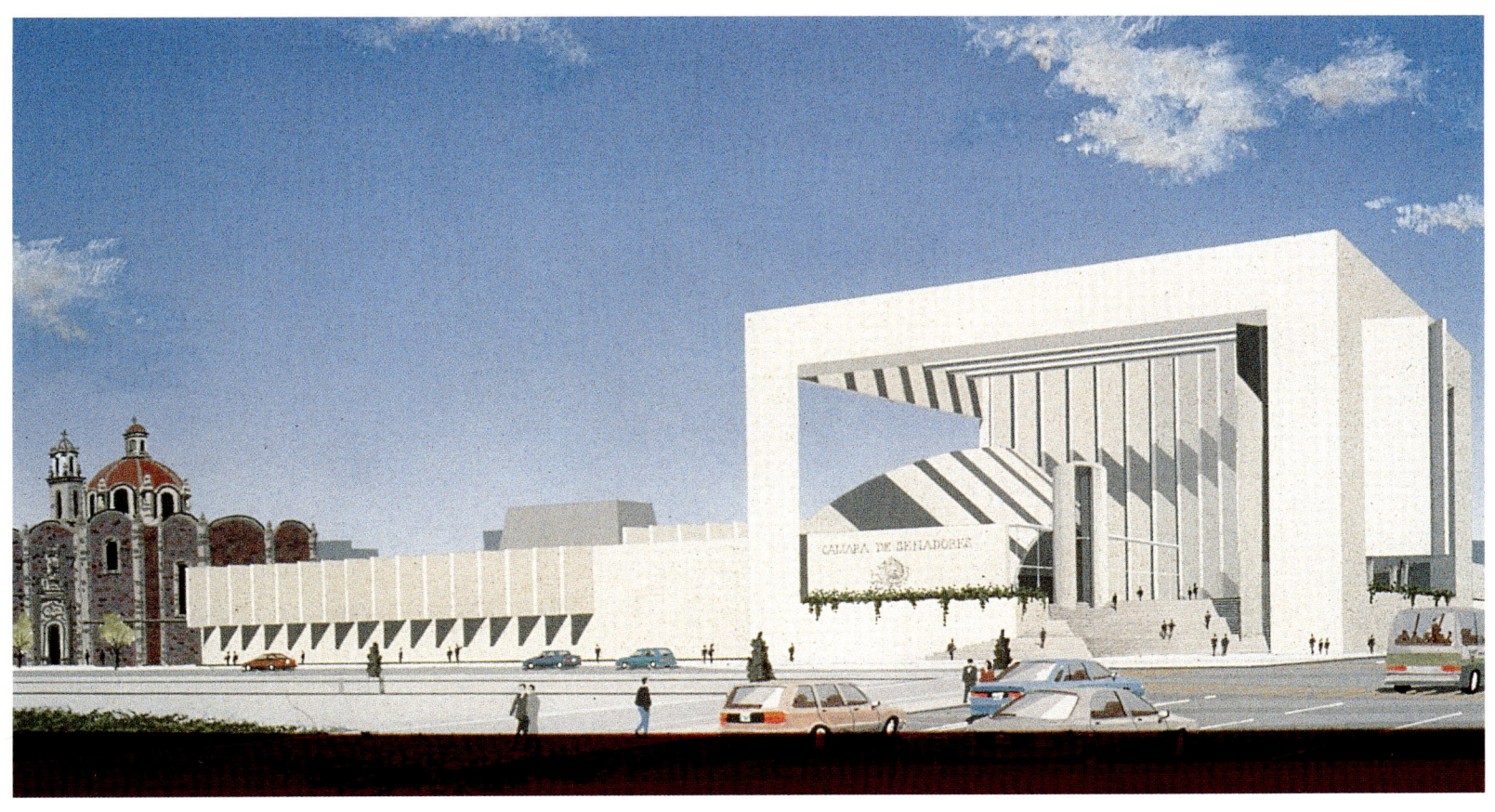

Mexico City, 1996

Amsterdam House

Architect
Teodoro González de León

Collaborator
Miguel Barbachano Osorio

Structural design
Diseño y Supervisión, S.C. "DYS, S.C."

Electric design
Constructora de Obras Electricas, "COESA"

Hydraulics and sanitary design
Garza Maldonado y Asociados, S.C.

Construction area
650 sq.m.

This single-storey house is built on a square plot of land. The various parts of the house are anchored across a diagonal linking them together in a clearly defined interior arrangement of each separate house function. It is interesting to note González de León's new approach in this project. This totally innovative way of designing architecture has nothing in common with his previous designs.

González de León has attempted to give each separate function its own peculiar form instead of trying to combine them into one single context.

This shows how González de León's style has progressively evolved as he now tends to create a sense of overall unity through structural design.

His most recent experimentation has hinged around differences, clear combinations of separate forms, and striking contrasts.

González de León is striving to create a new form of architectural expression lending even greater weight to his designs. It is also worth pointing out the different way he now organises his work.

In this case, for instance, he makes systematic, reiterated use of models to instantly create minor comparisons and contrasts of great evocative force. This is how González de León tries to find the right balance of forms in the proper three-dimensional perspective.

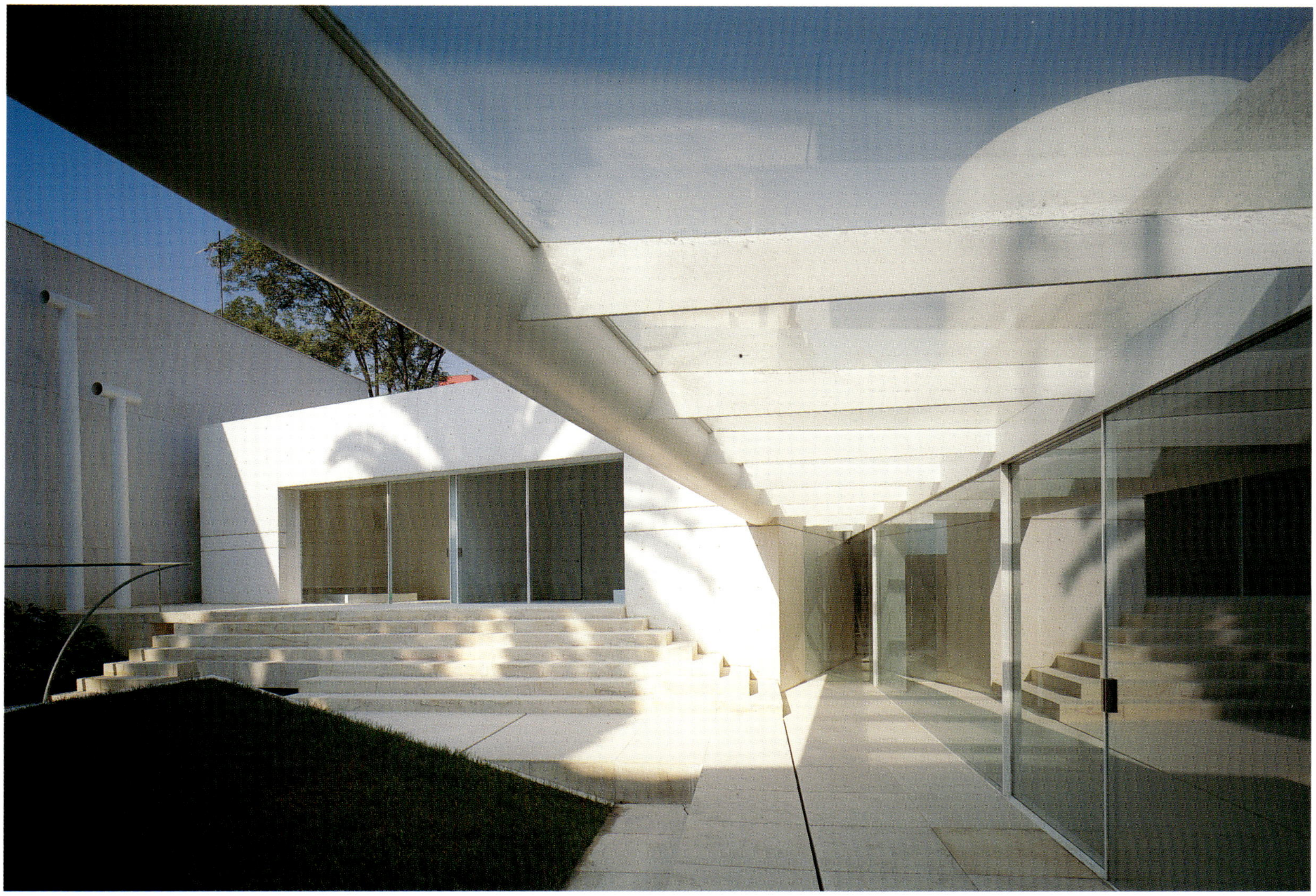

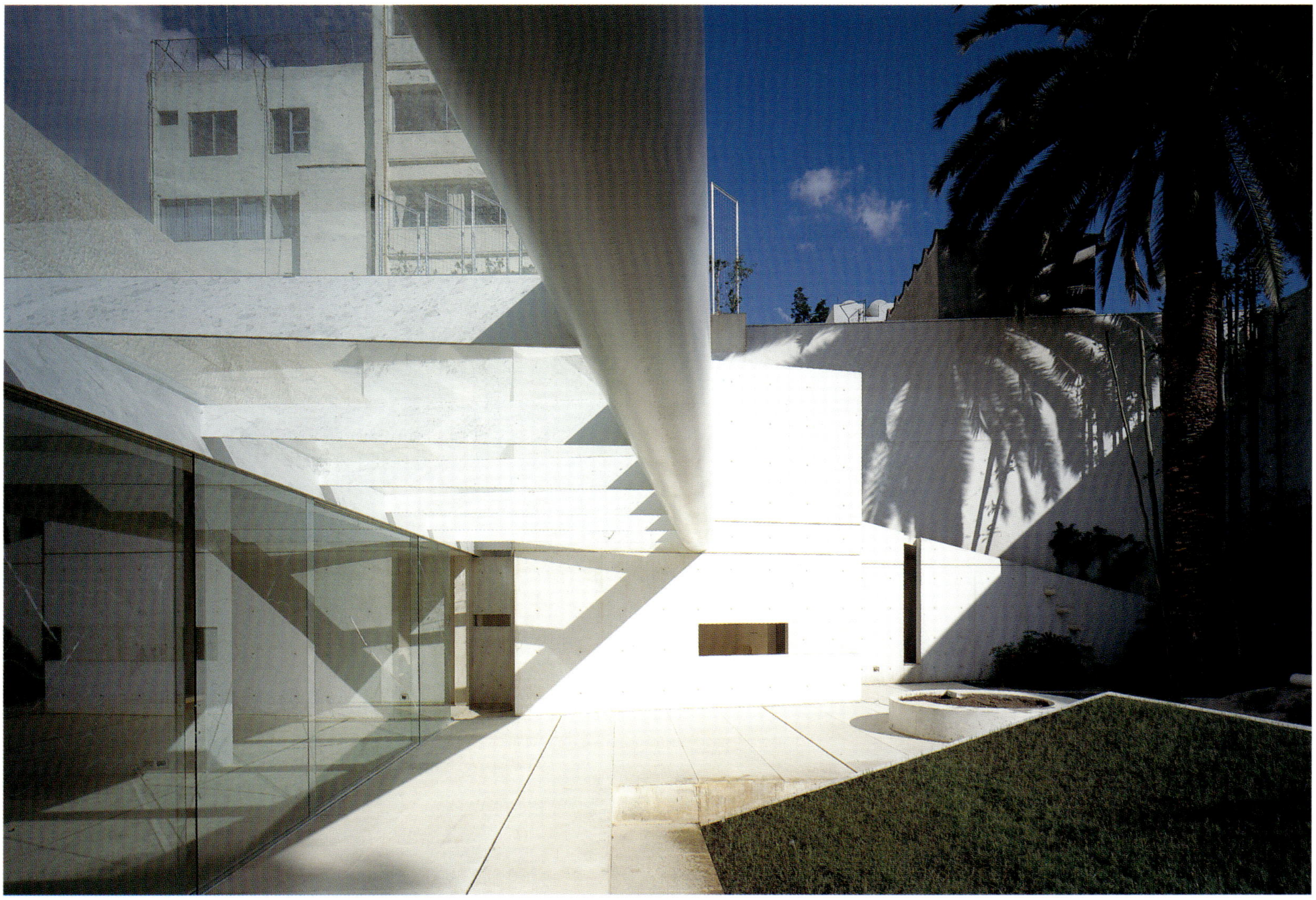

123

Left, plan of the roof level. Below, perspective view of the courtyard. Opposite page, details of the exterior facades.

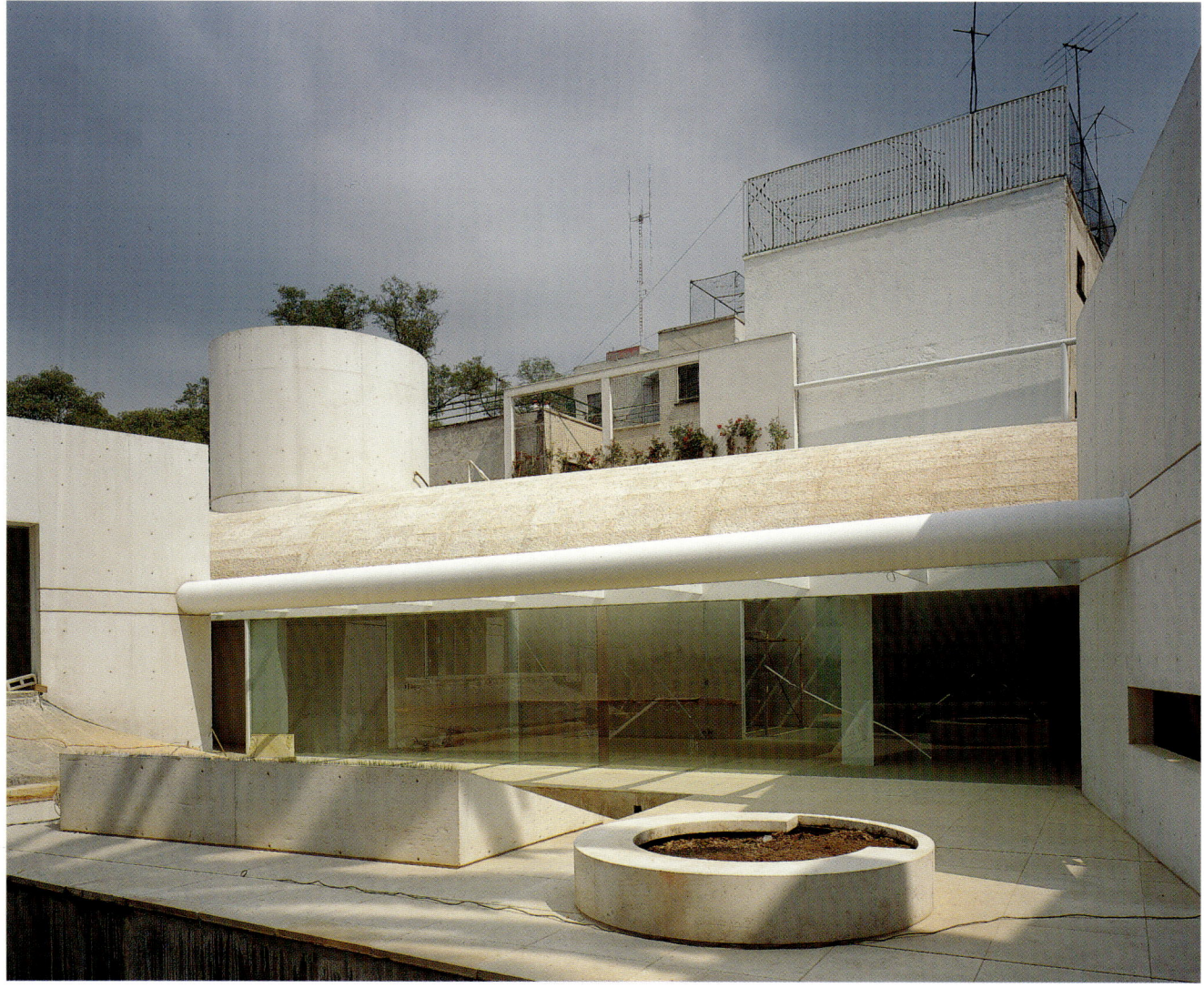

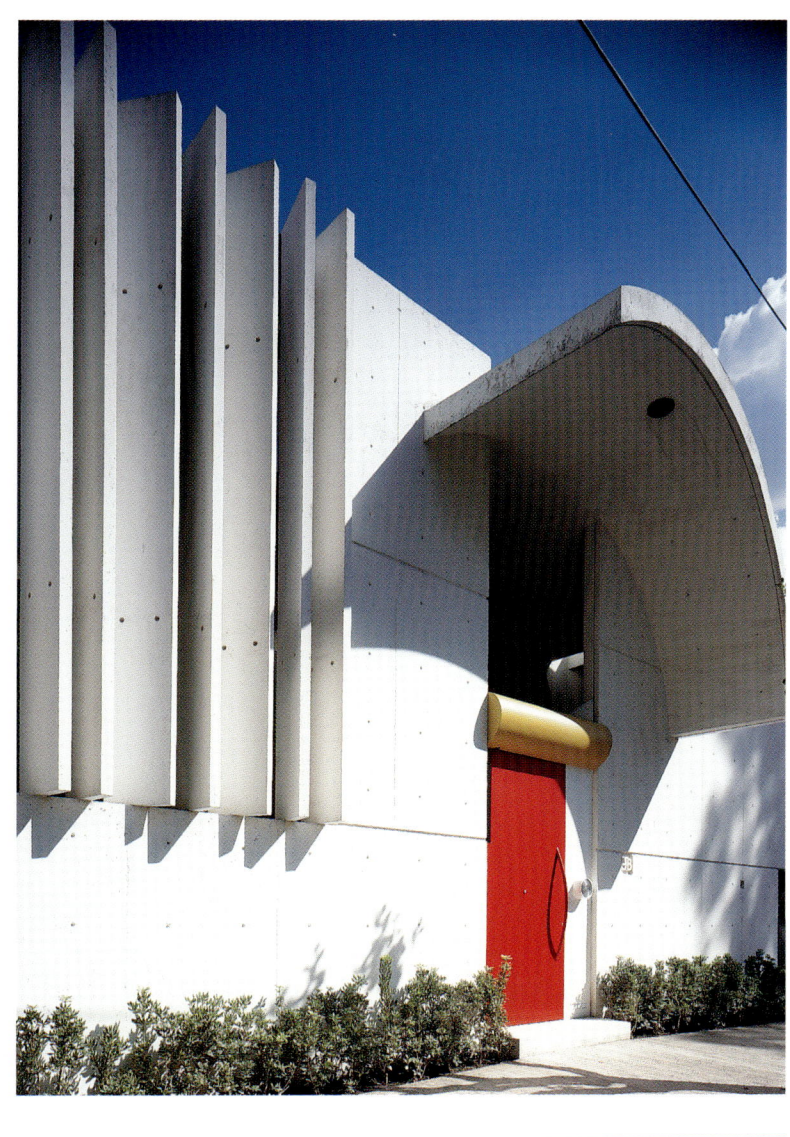
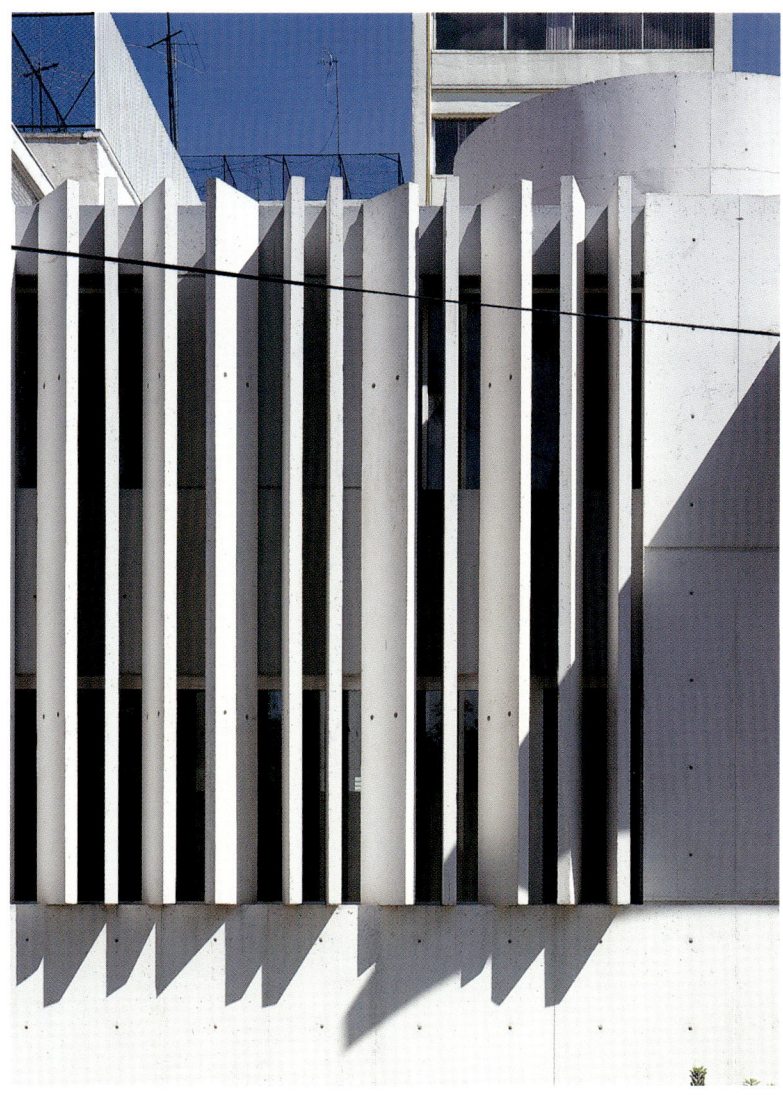
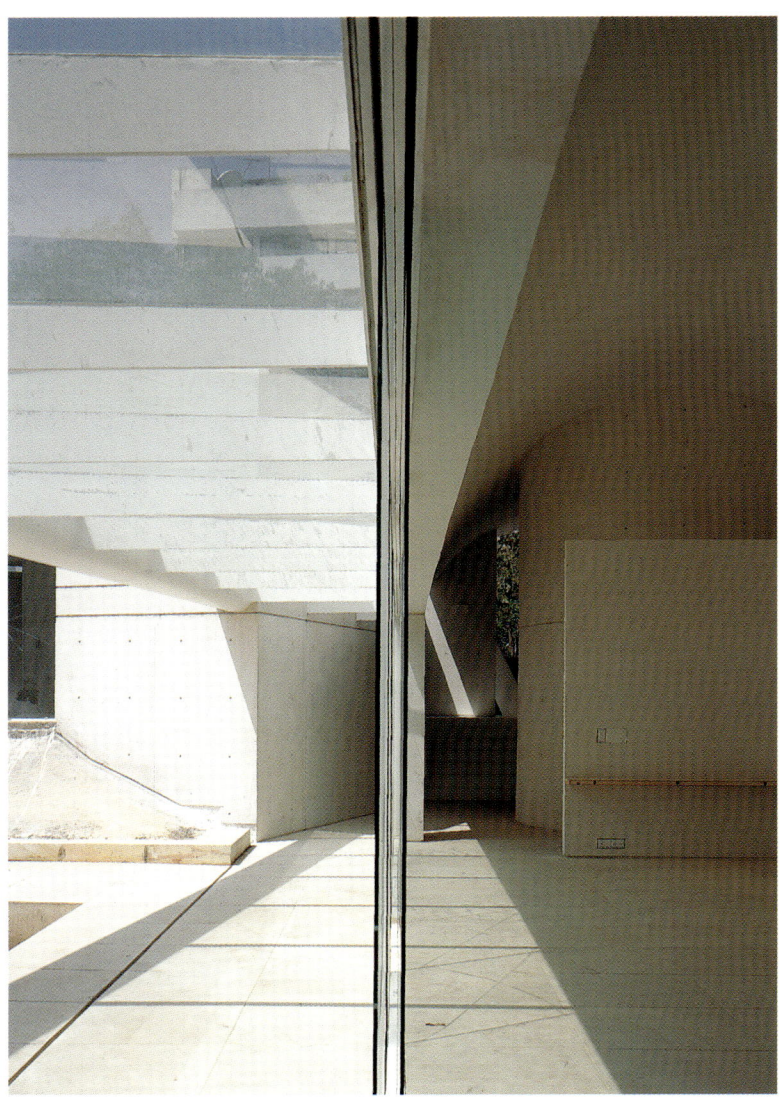
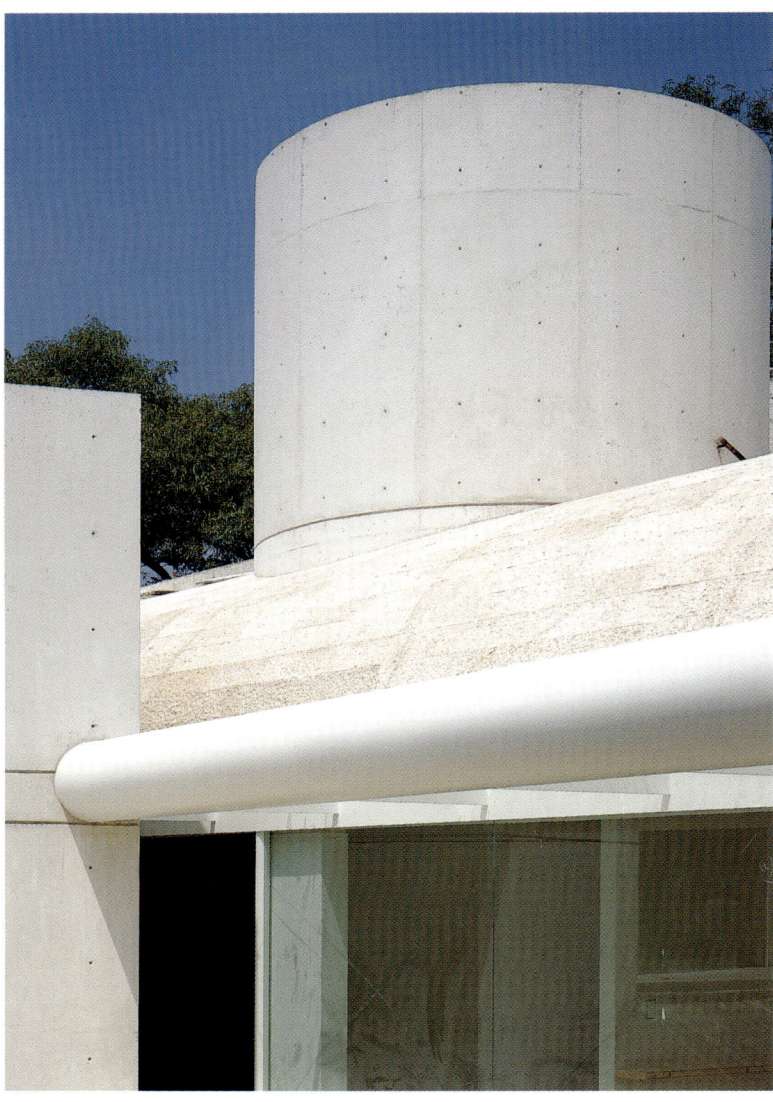

Mexico City, 1996

Insurgentes Sur Office Block

Owner
Telmex

Architect
Teodoro González de León

Collaborator
Carlos Gutiérrez Juárez

Structural design
Carrillo Ingenieros Consultores, S.A. de C.V.

Air-conditioning design
Acondaire, S.A. de C.V.

Electrical design
COESA Ingenieria, S.A.

Hydraulics and sanitary design
Garza Maldonado y Asociados, S.C.

Special installations
Red Uno

Construction area
45,000 sq.m offices
35.000 sq.m. parkings
80,000 sq.m. total

This building is still at the drawing board in Teodoro González de León's design studio.

The spiral-shaped office block is pervaded by a sense of continuity.

Here again González de León shows a surprising mastery of how to use new materials. Iron is actually the structural element that allows him to arrange spaces as effectively and flexibly as possible. A bearing structure made of reinforced concrete would have prevented him from designing such a light and airy building volume.

The main thing worth pointing out is the contrast between this new building and the projects he designed in the 1980's: the comparison shows that his mastery of architecture has turned him into an attentive narrator of the universal aspects of contemporary society.

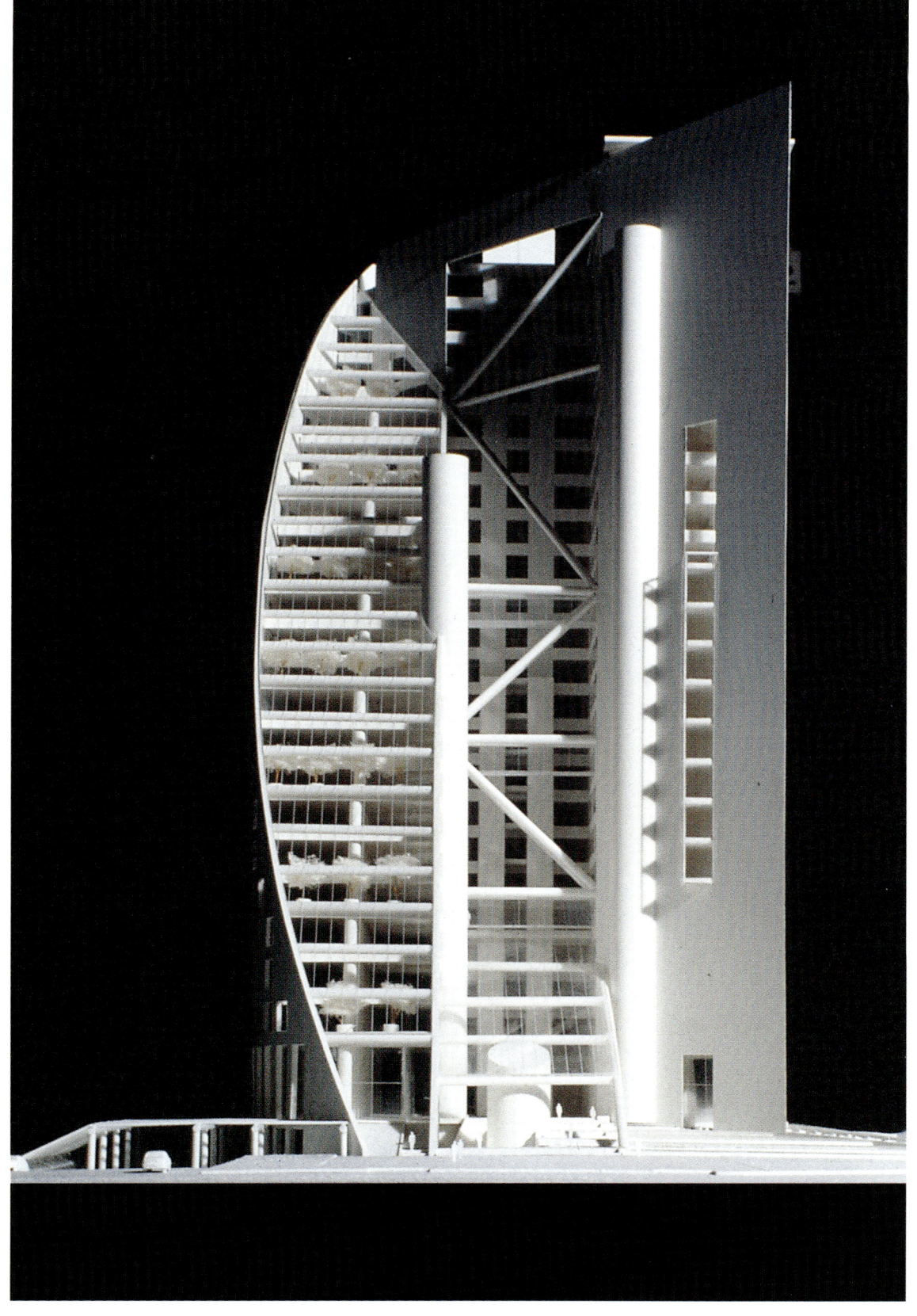

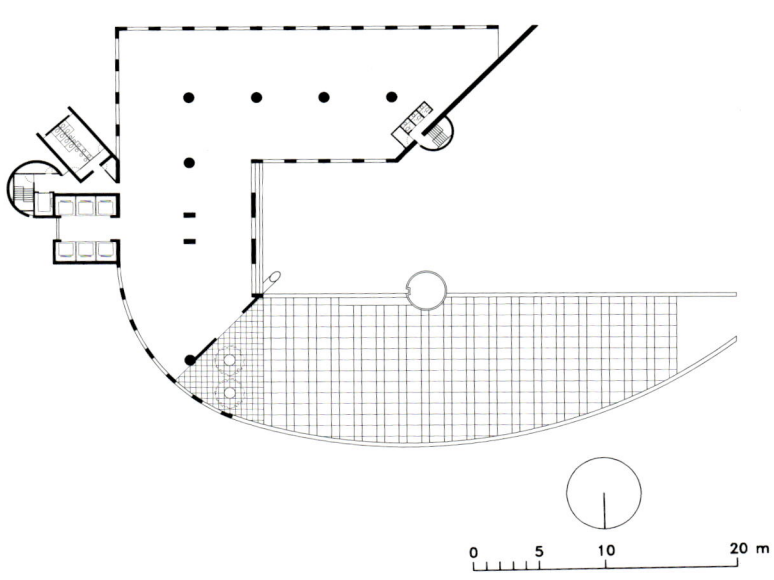

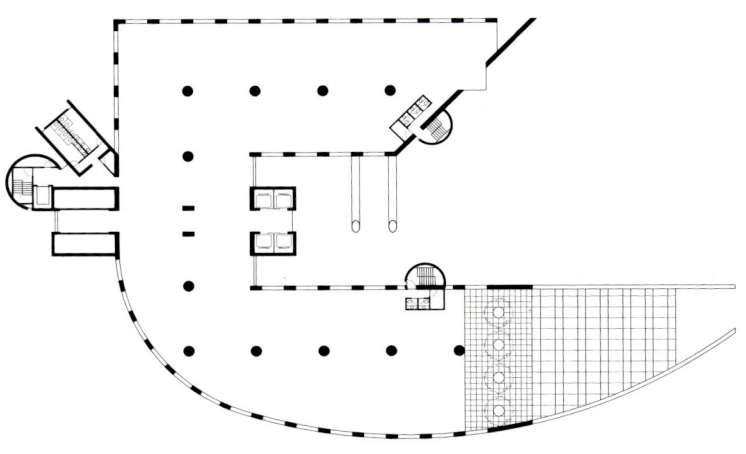

Above, typical plan of the middle levels. Top, typical plan of the upper levels, Right, Cad rendering of the building inserted in its context.

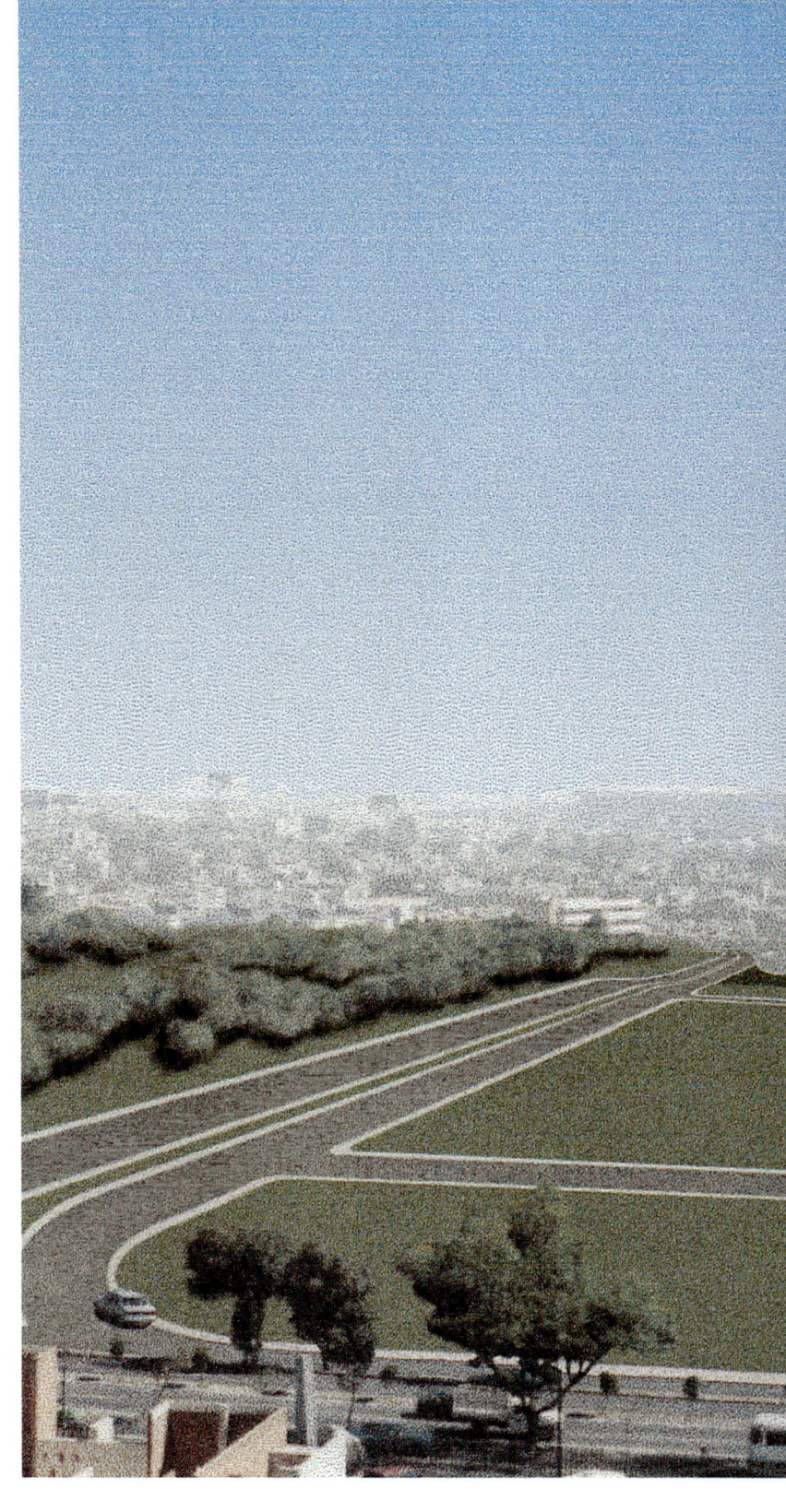

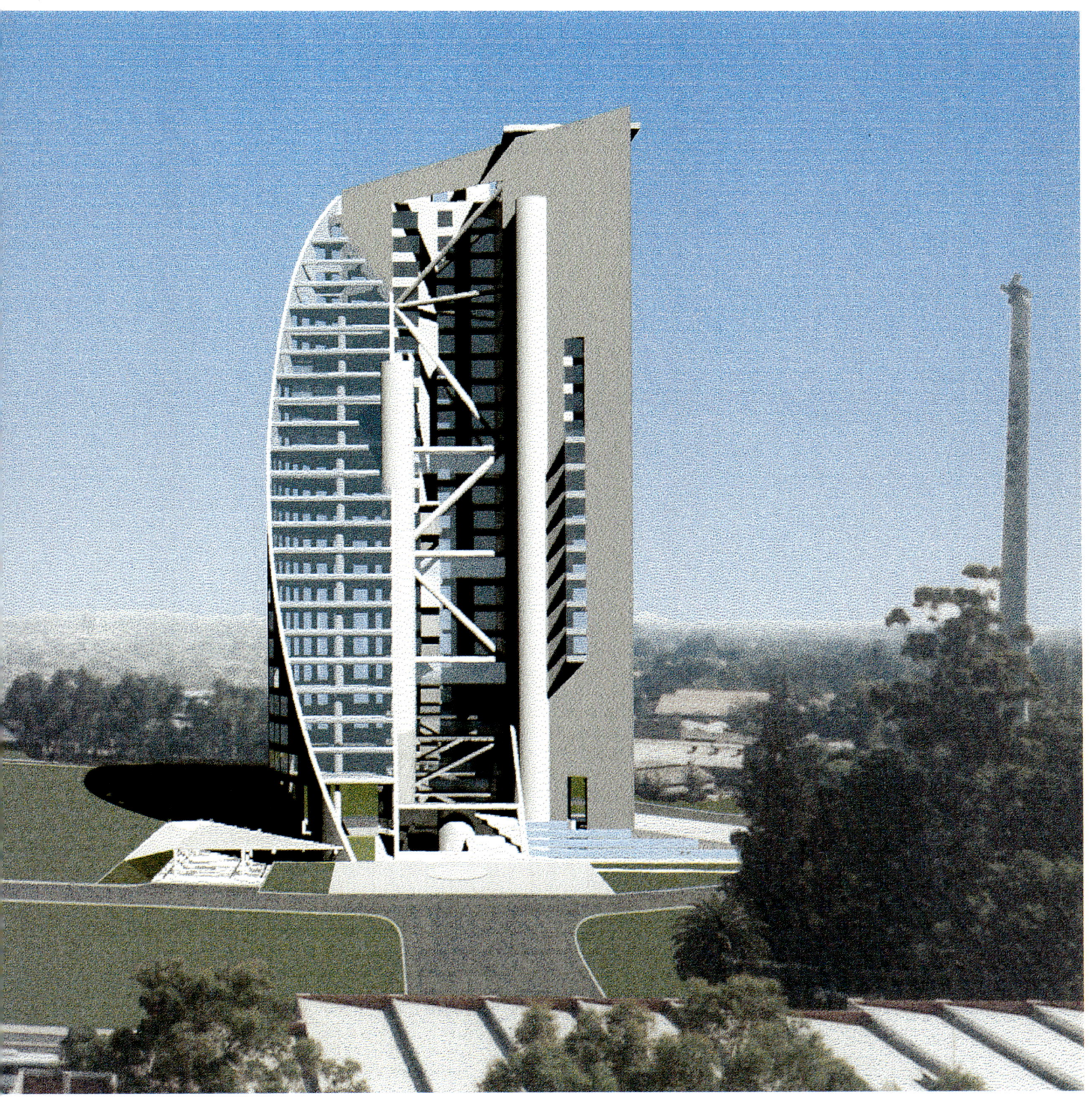

Cross section.
Opposite page,
Cad rendering showing
the entrance side.

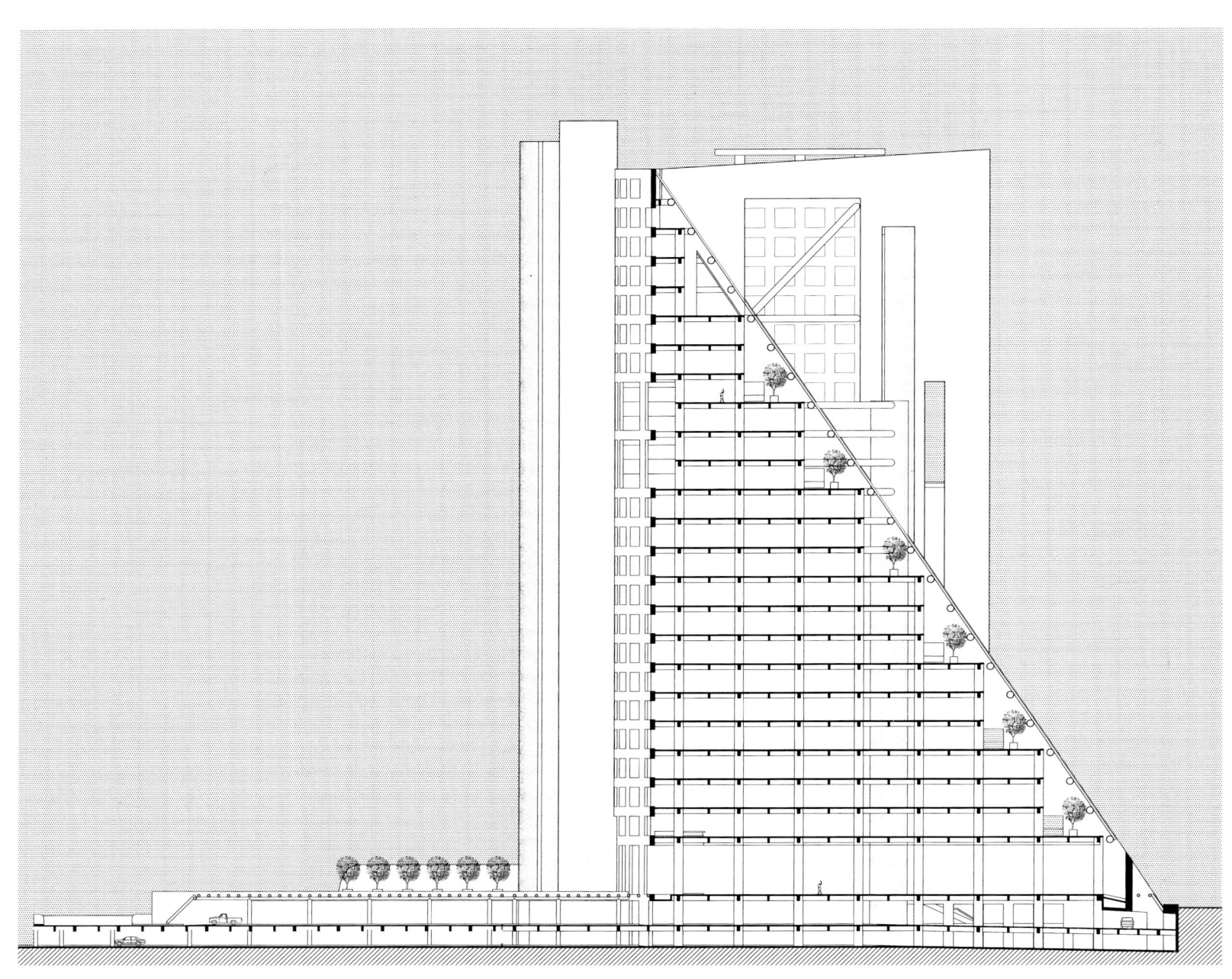

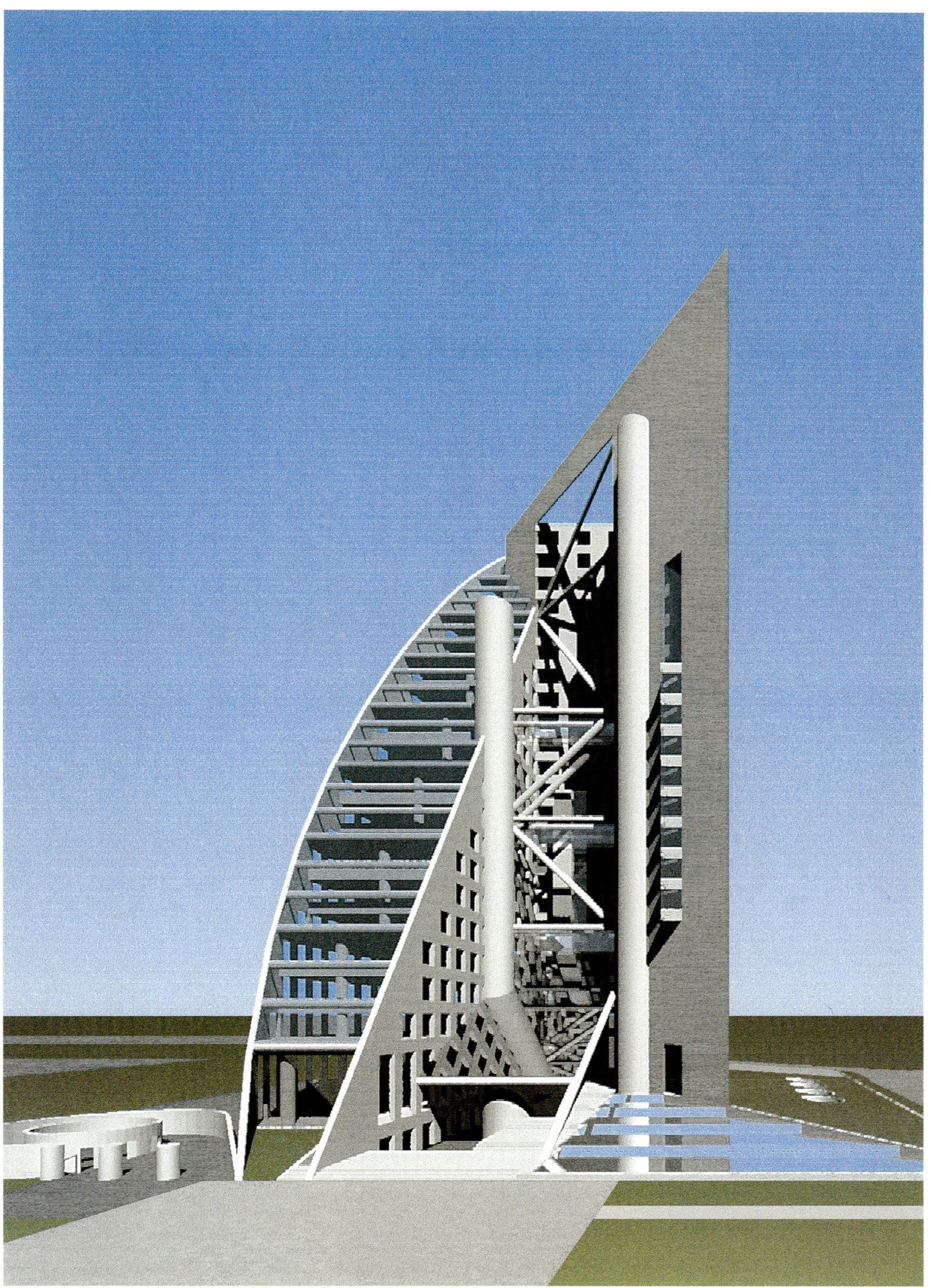

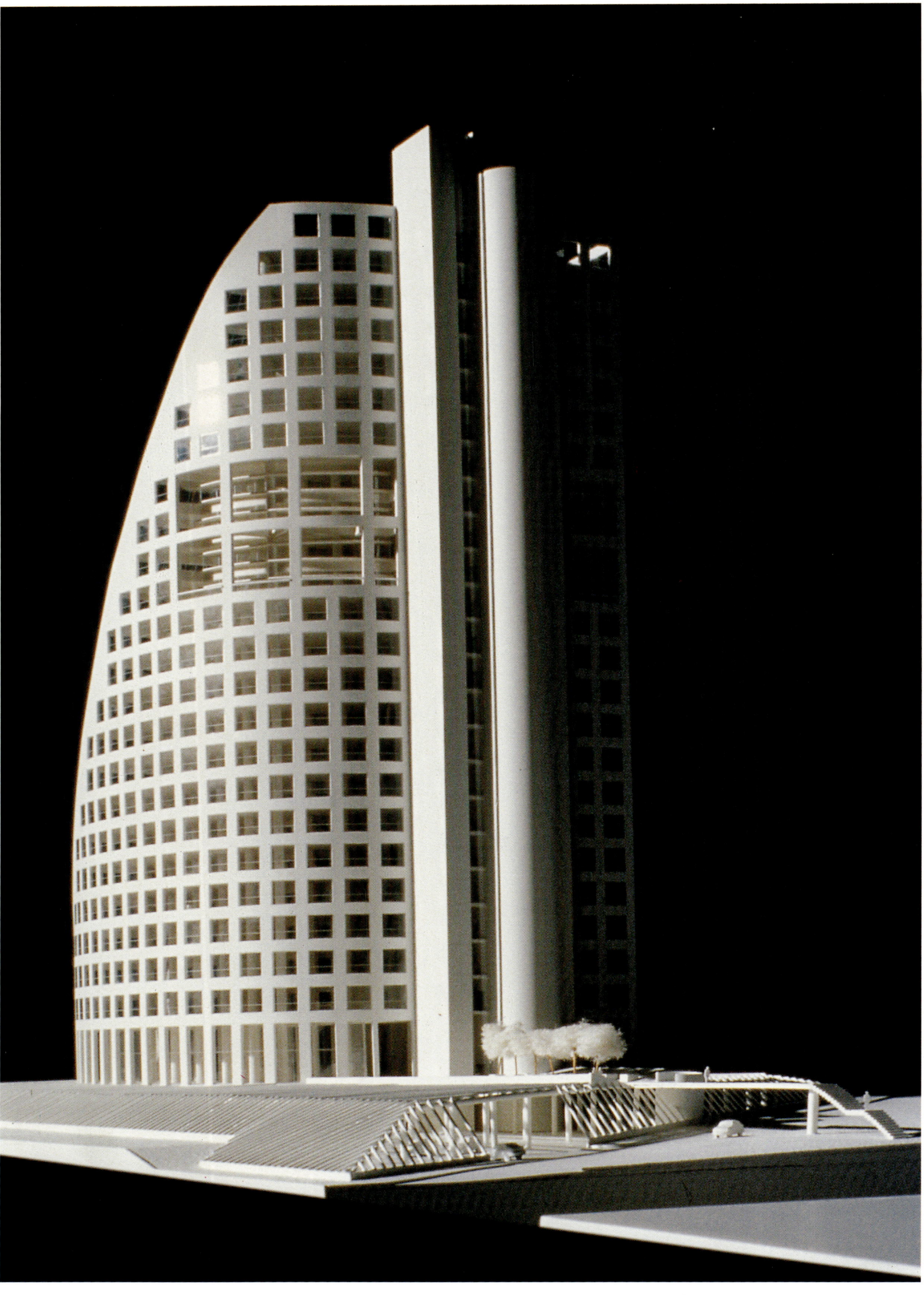

Opposite page, detail of the model showing the cylindrical structure housing the lifts and services. Right, the entrance side.

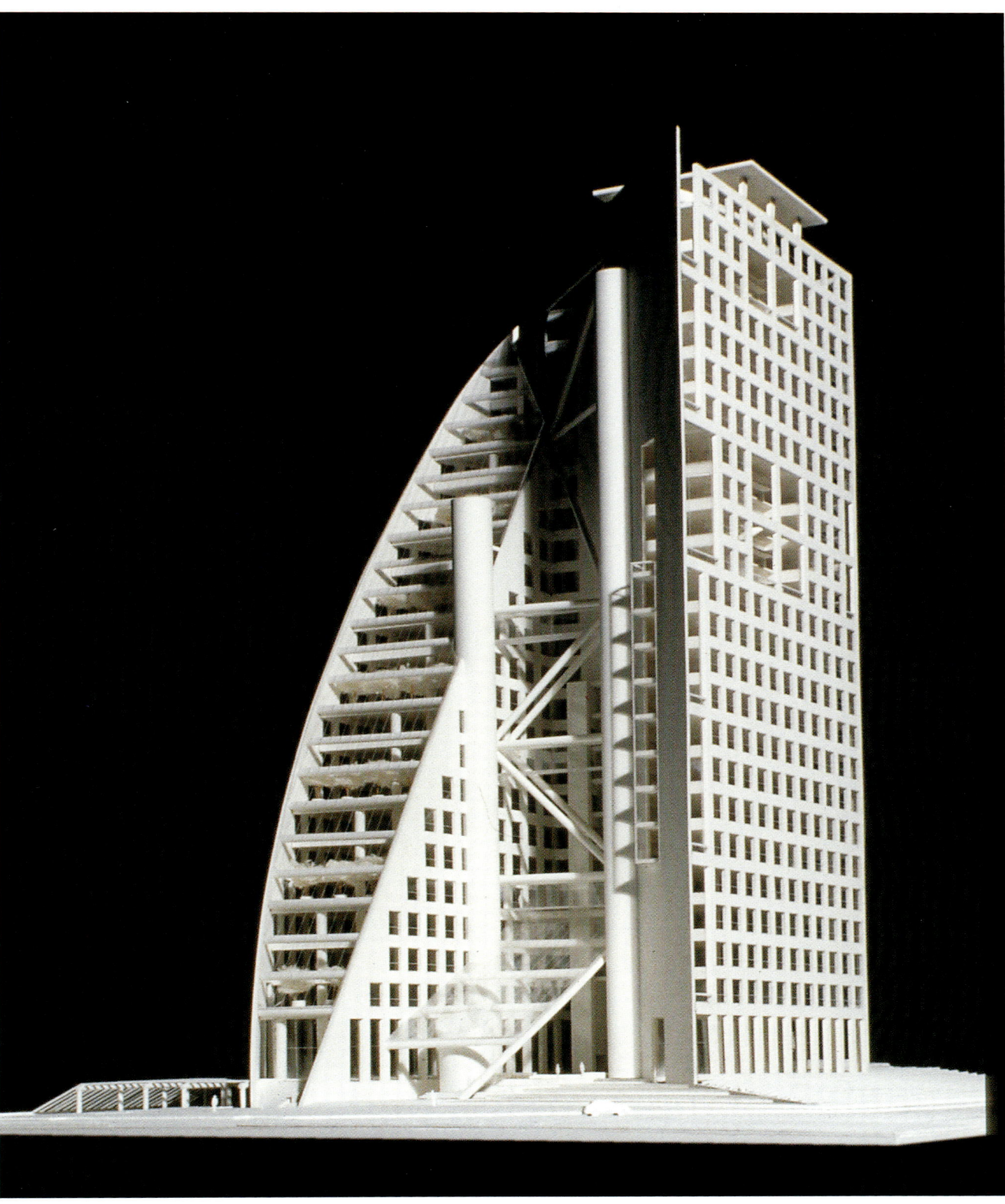

Views of the model of the office block which, like other projects designed by González de León, combines square concrete elements with curved glass and metal structures.

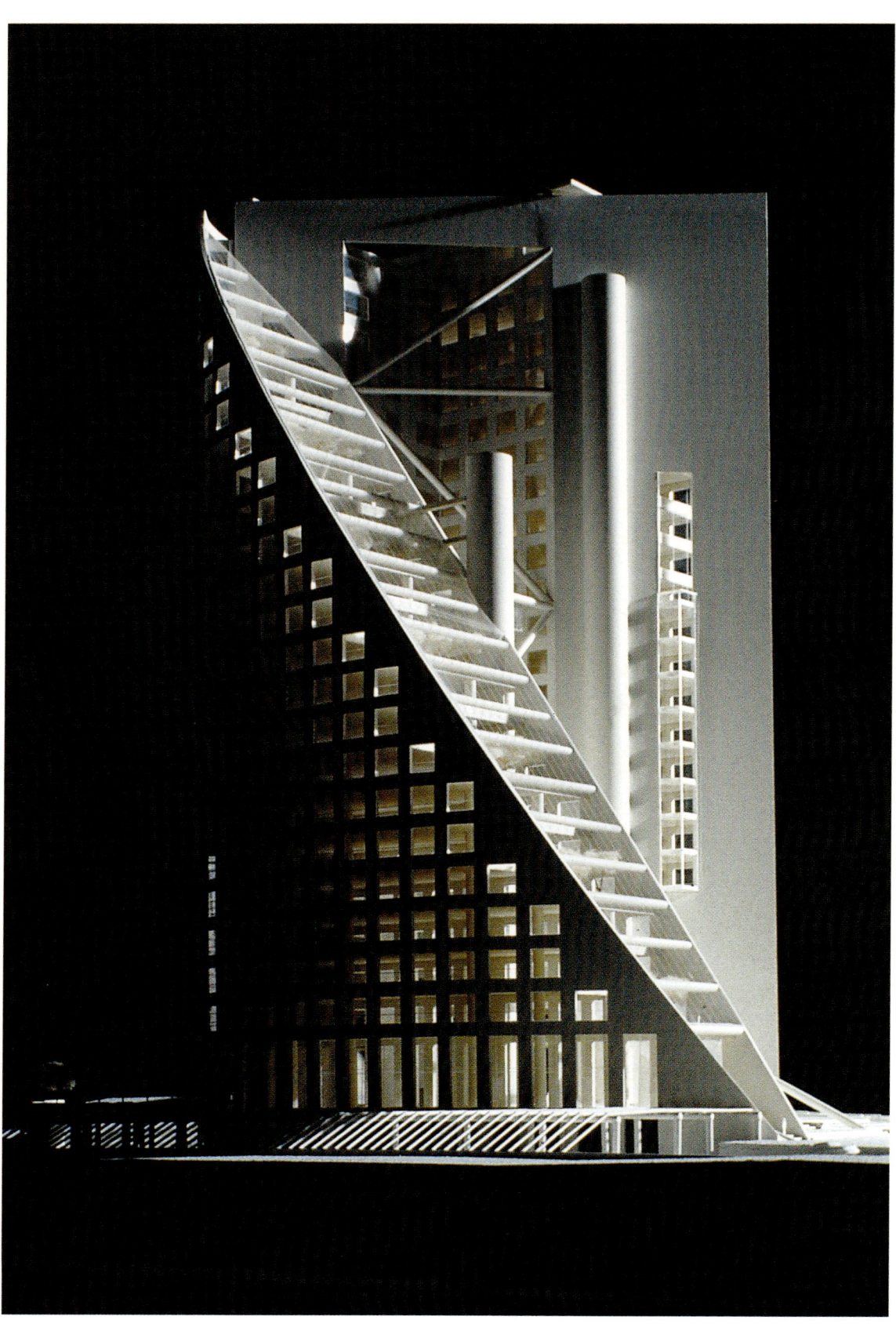

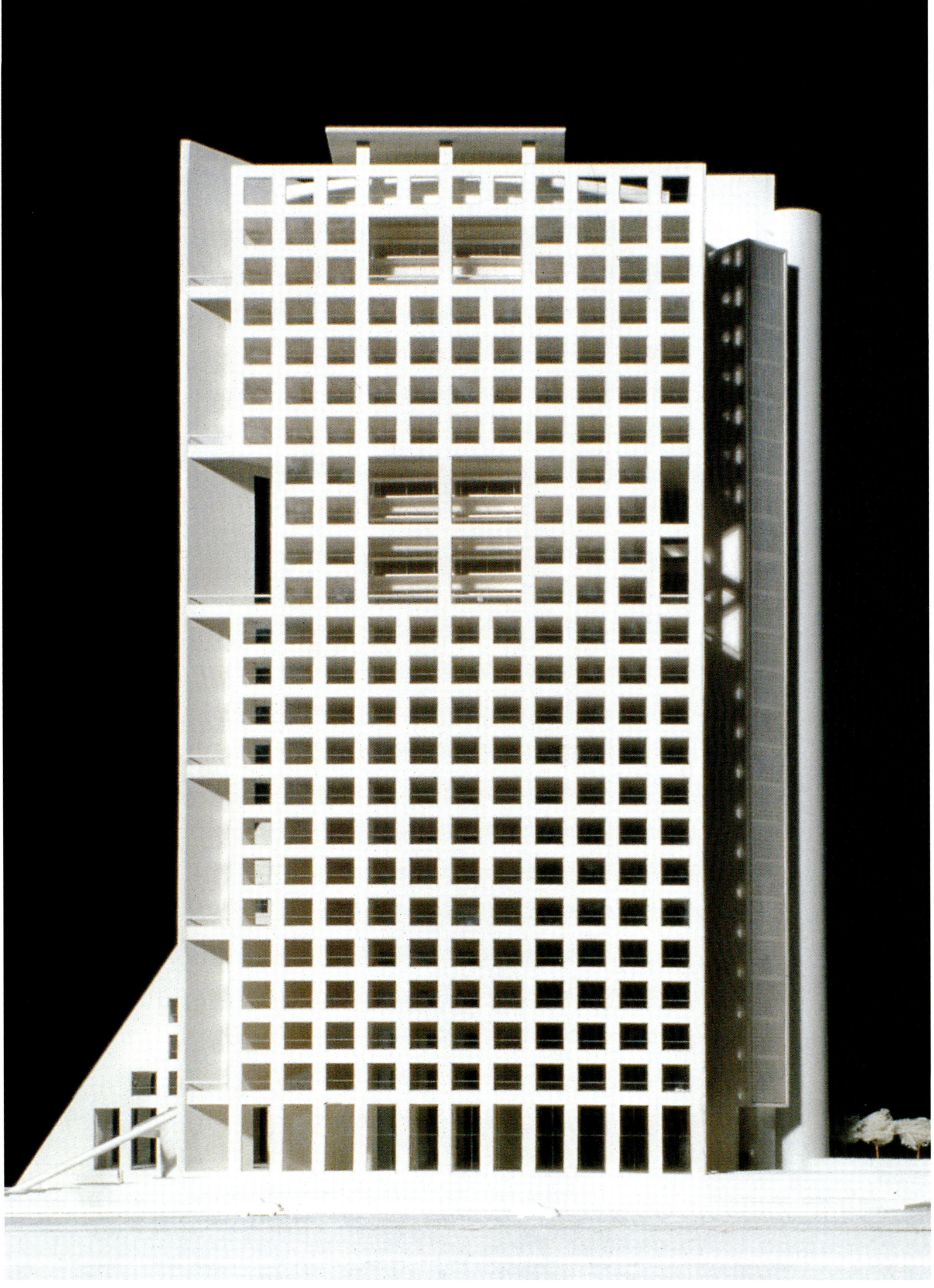

Berlin, Germany, 1997

Mexican Embassy in Berlin

Owner
Secretaría de Relaciones Exteriores

Architects
Teodoro González de León
J. Francisco Serrano

Collaborator
José Arce Gargollo

Project area
3,317 sq.m

Models
Rodrigo Márquez

Urban Image
The facade along Klingerhöfer Street is constructed out of a large portico with a triangular portal leading through to the entrance.

The portico and portal create a powerfully imposing urban image, featuring up-to-date plastic forms with no concessions to historicism (creating the image of a youthful, modern, rapidly developing country).

Two surfaces, one sloping and one curved, constructed out of white concrete sunscreens, form the portal. They also act as frame and facade. They give a sense of density to the lateral elevations and, on their own, give a fleeting sense of transparency when viewed from the front. The transparency is most accentuated on the inside.

Conventional windows, on the other hand, break up the various levels. The side street, Rauchstrasse, contains a second portico, which is the same height (18 m) but narrower.

The rear part of the structure contains a diagonal slash through the two upper levels, where the chancellery is located, generously lightening the corridors leading to the "Pocket Parq". The diagonal also contains the "necessary windows", opening up towards the south and west to let more sunshine into the building. The diagonal slash creates a spatial break in the narrow corridors marking the boundaries of the Master Plan. It widens the perspectives and creates a rich structural composition of cylinders and triangles on the interior facades.

Spatial Layout
The entrance portico leads through to a sequence of public spaces. A double bronze door leads into the visitor check-in area: a double-height space housing a cylinder with three openings.

The cylinder spatially symbolises the entire Embassy. An 18-metre-high open space organises the layout of pathways for both visitors and staff. This constantly-used space is the focus of the entire project. It acts as a reception area and multi-purpose room.

The cylinder is semi-suspended above a terraced garden terminating the lobby space and concealing the lavatories.

The structure is built over three levels at 3.30 m (40+2.90), above a basement at 1.20 m, and above the road and a basement used for the parking facilities and service rooms.

The top floor has a garden where the end sections of the two porticoes, cylinder and double-height ceiling of the Ambassador's private quarters are constructed.

The consulate and centre for the arts are located at the mezzanine level, above the large double-height reception area and multi-purpose room that come together on the ground floor near the library.

The chancellery is built over the next two levels.

The Ambassador has double-height private quarters offering an unblocked panoramic view.

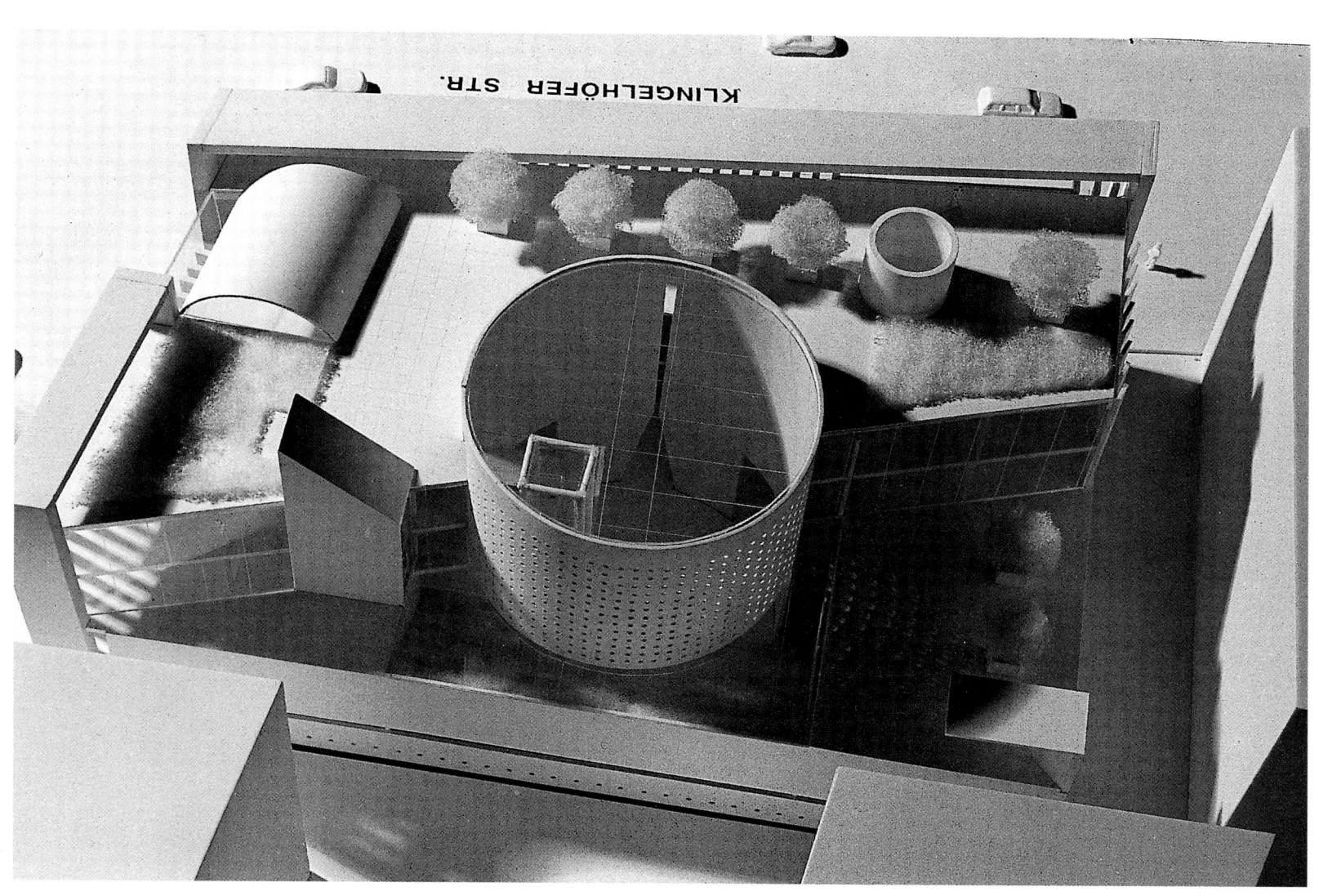

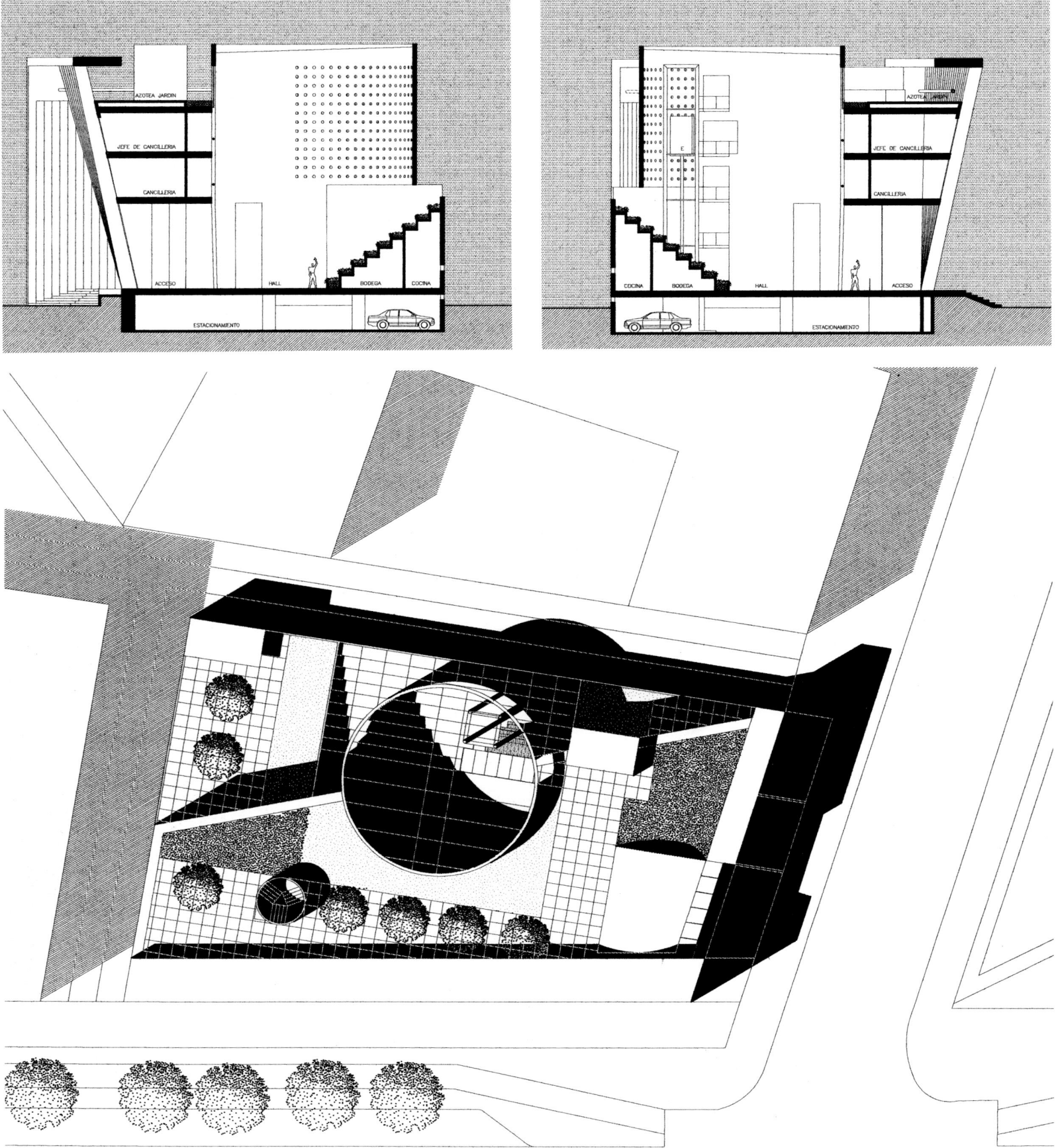

Site plan, and, top, cross sections.

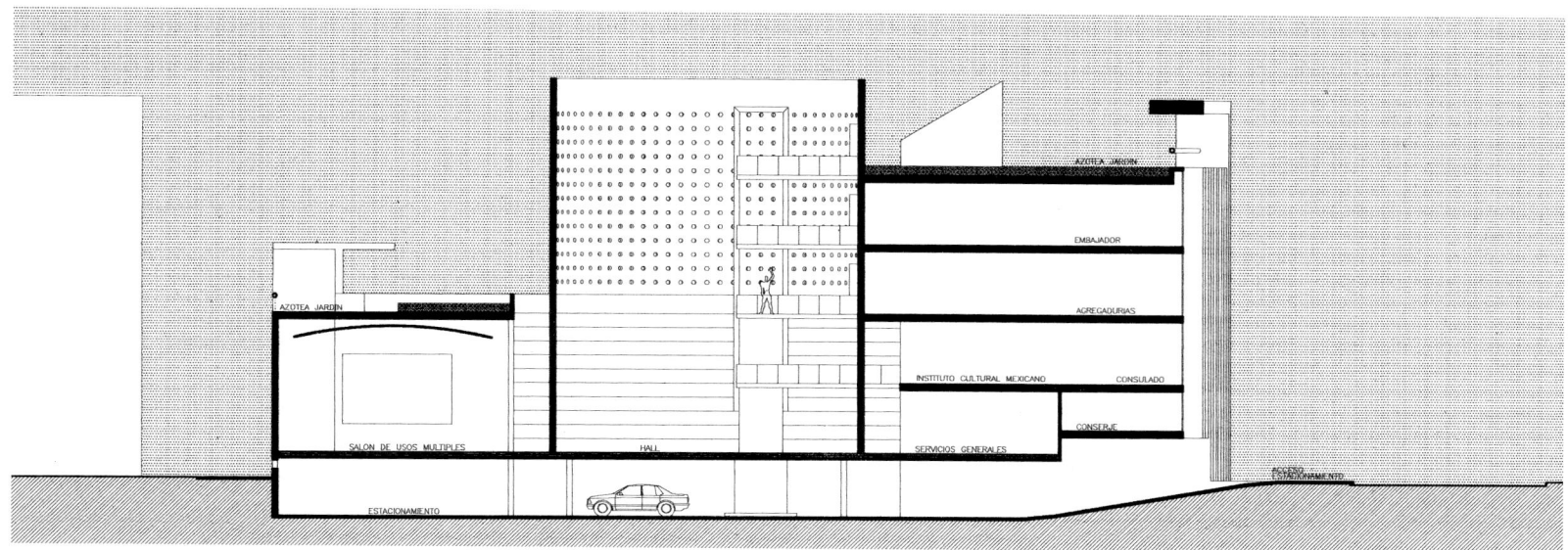

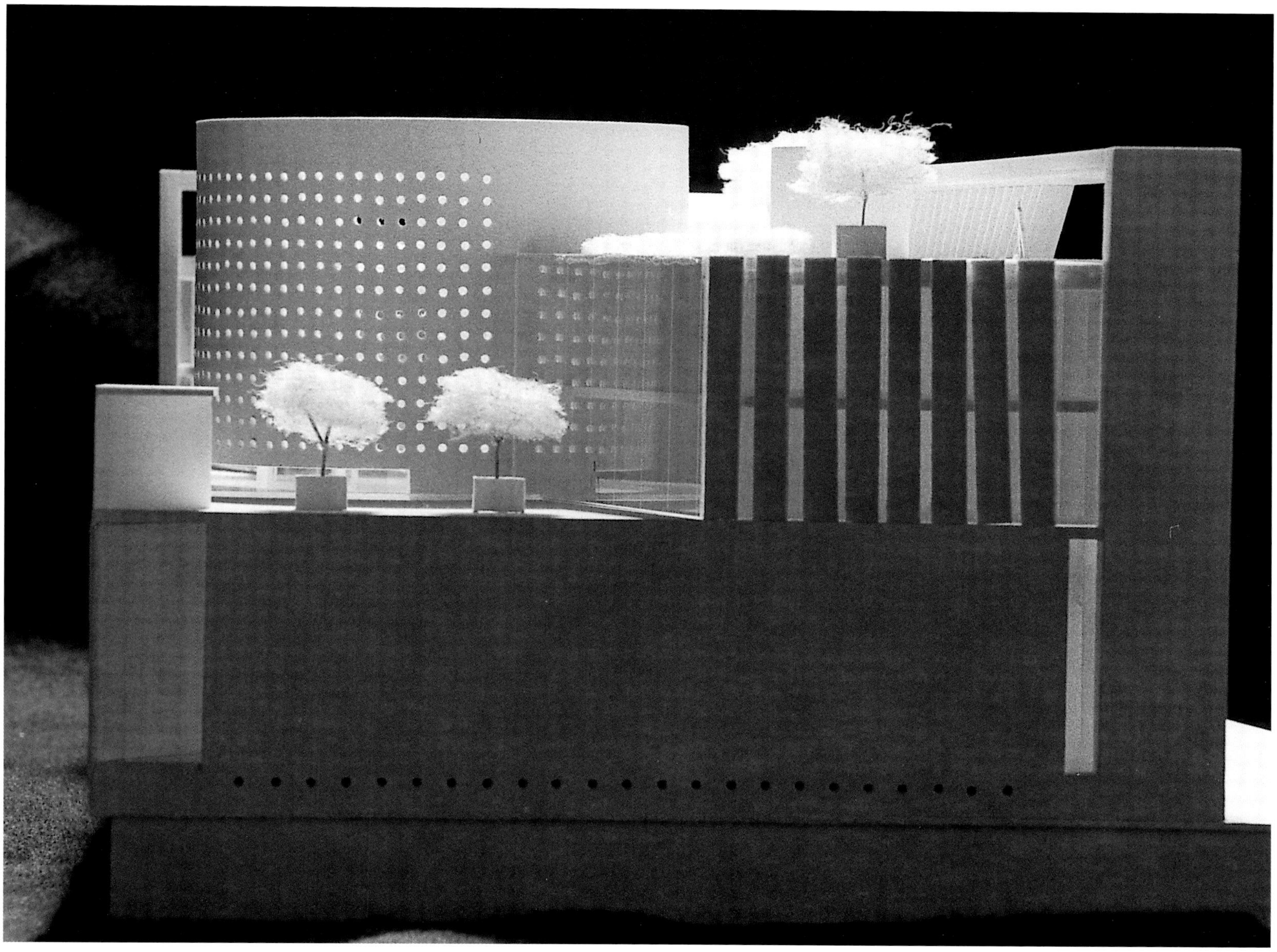

Model of the Embassy, and, top, longitudinal section.

From bottom up, plan of the first, second, and third level.

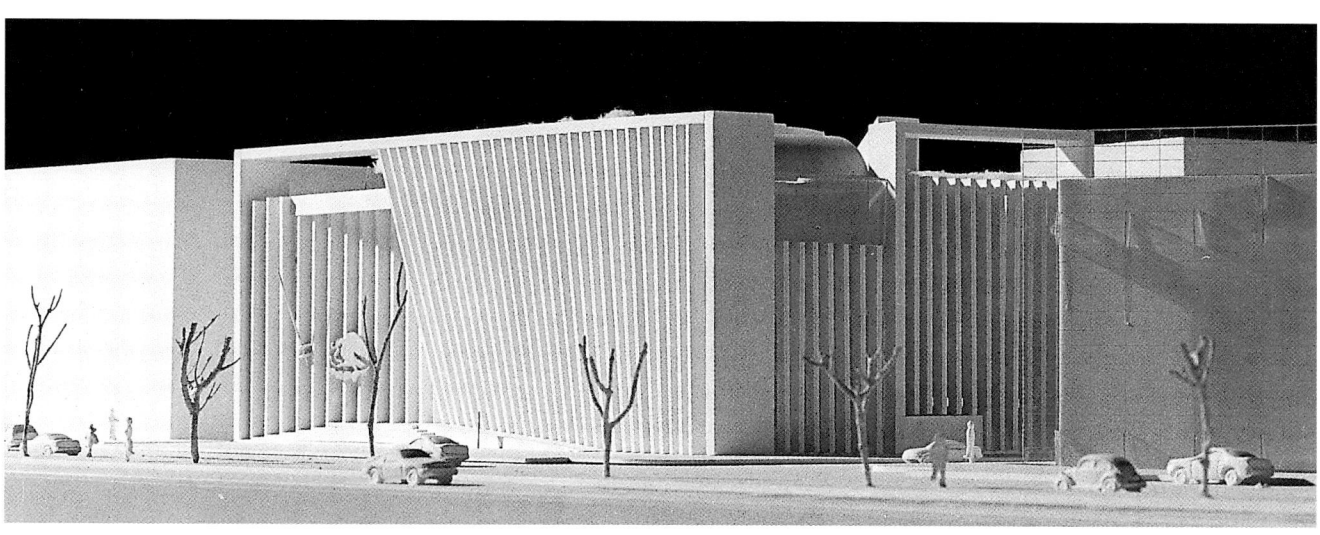
Two views of the model showing the entrance facade.

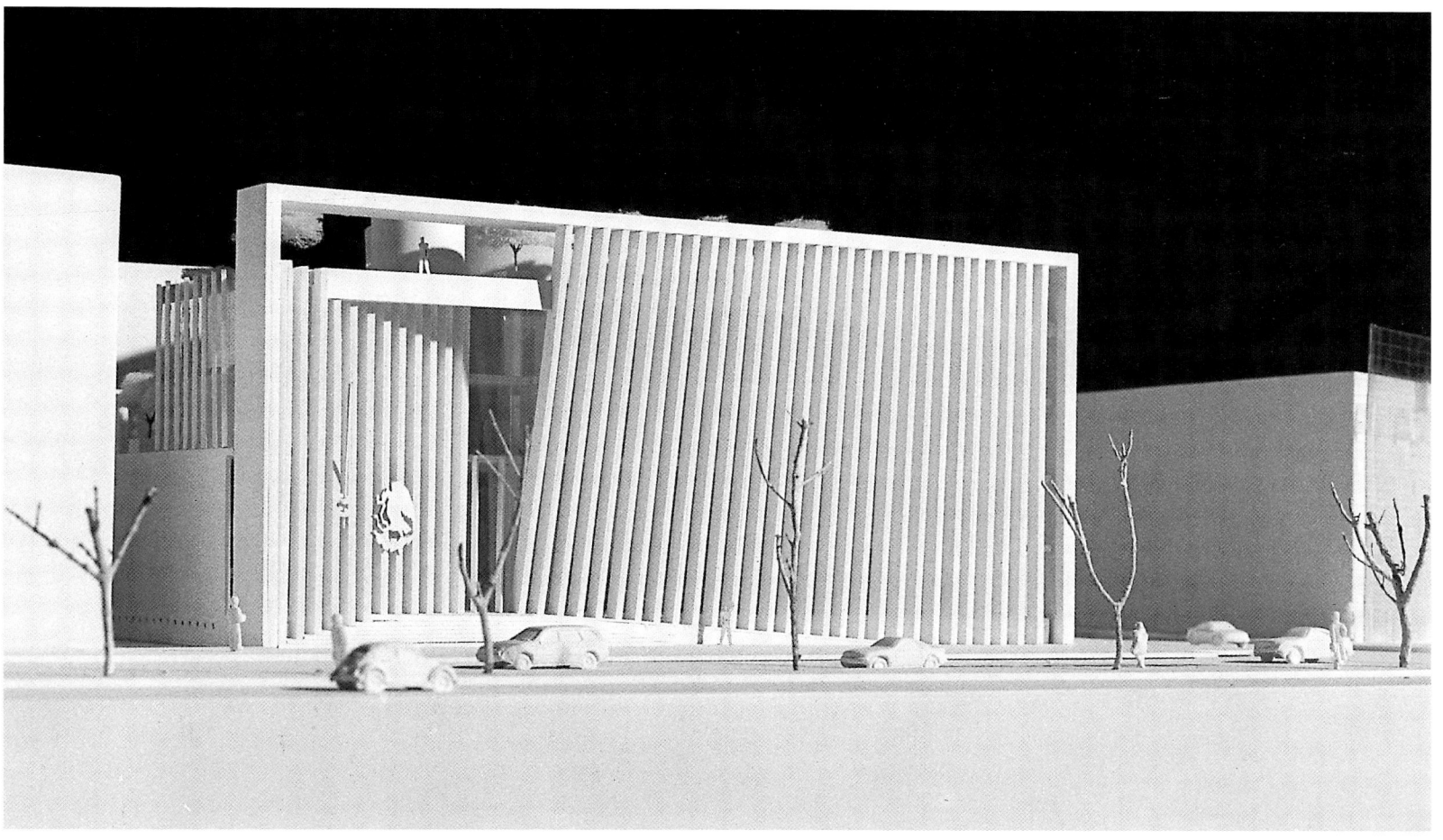

Selected works

1946
Author (in collaboration with Armando Franco and Enrique Molinar) at the winning project of the competition in the National School of Architecture for "Ciudad Universitaria" (National University of Mexico). This project served as a base for the main project of the university campus in Mexico City.

1966
"Escuela de Derecho" (School of Law), University of the city of Tamaulipas, Tampico, Mexico.

1968-71
"Unidad Habitacional Torres de Mixcoac-Lomas de Plateros" (housing unit), Mexico City, in collaboration with Abraham Zabludovsky.

1970-76
"Unidad Habitacional Vallejo-La Patera" (housing unit of 1760 apartments), Mexico City, in collaboration with A. Zabludovsky and A. Franco.

1972-73
"Delegación Cuauhtemoc" (government offices), Mexico City, in collaboration with A. Zabludovsky, and Jaime Ortiz Monasterio and Luis Antonio Zapiain.

1972-75
Mexican Embassy in Brasilia, Brazil, in collaboration with A. Zabludovsky and J. Francisco Serrano.

1973-75
"Oficinas Centrales del Infonavit" (office building), Mexico City, in collaboration with A. Zabludovsky.

1974-76
"El Colegio de México" (private university), Mexico City, won in a competition, in collaboration with A. Zabludovsky.

1975
"Torre Manhattan" (apartment tower - 25 floors), Tecamachalco, Estado de México, in collaboration with A. Zabludovsky.

1976-81
"Unidad Habitacional Ex-Hacienda de Enmedio" (housing unit), Mexico City.

1979-82
"Universidad Pedagógica Nacional" (building of the National Pedagogic University), Mexico City, in collaboration with A. Zabludovsky.

1981-82
"Museo Rufino Tamayo" (Rufino Tamayo Museum), Mexico City, in collaboration with A. Zabludovsky.

1982
Office Tower, Av. de Las Palmas, Mexico City, in collaboration with A. Zabludovsky.

1982-84
"Centro de Cómputo y Sala Bancaria de Nafinsa" (financial center), Mexico City, in collaboration with J. F. Serrano.

1983
International competition Tête Défense (project), in collaboration with J. F. Serrano, París, France.

1984-87
"Centro Administrativo de Gobierno" (administrative center for the government of the state of Tabasco), Villahermosa, Tab., Mexico, in collaboration with J. F. Serrano.

1985-87
"Parque Tomás Garrido Canabal" (renewal of the public park and zoo), Villahermosa, Tabasco, in collaboration with J. F. Serrano and Aurelia Nuño.

"Unidad de Servicios Turísticos y Culturales en Chichén-ltzá" (museum and tourist services) in Chichén-ltzá. Yucatán. Mexico, in collaboration with A. Zabludovsky.

"Biblioteca Pública José María Pino Suárez" (Public Library of the State of Tabasco). Villahermosa, Tabasco, in collaboration with J. F. Serrano.

1986-88
"Centro Minero Nacional" (National Mining Center), Pachuca, Hidalgo, Mexico, in collaboration with J. F. Serrano and Carlos Tejeda.

1986-89
"Oficinas Centrales de Banamex (ampliación)" (extension of the Central Building of Banamex), Mexico City, in collaboration with A. Zabludovsky.

"Centro Financiero Lomas de Banamex" (financial center), Mexico City, in collaboration with A. Zabludovsky.

"Centro Financiero Insurgentes-Encanto de Banamex" (financial center), Mexico City, in collaboration with A. Zabludovsky.

"Centro Financiero y Sucursal San Angel de Banamex" (financial center), Mexico City, in collaboration with A. Zabludovsky.

1987-92
"Palacio de Justicia Federal" (Federal Judicial Palace), Mexico City, in collaboration with J. F. Serrano and Carlos Tejeda.

1988
Hotel Sierra Continental (hotel project), Mexico City, in collaboration with J. F. Serrano.

1989
International Competition "Tribunal of the Sea" (project) in collaboration with A. Zabludovsky, Hamburg, Germany.

1989-91
"Auditorio Nacional" (renovation of the National Auditorium), Mexico City, in collaboration with A. Zabludovsky.

1990
Children's Museum (project), Mexico City.

1990-92
Building for "El Fondo de Cultura Económica" (publishing company), Mexico City.

1990-91
Plaza Rufino Tamayo, Mexico City.

1991-92
"Museo de Sitio en Tajín" (Site Museum of the archaeological zone of Tajín) Veracruz, Mexico.

1992-96
Mexican Embassy in Belmopan, Belice.

1993-94
Renovation of the building of "El Colegio Nacional" (building of the XVIIth Century), Mexico City.

"Conservatorio Nacional de México" (new building of the National Conservatory of Music) of the "Centro Nacional de las Artes", Mexico City.

"Sala Mexicana en el Musec Británico" (Mexican Gallery at the British Museum), London, England.

1993
"Museo de Historia de México" (Mexican History Museum projet), Monterrey, Nuevo León, Mexico, in collaboration with J. F. Serrano.

1994-95
Extension of "El Colegio de México" building, Mexico City.

Biography

1994

"Cámara de Senadores" (senator's chamber project), Mexico City, in collaboration with J. F. Serrano.

Renovation of 4 exhibition halls of the "Palacio de Bellas Artes", Mexico City, in collaboration with J. F. Serrano.

Corporative Center "Vasco de Quiroga" (project), Mexico City, in collaboration with J. F. Serrano and José Pintado.

Villa in Moscow (project), for the "International Dwelling Complex Interbau-Moscow", Moscow, Russia.

1995

Mexican Embassy in Guatemala (project), Guatemala, in collaboration with J. F. Serrano.

Footbridge over Picacho-Ajusco road, Mexico City.

Gymnasium and dressing rooms for El Fondo de Cultura Económica building (project), Mexico City.

1993-1996

Building for Hewlett Packard, Mexico City, won in a competition, in collaboration with J. F. Serrano.

"Arcos-Bosques Corporativo" (corporative center), Mexico City, won in a competition, in collaboration with J. F. Serrano and C. Tejeda (in construction).

1996-97

House in Av. Amsterdam, Mexico City (in construction).

Office building in Paseo de la Reforma, Mexico City (in construction).

Office building for Telmex in Av. Insurgentes Sur, Mexico City (in construction).

Puente de Santa Fe (highway two level bridge), Mexico City (in construction).

1997

Hotel Xaac, Carefree Resort (project), tourist resort Canún-Tulum, Quintana Roo, Mexico, in collaboration with J. F. Serrano.

Mexican Embassy in Berlin won in a competition in collaboration with J. F. Serrano, Berlin, Germany.

Teodoro González de León was born in Mexico City on May 29, 1926. He graduated at the School of Architecture of the National University of Mexico (1942-47). Parallel to his studies, he began his professional life at the studios of notorious Mexican architects of the time: Carlos Obregón Santacilia, Carlos Lazo, and later, Mario Pani (1945-47). He obtained a scholarship from the French government and worked in Le Corbusier's atelier during eighteen months (1947-48). He participated in the construction of the Unité d'Habitation in Marseilles and was in charge of the building of the Manufactures St.Dié, France (1948-49). In the early fifties, he went back to Mexico; since then, he has developed an uninterrupted professional activity; first, in many urbanistic projects and buildings of popular housing units and later, in large public and private buildings.

He has been awarded with the following honors: Emeritus Academician of the "Academia Nacional de Arquitectura" (National Academy of Architecture) and the Arts and Science National Prize of Mexico, Honorary Member of the American Institute of Architects, Member of the "Academia de Artes" (Mexican Academy of Arts) and of the Colegio Nacional (National College, Mexico), Member of the International Academy of Architecture. He also received several prizes such as: First Latin American Prize at the Biennial of Architecture in Buenos Aires (1989), several prizes at the Biennial of Architecture of Mexico (1990,1992,1994 and 1998), Grand Prix of the International Academy of Architecture in the Biennial of Architecture in Sophia, Bulgary (two times: 1989 and 1994), International Honorable Mention at the IX Panamerican Biennial of Architecture, of Quito, Ecuador, and Grand Prix at the II International Biennial of Architecture of Brazil (1994).

His architectural works and paintings were recently exhibited at the Rufino Tamayo Museum. The exhibition was called "Ensamblajes y Excavaciones - La Obra de Teodoro González de León 1968-96".